FROM PRISON
TO PULPIT

FROM PRISON TO PULPIT

My Road to Redemption

THE REVEREND VAUGHAN BOOKER

WITH

DAVID PHILLIPS

CADELL & DAVIES
NEW YORK

Cadell & Davies™

An imprint of Multi Media Communicators, Inc.

575 Madison Avenue, Suite 1006
New York, NY 10022

Cover design Tim Ladwig and Jim Hellman.

Cover photo by Rick Potter.

Library of Congress Cataloging-in-Publication Data:

Booker, Vaughan P. L. (Vaughan Palmer Lorenzo), 1942-
    From prison to pulpit: my road to redemption / Vaughan P. L. Booker, with David Phillips.
        p.   cm.
    ISBN 1-56977-860-4: $19.95
    1. Booker, Vaughan, P. L. (Vaughan Palmer Lorenzo), 1942-
2. Episcopal Church—Clergy—Biography. 3. Murderers—
United States—Biography. I. Phillips, David. II. Title.
    BX5995.B62A3   1994
    283'.092—dc20
    [b]   94-39626
                                                              CIP

10 9 8 7 6 5 4 3 2 1

Printed in the United States of America at Berryville Graphics, with special thanks to Jackie Rhine.

Contents

FOREWORD   vii

CHAPTER ONE:
   "You shall not murder."   1

CHAPTER TWO:
   "Let the little children to come to me..."   16

CHAPTER THREE:
   *...the wedding was turned into mourning and
the voice of their musicians into a funeral dirge.*   30

CHAPTER FOUR:
   *...he has shed blood, and he shall be cut off
from the people.*   60

CHAPTER FIVE:
   *"...to give light to those who sit in darkness
and in the shadow of death..."*   79

CHAPTER SIX:
   O LORD, in your justice preserve my life.   97

CHAPTER SEVEN:
   "...I was in prison and you visited me."   120

CHAPTER EIGHT:
   *...let them first be tested; then, if they prove
themselves blameless, let them serve as deacons.*   142

CHAPTER NINE:

*...to those who repent he grants a return,
and he encourages those who are losing hope.*   169

CHAPTER TEN:

...perfect love casts out fear.   185

CHAPTER ELEVEN:

*"Ask, and it will be given you; search, and
you will find; knock, and the door will be
opened for you."*   202

CHAPTER TWELVE:

*I will study the way that is blameless.
When shall I attain it?*   220

CHAPTER THIRTEEN:

...you are my refuge in the day of disaster.   241

CHAPTER FOURTEEN:

*"Look, the men whom you put in prison are
standing in the temple and teaching the people!"*   252

CHAPTER FIFTEEN:

*"For I have come to call not the righteous
but sinners."*   279

Foreword

I am not proud of the events which led to my incarceration. Never in my wildest dreams would I have imagined that I could murder someone, let alone my own wife, the mother of my children, and in such a horrible manner.

So why write a book? It would seem to just put further attention on what would best be forgotten.

I cannot bring Angie back. If I could, nothing would make me happier. There are some things you do in life which cannot ever be reversed, and taking someone's life is obviously one of them.

Many, many people have helped me put my own life back together. Through God, their efforts and mine, I have not only been able to turn my life around, but am now in a position, and have been for some time, where I can return that help, if not to the people who gave it, then to others who need it.

My main purpose in writing my story is to show others that, no matter what you have done, there is hope. Through faith, with much help both human and divine, as long as the willingness is there, one can turn one's life around and become a useful member of society; one can learn to be at peace with oneself; one can repent; and one can be redeemed.

If, through this book, others in different situations (not nearly as drastic as mine I hope—but even those), can find a glimmer of hope, then the book will have been worthwhile. And if it helps convince people that they should face their problems or turn to someone for help before they are overwhelmed by their own insecurities, then that will make it more worthwhile. Domestic violence, any violence, is not a necessary part of life and I would hope that no one need to go through what I did, causing untold grief and hardship to many, to find that out.

In this book we have tried to present a complete picture. You will hear many voices from my past and present. Many people have been interviewed—not by me—and their words are set forth accurately. Our aim has been to give the reader a full picture of my life, my crime, my punishment, my repentance, redemption and eventual acceptance to the clergy.

Not everyone, by any means, feels that I should have been allowed out of prison. There were many who opposed my acceptance to the priesthood. There are people who have never forgiven me for what I did. We have tried to include these voices and not present a one-sided picture. Only with the truth can you, the reader, judge for yourself and, I hope, learn something.

The book touches on many aspects of life in this country from the 1940s through to the 1990s: growing up as a middle class black youth in Philadelphia; the church; the justice system; the penal system and life in jail, rehabilitation versus mere punishment; corporate America; marriage, family, children, domestic violence and tragedy, and domestic peace; racial issues; religion, God, repentance, forgiveness and redemption, and what these mean in everyday life.

It is a true story. It happened and is happening. It could happen and will happen to others.

My only hope is that the lessons I have learned slowly and painfully can be learned quickly by others, without the toil, the grief, and the tragedy.

Vaughan Booker, Rector
Meade Memorial Church
Alexandria, Virginia

CHAPTER ONE

"You shall not murder."

(Exodus 20:13)

No shot rang out. No screams were heard. It was a relatively silent murder. The bow and arrow is a relatively silent weapon.

It was very early on the 23rd of October, 1967. Inside the duplex on North 57th Street in Philadelphia the only witnesses to the crime were Annabelle Booker, the victim, and myself, Vaughan Booker, her husband, who killed her. Our children, Kimberly, aged three, and Vaughan, Jr., who was called Tawney, aged one, were asleep in their own room.

When the police arrived Angie (Annabelle) was dead.

The details surrounding the incident are still somewhat cloudy and aspects of it will continue to be mysterious, even to me, probably until the end of time.

Certain facts, however, are known. Three years later when the case eventually came up for trial, evidence was presented to three judges in the Court of Common Pleas, First Judicial District of Pennsylvania. The official version of the crime was given at that trial and agreed upon, at least by the judges who heard the case.

Detective Thomas Fredericks, the first witness for the Commonwealth, provided the following testimony under oath:

On Monday, October 23, 1967, I was working the twelve to eight tour of duty, twelve o'clock midnight to eight A.M. At approximately 6:08 A.M. I received a call in a male voice which said, "I just killed my wife." I said to him, "Where do you live?" He said, "1831 North 57th." I said, "What is your name?" He said, "Vaughan Booker." I said to him, "How did you kill your wife?" He said, "With a bow and arrow." I told him I would dispatch a police car to the house. He hung up. I sent a wagon, a sergeant, and a radio patrol car.

Dr. Marvin E. Aronson, Assistant Medical Examiner for Philadelphia, also testified at the trial. Mr. Ivan Czap, the Assistant District Attorney and Prosecuting Counsel, questioned him.

Q: Dr. Aronson, did you have under your examination the body of one Annabelle Booker, now deceased?

A: Yes, sir.

Q: Would you state when and what your findings were with respect to the pathological diagnosis?

A: My examination of the body of Annabelle Booker commenced on the 23rd of October, 1967, at 1:30 P.M., Daylight Savings Time, at the office of the Medical Examiner. I noted that the body was 5 feet 6 inches in height and weighed 107 pounds. The remarkable feature of my examination was that there were five arrows piercing the body of the deceased. In my description of these I shall refer to numbers which are arbitrary numbers, because I have no way of knowing in fact which were inflicted first.

I noted first that on the right front part of the neck at the area which I am indicating now on my own body, bearing in mind that I am obese and the deceased was

not, there was an arrow 29 inches in length and blue
colored. This entered the skin through an incision
which was cross-shaped. This arrow went from front to
back and from below upward, the direction which I am
indicating now, I hope I am indicating—with my pen,
at an angle of 45 degrees without deviation to right or
left. I subsequently removed the arrow.

Judge Robert N. C. Nix, one of the three judges, also questioned Dr. Aronson:

Q: How deep did the arrow penetrate?

A: This arrow penetrated a distance of approximately two
inches into the bone of the vertebral column, a total
distance of two and a half to three inches into the skin
of the deceased.

Dr. Aronson went on to describe, in the same gruesome
detail, four other arrows he found in the body of the 27-year-
old Annabelle Booker. Each of them was 29 inches long,
three of them were hunting arrows with razor sharp, cross-
shaped points, the other two were target arrows with conical
metal tips. He explained that three of the arrows had pierced
the neck and embedded themselves in the bone of the spinal
column, all very close to each other. The fourth arrow had
entered the body approximately three-quarters of an inch
above the left nipple and penetrated into the abdomen wall,
incising the stomach and the liver, leaving a pool of approximately one-third of a quart of liquid blood in the abdominal
cavity.

The fifth arrow entered the body on the right side at a point
approximately two and a half inches above the front of the
pelvis and exited at a slightly lower point on the left side. Dr.
Aronson demonstrated to the court with his pen, reminding
them again that he was obese and the victim was not.

Aside from these findings of significant findings, he found

no evidence of significant disease, no presence of drugs or chemicals....

Such was the substance of Dr. Aronson's testimony.

Officer William Harris was the first police officer on the scene of the crime. He added his account:

> Your Honor, when I arrived at 1831 North 57th I observed a Negro male standing on the steps of 1831 North 57th Street. Approaching the location I observed this Negro male, who was identified as the defendant, Vaughan Booker, and because I made an incorrect notation of the address, I asked him was this 1837 N. 57th Street, and the defendant answered, "No, this is 1831. I just killed my wife." Then I asked the defendant, "Where is she?" And he led me upstairs to the rear bedroom where I observed a Negro female lying in bed identified as Annabelle Booker, the deceased lying in bed, with this female having five arrows protruding from her body. I then requested the defendant to come into the adjoining room and I waited until a wagon crew arrived....

Mr. Czap continued questioning:

Q: Officer, did you determine who else was present in that apartment? This was the second-floor apartment?

A: Right.

Q: You said a Negro male. Is that Negro male here in court?

A: Yes, he is.

Q: Is that Vaughan Booker, the Defendant?

A: Yes, it is.

Q: Did you determine who else was in the apartment besides Mr. Booker?

A: Yes. I asked, as I recall, asked the defendant was there anyone else in the house besides himself and he said his two children.

Q: Were his two children there?

A: His two children were in the bedroom.

Judge Nix then interjected, "The same room where their mother was?"

"No," the officer answered, "the adjoining bedroom."

Officer Harris went on to identify the 60-inch wooden bow with a 47-pound pull (referring to the force measured to pull it back to release the arrows) and the 53-inch string, the quiver and the arrows. Yes, he had seen all these in the house in addition to the Negro male and Negro female already described. (This was 1970 and "Negro" was still part of the language.)

Under cross-examination he testified that I had appeared composed when he first saw me, not in a state of shock. After a few more questions he was excused.

Lieutenant Kachigian was not present at the trial but his statement, read by the Assistant District Attorney, Mr. Czap, was admitted as evidence. "The relevant part of what his testimony would be is that he did see Vaughan Booker, the defendant there, and did see the deceased, Annabelle Booker, lying in the bed face up."

> Upon my return to the kitchen Mr. Booker asked me for a cigarette and then asked me if I would check his children in the front bedroom. He stated that he had tried to kill his son by strangling him, but that he had given the boy respiration and he thought he was all right. I checked the front bedroom and found both his son and daughter alive and apparently in good health. At this time I observed writing on the wall.

"Your Honors, now I will read from a photograph of the writing which will be offered in evidence.

"These were the words found on the wall in the children's bedroom, next to the crib where Vaughan, Jr., aged one, slept:

I TRIED TO KILL MY CHREDRIN. MY SON FIRST WITH STRANGULATION. MY DAUGHTER I DID NOT. I TRIED TO STRANGLE MY SON. I THOUGHT HE WAS DEAD, BUT I REVIVED HIM. I HOPE. THANK GOD. I LOVED MY FAMILY. I DON'T KNOW WHAT TO SAY.

Shortly after I was arrested and taken to the local police precinct, I was questioned by Detective Joseph Schimpf. A statement was typed up by Frances Erline, at the time the clerk-stenographer of the Homicide Division. Detective William Thompson was also present. Both detectives appeared in court.

There had been an attempt to suppress the statement at an earlier hearing before Judge Meade, but the petition was dismissed. With my agreement, based on the advice of my counsel that it would not harm my case, the full statement was accepted as evidence at the trial.

The confession is included here, although information I revealed later raises serious questions as to its factualness.

I was read my rights. The following statement is published as-is, spelling errors and all.

Q: Are you willing to answer questions of your own free will, without force or fear, and without any threats or promises having been made to you?

A: Yes.

Q: What is your full name, age and address?

A: Vaughan Palmer Lorenzo Booker, 25 years, I live at 1831 Apt. A, North 57th St.

Q: What is your occupation; where do you work?

A: I'm unemployed.

Q: Are you related to the victim, Annabelle Booker?

A: Yes I am, I'm her husband.

Q: Do you know why you have been arrested?

A: Yes I do, because of the murder of my wife.

Q: I want to inform you at this time, that Annabelle Booker, has been pronounced dead from injuries received from a bow and arrows, on Monday, October 23, 1967, at 9:45 AM, by Dr. Aronson. Do you understand this?

A: Yes.

Q: Vaughan, will you go on in your own words and tell us what you know concerning this incident? We may interrupt you at any time with a question.

A: At approximately 4 AM, I went to my home and proceeded to the bedroom, found my wife asleep at this time, proceeded to the bathroom, during this time she awoke. After this I proceeded to the front room, the closet, and retrieved my bow and arrows and I proceeded to the bedroom again, strung my bow, took out one arrow and at this point my wife and I started talking.

Q: Why did you and your wife talk about?

A: We just had a general conversation, it was very short and we had smoked a cigarette together. After this time I pulled the bow back and the first arrow apparently struck her in the chest. She did say something after that but I don't remember exactly what it was. I then was aware of the pain and agony she was in so I went to my quiver and pulled out another arrow, this second one striking her in the throat. She still seemed to be in agony so I went to my quiver again, pulled out another arrow and struck her again in the throat. I then proceeded to my children's room with the vain attempt of first destroying my son, my daughter and then myself. I then at this time proceeded to choke my son, found that he was loosing his breath and his life at the same time, and then proceeded to administer mouth to mouth resuscitation to revive him. I succeeded in reviving him, put him in my daughter's bed, transferred my daughter to my son's bed. She woke up and said, basically, "What am I doing in my brother's bed?" I transferred my son back to his bed, my daughter back to her bed, she asked me, "Where's my mommy?" and I said, "She went away." I then went to the front room to find a pencil to go back and write on my children's wall exactly what I had done. And after not having the ability to think, I proceeded to my mother's house, she lives across the street, rang her bell, waited until she was comfortably indoors, and told her what had happened. She, in a mild sate of hysteria continued upstairs, told my father what had happened, then they both started talking and she said to my father, "Call the police" and being the phone isn't connected, my father said to me, "Go out and call the police yourself." I did call the police, went to my next door neighbor, rang her bell and made her aware of what had happened. She being in slight shock herself, said wait until I get dressed, and at this time I saw a police car passing by, hailed to him to acknowledge that I knew of his presence and then he arrived and I was taken into custody. Of course the police came upstairs, and then I went upstairs at this point, I went in and looked at my wife and I came into the kitchen of course, this was prior to my being taken into custody, the police came in and asked me my name and asked me to sit in a kitchen chair, I was handcuffed and taken into 61st and Thompson put then in a cell then brought to the homicide division.

Q: What reason did you have for doing this?

A: Well it was something I thought about doing for a long time. We've had bickering, arguments, over cleanliness of the house, the care of the children, I guess you could say we had basically economical problems.

Q: You mean that you weren't satisfied with the way your wife kept house and took care of the children?

A: As far as the basic well being of the children, she was a good mother, hygienically though, she never kept a very clean living quarters for the children, herself and myself.

Q: When you and your wife talked and smoked a cigarette, was there an argument at this time?

A: No.

Q: How far did you have to go to get your bow and arrows?

A: Past the children's room, past the kitchen and into the front room.

Q: When you hit your wife with the first arrow, she said something, do you remember what this was?

A: It was something like "Oh, Shirley," which is the lady downstairs.

Q: You then said you put two more arrows into her throat.

A: Yes.

Q: When I viewed the body, there was five arrows, did you shoot three or did you shoot five?

A: I remember shooting three arrows.

Q: Of the arrows you shot, did you or she break any in half?

A: I don't remember any being broken.

Q: You attempted to kill your son, your daughter and yourself, for what reason did you want to do this?

A: Instead of having my children to suffer, I would take them out of their misery at the present time. In other words I didn't want them to suffer for a lifetime for what their father did.

Q: You said you went to the front room to find a pencil to go back and write on the children's wall, exactly what you had done, did you in fact write anything on the wall?

A: Yes I did.

Q: Do you remember what it was, Vaughan?

A: Not exactly.

Q: What type of arrows did you use?

A: I used two hunting arrows and one field or target arrow.

Q: What's the difference between a hunting arrow and a field or target arrow?

A: The hunting arrows I had were three prong, razor tipped; a field or target arrow has a sharp non-razor edged point.

Statement interrupted at 10:50 AM to allow defendant to get a drink of water.
Statement resumed at 10:55 AM.

Q: Vaughan, how far away from your wife were you when you fired the arrows?

A: Due to the force of the bow, I stood at the door, maybe eight feet.

Q: What is the pull of the bow?

A: It's a 47 pound pull and I pulled it to its maximum.

Q: Prior to going home at 4 AM, where had you been?

A: At the Republican Club, 52nd and Vine.

Q: When is the last time you were home?

A: I left the house Saturday night somewhere around 9:30 PM, I called my former employer, Howard L. Scott, I was a salesman for him at Lavender House Products, beauty supplies, at 9th and McIlvaine St., Chester, Pa., he said he was coming in town so I went in town to have a couple of drinks and relax. I went to the Liberty Bar, 15th and Samson, I had a beer in there and left, I went to the Mystic Club, 1418 Spruce St. I met a friend of mine named Carmen, in there, I don't remember his last name. I had two beers then went home with Carmen to his house, it's somewhere in the northwest, I don't know where because he drove me in his car. I stayed at his house Saturday night, Sunday we watched the football games and I drank a couple of glasses of wine. Around 11:30 Sunday night, Carmen drove me to Devon, we went to the Devon Club, I had two beers, then Carmen drove me to the Republican Club, I had three beers in the Republican Club. After that I was ready to go home. Carmen drove me to my home, I got out of the car and he drove off. I went home and this is when the incident occurred.

Q: When you came into the bedroom with your bow and arrow, did your wife ask you why you had it?

A: She said, "What's on your mind" or something to that effect.

Q: Did she have any idea of what you were going to do?

A: No, I had no idea myself.

Q: In what position was your wife when you fired the first arrow?

A: I'm almost sure she was sitting on the bed, and the force of the first arrow knocked her back. She moved and thrashed around a bit and tried to get up and I let the second one go and it hit her in the neck. She was still in apparent agony, that's why I fired the third one.

Q: Where did you get the bow and arrows?

A: I got them about two years ago from a friend in a swap for a bull whip. I've always been interested in archery and I had several bows in the past. I have always been interested, I got a boy scout merit badge for archery and had practiced target shooting.

Q: When is the last time you had an argument with your wife?

A: It was sometime last week and for the same reasons as before, unclean house, and economic reasons.

Q: Did you ever hit your wife before or did she ever hit you?

A: Yes we've had arguments where we've exchanged blows, not violently me being 160 pounds, and her being quite small, I could handle her with a slap or two, I've never punched her or anything like that.

Q: Who does Carmen live with?

A: He lives alone.

Q: Is he a homosexual?

A: If he is a homosexual, he never approached me in a homosexual way.

Q: What is your opinion as to whether he is or not?

A: I think he had tendencies to being a homosexual.

Q: How had you intended to kill yourself?

A: I was going to slash my wrists.

Q: Were you drunk?

A: No.

Q: When you were brought to Homicide Headquarters did anybody warn you orally of your legal rights?

A: Yes, a detective read me all the warnings from a little yellow card.

Q: Is there anything further you wish to add to this statement?

A: No.

Q: Can you read and write the English language?

A: Yes.

Q: How far did you go in school?

A: I finished High School, Overbrook and went to Temple Prep. where I graduated from and then took a couple of courses at St. Joseph's College.

Statement finished: 11:55 AM, Monday, 10/23/67.

Apparently this is what I told them. I signed the full statement at the end and on each page, but I did not read it before I signed it. The confession was witnessed by both detectives and the stenographer-clerk. Then I was taken to a Philadelphia Detention Center and locked up in isolation under 24-hour suicide watch.

Later I revealed information which threw a different light on the whole incident; but the incontrovertible and irreversible facts were that Angie was dead, killed by my own hand, and that I was behind bars.

My parents, Lorenzo (Sam) and Mary Booker, my sister Delphine, their friends and acquaintances all had similar reactions. This was their Vaughan, the same Vaughan who had had, in many ways, a model childhood: a succession of achievements at school; the only Eagle Scout produced by my troop; an altar boy at St. Augustine's Church of the Covenant in Philadelphia from the age of 8; a person who loved animals and couldn't stand to see them hurt. This was not a drug addict, a gang member, a child from a broken home, or a former juvenile delinquent. This was a young man who had already tasted success, who had had a stellar youth and who had a bright and promising future ahead.

The victim's family was, of course, more shocked. How could their Angie, the vivacious girl who was loved and respected by parents, family and friends, have been taken away from them so suddenly and cruelly at the age of 27? A future without her could never be the same for them.

Feelings of anger, hatred, and revenge toward me, the man who had committed the heinous crime, mingled with the shock and grief of sudden bereavement. What else can one expect in the wake of a murder?

———

It's a warm Wednesday afternoon in June. The year is 1992, 25 years after the murder. The organ music provides a beautiful, holy backdrop to the procession of acolytes, deacons, and priests as they walk up the aisle in the Episcopal Church of St. Alban's in New Brunswick, New Jersey.

Bishop P. Mellick Belshaw, in his cape and miter brings up the rear. And there, in their midst, I stand—Deacon Vaughan Booker—the same Vaughan Booker who, a quarter of a century before, had pulled back the bowstring and let fly the arrows that took Angie Booker's life.

This is a special day at St. Alban's and one of the most significant days in my life—just as significant as that tragic day when I killed my wife. For the service at St. Alban's, attended by friends, family and supportive associates from my prison days, my corporate days, my seminary days and my childhood, is my ordination as a priest in the Episcopal church.

Bishop Belshaw reads in solemn voice from the Rite of Holy Orders:

"Therefore if any of you know any impediment or crime because of which we should not proceed, come forward now and make it known."

My heart skips a beat. But no one in the congregation stirs or says a word. He looks around. Silence. The service continues.

The vows recited, the priest's vestments donned, the hands of the bishop and the attendant priests laid on my head, the ceremony over, I break down and weep tears of joy and other emotions, very real but hard to name.

CHAPTER TWO

*"Let the little children
to come to me..."*

(Matthew 19:14)

The three judges handed down their verdict on Friday the 13th of February, 1970. Before the sentence was passed, Judge Nix, the only black judge on the panel, addressed me, the defendant, directly:

> You were a young man who had all the promise.
> God had endowed you with many, many gifts
> that many youngsters don't have, and it's unfortu-
> nate that this incident, these few hours, marred
> what was otherwise an excellent life. Certainly
> we cannot in our limited facilities understand the
> working of the Divine. I am sure, however, that
> there is some reason that this happened, and I
> hope that you profit by it.

God had indeed endowed me with many gifts and had fea-tured extensively in my life prior to the murder.

"It was September 17th, 1942 when Vaughan was born—the hottest day in the year," recalls my mother, Mary Booker. "I wasn't enthused over a son or a daughter. It really didn't matter to me one way or the other. My husband Sam was

thrilled. He was the one that was running out telling everyone, 'Mary gave me a son! Mary gave me a son!'"

I had a sister Delphine, 18 months my elder, nicknamed
Putie. I rapidly became Giggle. "He was sick all the time,"
says my mother. "He threw up constantly. We didn't know if
he was going to last 24 hours at a time. So I called him
Stinkin'. Putie called him Geekin'. Somehow that turned into
Giggle. Giggle he remains to this day. When he comes home
it's not Vaughan, it's not Reverend and it's not Father—it's
just plain Giggle."

My parents, Mr. and Mrs. Sam Booker were well respected
in the neighborhood. My maternal grandparents, Mr. and
Mrs. Archer, lived nearby, also respected members of the
community. Dad (Lorenzo Samuel Booker) was a master car-
penter. He always worked, although life for a black man in
those days was tough; he couldn't even join the union. Later,
in 1957, he would go into business with his brother and my
family would move to a better home in West Philadelphia.

My mother used to dress my sister and me in matching
maroon and white outfits, Putie in a dress and me in shorts.
We became the Putie and Giggle show.

People would see us coming and know we were Mr. and
Mrs. Booker's son and daughter, Mr. and Mrs. Archer's grandchildren. At that time there was a true sense of community
where people knew each other and interacted. People spoke to
each other and looked at each other. There was eye contact. I
can remember you didn't live in fear. We used to walk to a lot
of places. Now the area where I grew up is a war zone. The
scourge of drugs and other factors have taken their toll.

We certainly weren't poor. We had good food, nice clothes
to wear and my father always had a car. But we were middle
class more by philosophy than by economics at that time.

My sister Delphine's memories of our childhood and the
way we were brought up help add to the picture.

My parents were strict. When Daddy said, "Be home by 11," that's what you did. Mom was more or less the head honcho as far as our discipline was concerned. Sometimes we would say they were mean because we weren't allowed to do a lot of things or go a lot of places that a lot of the other kids went and did, but that was the way they were. They said "No" and that was the final answer.

They brought us up to do the right thing and to grow up and be respected citizens of the world, to be Christians, not just to follow the crowd. If someone was doing something wrong and they were going to the right, you went left. They were very strict, but I appreciate it now.

As children we were sent, rather than taken, to church on Sunday. We were allowed to involve ourselves in church-related activities and, for us kids, this had the added benefit of providing us with plausible reasons for getting out of the house.

We went everywhere together. When Putie first entered kindergarten, I was so upset at having to leave her that her teacher let me stay in the class to calm me down.

I couldn't wait to get enrolled in school. Douglass Elementary School, named after Frederick Douglass, was all black. I liked everything about school. I loved to write and I loved to read. As I got up in the grades I became a member of the safety patrol, then I was assigned as a sergeant, then I became a lieutenant, then ran for captain of the safety patrol and won.

We had to make our own slogans. I ran with another guy, Alonzo Lofton, and we had a little saying: "Rain or shine, sleet or snow, Vaughan and Alonzo are on the go." Typical stuff kids come up with. I was also the health representative for my class and ran track for my school. As far as grades were concerned, I usually received *A*'s and *B*'s.

But the crowning glory of elementary school came at graduation. The entire school was assembled and our parents were there. Every year an Outstanding Student Award, called the Pointdexter Award, was given to the best students (one girl, one boy) graduating that year. No one knew ahead of time who was going to win it and the kids were very competitive.

Of course all the family was there. Then the principal announced that a little girl called Peachy and Vaughan Booker had won the Pointdexter Award. Naturally I was thrilled, and nervous. I went up and received my framed certificate and the savings bond that went with it. What a way to end my elementary school career.

Vacations were often spent upstate in Pennsylvania Dutch country with my grandparents at Lewiston, out in the country. I can see the house so vividly. They didn't have running water, so my grandmother used to take hot water and pour it into the tub until there must have been two inches of water in it, and then she would scrub us. I remember playing with wooden toys they had. We would go for walks down to the Juniata River and we would run through the cornfields by my grandparents' house. It was just a wonderful atmosphere and a really pleasurable part of my childhood.

There was another side to my childhood, however. One which I never talk about. From the earliest times I can remember, my parents used to fight. My father used to drink and he used to stay out a lot. The arguments were about this and I can recall the subject of other women coming up. I never saw any, but I was a child.

I remember my mother taunting my father. She knew how to push his buttons and she would do so. There was a lot of physical violence and I remember one time when it got so bad that my father hit her and pushed her down the stairs.

This was not just an occasional circumstance. It was fairly

routine. Putie and I would be terrified and would want them to stop. We would try to console each other because often enough we had only each other. Going to our grandparents' house was a relief. I can remember my grandmother holding me as a child, but never my mother. I don't recall her telling me she loved me. There was very little affection or positive emotion in our house.

My mother was an angry person and often that anger would turn against us. She used to wear a heavy ring and I got used to sideswipes with this ring, often for reasons which I could not fathom.

We were not allowed to make mistakes. As a kid I wanted to experiment with my handwriting and on one report card I got an *I* for "Needs Improvement." I was used to getting the *O*'s for "Outstanding" and the *S*'s for "Satisfactory." I was so distraught and so scared of being brutally beaten when I took this report card home that I swallowed some roach poison to try to kill myself. This was when I was still at my elementary school.

Another time I was pulling groceries or laundry in my wagon and came to the curb and overturned it. My mother's response was to kick me.

To all outward appearances we were the model family and what went on at home was kept strictly under wraps. We were seriously threatened about what would happen if we ever breathed any word of the domestic violence and general dysfunction outside the house, even to my grandparents. My mother's favorite saying was, "I brought you into this world, and I will take you out of it."

So we never talked to anyone about it. Even now my sisters and I are very protective of our mother and still try to keep up a facade of a happy childhood and a normal home life. Since I have been out of prison I have become close to her and tried to reconcile some of these differences, but she still denies that any of this ever went on. I have done my best to honestly reveal my feelings to her and there's no more I can do on that score. My bitterness about it has gone and it's important to me, after all the trouble the family has been through, to maintain some sort of an appearance of having had a normal, happy family life. On the other hand, I can't discount the effect this aspect of my childhood had on me.

My response at the time was to look for any excuse to be away from the house, something that would continue all the way up to, and including, my getting married.

I am sure my introduction to the church came through my grandparents who were good Christian people of strong faith.

At the age of eight I had become an altar boy at the Episcopal church of St. Augustine, where my Uncle Charles served as a deacon before he went on to becoming a priest and was assigned his own parish. Uncle Charles was a role model for me. My mother remembers me coming home at an early age saying I wanted to be a "churchman" but she didn't pay it any attention because on another day it would be a fireman or a doctor, a veterinarian or almost anything. Nevertheless, I remained active in the church throughout my youth, as an acolyte and was elected president of the teenage canteen at St. Thomas, one of the church's organizations for young people.

I started off as a torch bearer. I remember leading the procession, dressed in my red cassock and white surplice, and this really meant something to me, with my grandparents and family in the congregation and my uncle Charles a deacon at the church.

The next year I had grown a couple of inches so I could be trained to carry the cross. Carrying the torch was significant, but carrying the cross...For a child, this is the cross of Jesus, and in my theological mind of a nine or ten year old, there was no greater thrill than being able to carry the symbol of our Lord.

I loved the pageantry and the beauty of the service as much as I loved anything. At a service like this, God just had to be there. With this beautiful music playing and the incense and the reverence, it wouldn't occur to you to think an evil thought in that place, because God had to be there.

I also remember I used to sneak the wafers for the Eucharist—they weren't consecrated but I would always cross myself—and I thought these little pieces of cardboard-like stuff would add something to my "holiness."

Although we were taught to live by the Golden Rule and other biblical tenets, I don't think, looking back on it, that there was enough emphasis placed on taking that same feeling with you wherever you went. We were just told that that's what we were supposed to do, but we were never told how.

My service as an acolyte continued throughout my childhood and youth, from St. Augustine to our new church in West Philadelphia, St. Thomas, and as far as my Uncle Charles' parish church in Chester, south of Philadelphia.

The church led me into other activities as well. It was through the church that I found the Boy Scouts. I took the oath at the age of 11 when I joined Troop 357 through St. Augustine's church.

My activities with the Boy Scouts became another major love of my life. I learned to appreciate the environment and nature and to care for God's creatures. There is a passage in the *Boy Scout Handbook* which seemed to apply very much to me.

> *When you are a Scout, forests and fields, rivers and lakes are your playground. You are completely at home in God's great outdoors. You learn to notice every sound, to observe every track. Birds and animals become your friends. You master the skills of walking noiselessly through the woods, of stalking close to a grazing deer without being noticed, of bringing a bird to you by imitating its call.*

My mother remembers, however, when "God's great outdoors" started to come indoors, much to the alarm of Putie and herself. One time I brought home a white rat, my new pet. It had been missing around the house for some time when suddenly it came out from behind the radiator and scampered right over her shoulder.

On another occasion I brought home a box with a snake in it. The snake had just had babies. I asked my mother and sister to look after it while I went out, deposited the box on the dining room table, and left the house. They told me later that they had been in the bedroom when they heard a soft thud in the dining room. My snake had made her way out of the box and was roaming free around the dining room floor. My mother hid in the bed, which was not the best place since reptiles on the loose tend to look for warmth.

I learned to love all animals, and I do to this day. Scouting for me, however, went far beyond God's great outdoors and the creatures therein. It became a full time endeavor. While other kids were off doing what kids do on their summer vacations, I would be working on my next merit badge.

I remember the summer when I was 14. I worked really hard to get my swimming and lifesaving merit badges. These were the only required badges for Eagle Scout that I still lacked. I spent most of that summer in the pool and I went from being a mediocre swimmer to becoming a Scout lifeguard.

I focused on swimming and I learned all the strokes: the Australian crawl, the elementary back stroke, breast stroke, side stroke, the trudgen and so on.

Then came my test. I had to rescue the chaplain, a gentleman by the name of Father John Bieberbach. He was 6' 1" and weighed 240 pounds and here there I was, this skinny little guy, and I had to go in and actually rescue him and swim him back to the shore. This meant jumping into the water feet first, keeping my eyes on the "victim," and swimming towards him; then surface diving to grab him by the knees and turn him around; then putting him in a cross-chest carry and swimming him 25 feet to the shore—no mean feat!

That was just two merit badges. But I had decided to become an Eagle Scout (no one from Troop 357 had ever achieved that honor in the troop's 25 year history). I went on to gain 46 merit badges—the requisite number for Eagle Scout was 21. In addition to the badges, the requirements for Eagle Scout included 6 months as a Life Scout, active leadership in a troop (such as patrol leader, senior patrol leader, etc.) and completion of a service project helpful to the Scout's church, synagogue, school or community. The Scout must also satisfy the Scoutmaster that he lives up to the Scout Oath, Law, motto and slogan.

I remember for the awards ceremony we were in the auditorium of a major department store in Philadelphia and I was so excited. There were 40 or 50 other Scouts from around the city, all there to receive the Eagle Scout badge, and all our parents.

To begin with we were backstage, all in neatly pressed uniforms with our neckerchiefs and all of our badges and awards. I happened to be the only black scout there but that wasn't uncommon and it didn't bother me.

I was anxious because the spotlights were so bright that I couldn't see if my parents were in the audience and part of the ceremony is your mother also has to come up to get a miniature Eagle Scout badge pinned on her.

Finally the moment came when I was announced and I had to go forward and receive my badge and everyone in the audience was applauding.. Then my mother came onto the stage and I pinned her badge on her.

I went on in scouting to work in camps and was even on the nature staff of one camp. I remained active until I was 17. In theory I went from being a kid to being an adult.

But I was an achiever. There was a better life out there and

I knew it. It's not bad when people ask you to stand up and say, "Look what a wonderful thing this young man has done." I didn't feel I had to be better than others, just the best that I could be. If Eagle Scout was the highest goal, the furthest you could go, then that's where I wanted to go. It wasn't just that I wanted my parents' approval, as the psychologists would say (and did say later on), but I wanted my own approval too.

At the time, I paid scant attention to the fact that one of the merit badges I had earned was for archery, an activity that ten years later was to play such a significant and fatal role in my life. Or to the fact that, to earn my lifesaving badge, I learned to administer artificial respiration, a skill I would later use to restore my baby son's breathing after nearly choking the life out of him with my own hands.

No, back in 1957 I was simply making myself and my family proud by being the best Scout I could be: trustworthy, loyal, helpful, friendly, courteous, kind, obedient, cheerful, thrifty, brave, clean and reverent.

At Gillespie Junior High, I continued to excel and went on to become president of the entire school. My mother says that peer pressure began to take a toll on my grades, however. This is not what happened. I remember it quite clearly. We were not allowed to make mistakes as children. We had to be perfect. In order to avoid making mistakes with my homework, I simply stopped bringing work home. That was my way of avoiding the consequences of my mother discovering errors in my work. This, of course, had quite an effect on my grades. Not that I became a bad kid in general or got into a lot of trouble. My sister remembers the extent of my criminal activities: I broke a basement window when I and some other Scouts were playing about. My punishment consisted of paying for the damage. Hardly delinquency, certainly by modern standards.

By the time I went to Overbrook High School, I had also become interested in girls and dances and having fun but my academic prowess suffered. In the '60s the opportunities for black students going on to college were not what they are now. Because expectations were lower no one was particularly alarmed at my faltering grades.

I became a track star, representing my school in local competitions. On the first occasion that I took a time trial at hurdles I beat the person who was number one in the school, even though I had never run hurdles before. I had the second best time of any schoolboy in the whole city of Philadelphia in high and low hurdles. We used to go to track meets and had a traditional rivalry with Bartram and West Philadelphia high schools.

There was one meet at Bartram High where I was the lead-off for the hurdle relay. There were four men to a team, each had to run 120 yards of high hurdles. All our school supporters were there and there was quite a crowd to cheer us on, including the usual bunch of pretty girls among the spectators.

The starting shot was fired and we were off. I was over the first hurdle like a bullet and then, on the second one, the worst thing that could have happened, happened. I hit the top of the hurdle and knocked it over, and down I went with it. We used to run on cinders so I was hurt quite badly with blood everywhere—in fact I still have the scar. It looked like we would lose, and if we didn't qualify for the relay we wouldn't have a chance of winning the whole meet.

Just then the adrenaline kicked in and I got up and started running again. The crowd was going crazy which spurred me on. I was running faster and faster, not even feeling the pain in my leg, and I gradually caught up to the others in the race, finished the 120 yards, and tapped the next man on the shoulder so that we could continue the relay. I had made it. I collapsed by the side of the track. We went on to win the relay and the whole meet, but only by a few points. If we had dropped out of the relay we never would have won.

To my shame at the time, I did not graduate from high school with the rest of my class and had to repeat several subjects in order to get my high school diploma. I had spent too much time having fun and now I had to pay the price. This I did in the evenings at Temple Prep, not wanting to go back to Overbrook. After all, I had an image to maintain.

Already, before leaving Overbrook in 1960, I had begun to work and earn a living. By the time I was 17, I was working in a pharmacy. My entrance into the employment of Claude Klinger Clark, owner of the drugstore at 5700 Haddington Street, was not the usual one, however.

I went to buy something at the drugstore one day and it was really crowded with people milling around looking for things. So I started helping them find what they were looking for, pointing things out on the shelves and so on. Mr. Clark, "Doc" as we used to call him, noticed that and he was impressed, so he asked me if I would like to work there. As it happened, I was looking for a job, although that hadn't been my intention in helping out.

I started work as a Pharmaceutical Distribution Manager (which meant I was a clerk) and later Claude advanced me to a real management position where I had to open the store, and when he went on vacation I would be in charge of opening and locking up and other such activities which required a higher level of responsibility than that of a mere clerk.

He started me off at $50 a week which was a lot of money then, so I could afford nice clothes. My dad had recently bought a new, white '59 Chevy with big fins, and because he also had a truck that he would use, he let me drive the Chevy. So I became the guy with the white Chevy.

Those were the days. Years later, Claude Klinger Clark appeared at my murder trial, a character witness for the defense. He was questioned by Mr. Della Porta, one of the two lawyers assigned to defend me.

Q: Among these friends and acquaintances, what was his reputation for being an honest citizen?

A: Always had the feeling that it was very outstanding.

Q: What was his reputation for being a truthful citizen?

A: I've had that feeling because I had to depend on truth and honesty.

Q: How about his reputation for being a peaceful, loving, law-abiding citizen?

A: He had occasions to—you know, customers come in and become irritable. He could pacify them. He seemed to be very nice with the customers.

Judge Lagakos then asked:

Q: Do you know what his reputation was among the people who knew him for being a peaceful and law-abiding citizen?

A: All the ones that I would talk to—you know, I would check with the customers and say, "How do you like Vaughan?" And they always spoke very highly of him.

Mr. Della Porta tried to continue this line of questioning.

Q: Aside from his reputation among all the people that you knew knew him, how did you yourself find him as an honest, law-abiding good guy?

MR. CZAP: Objected to.

JUDGE NIX: Sustained. It is the reputation that is relevant for this purpose.

Q: Would you, Doc, be disposed today to hire Vaughan as your employee or your assistant or anything that you could trust him with?

MR. CZAP: Objected to.

JUDGE NIX: Sustained.

MR. DELLA PORTA: From the reputation that he enjoys in the community, will you trust him with your life?

MR. CZAP: Objected to.

JUDGE NIX: Sustained.

But that was much later. For now I was the guy in the white Chevy; the 17-year-old whom the girls used to come and check out; the young man who looked and dressed as if he had just stepped off the cover of *GQ;* the ambitious young man with a tremendous ability to focus his efforts and achieve the things he set out to achieve.

Then one day, into the drugstore walked Beverly.

CHAPTER THREE

... *the wedding was turned into mourning and the voice of their musicians into a funeral dirge.*

(1 Maccabees 9:41)

Beverly Gray was 14 years old. She was 5' 8" and had been that tall since she was 12. This in itself posed certain problems. Children can be cruel and she was subjected to more than her fair share of ridicule on account of her height. Her parents, however, had taught her to be proud of herself and she walked tall.

Bev was 14 when she and her friends first used to come to the drugstore where I worked. They would act nonchalant while in the store and then start giggling as soon as they walked out.

But to me, Beverly Gray was not just a silly, giggling girl. She thought she was tall and lanky and skinny, but I thought she was beautiful. I had had a lot of other girlfriends but Beverly was the first young lady I was ever involved with where my heart would skip a beat, and where I felt real love. In fact my heart skipped a beat the first time I saw her in the pharmacy. She was a very attractive, well dressed, pretty girl.

Not all pre-arranged matches are a failure from the start.

Mrs. Gray was concerned that her daughter had no one to escort her to the junior high school hop. Her maternal eye had also noticed the young man at Clark's drug store. So she called Mrs. Booker, wondering if I would be willing to accompany Beverly to the dance. The date was arranged.

Beverly remembers that her reaction was mixed. On the one hand she was annoyed that her mother had arranged a date for her and she acted annoyed. On the other hand she was excited at the thought of going out with a 17-year-old boy while all her friends were going to the dance with boys from the junior high school—boys that they saw every day.

The dance was a great success and we had a wonderful time. I asked Mrs. Gray if I could take her daughter out again and Beverly's mother was thrilled. We would go to the movies, play tennis, go to museums together, and spend time with each other's families.

I remember going to New Jersey with her family and staying with them, and I recall the time we went to see *Psycho* on the Boardwalk back in 1959. Beverly was petrified and she held me tightly...it was wonderful!

We became fast friends. Our relationship brought the two families together and they became quite close. As the relationship blossomed, everyone, including Bev and I, assumed that we would get married in due course. To me, Mrs. Gray was like a surrogate mother and I spent a great deal of time with the Gray family. To Beverly, the future was clear.

> When you're sixteen and you really care for someone and you think that person really cares for you, you think it's going to be like Cinderella and it's going to last forever. I seriously thought that Vaughan and I would marry and have the house with the white picket fence and the 2.5 kids. I really did. I sat all day in school and wrote his name on my books.

We talked about the future. I realized that he was older and I was still young, but we talked about becoming Mr. and Mrs. and the things we would do and the type of children we would have—those silly things you talk about when you're children and you're in love: the wedding and all that.

If only life were that simple. Before too long, another factor entered the equation.

I first met Annabelle (Angie) Banks when I was 17. At that time I was still going out with Beverly.

One day my friend Alex and I, both in our three-piece suits, went to a coffee house called the Amber Glass. This was at the tail end of the beat era and the coffee houses were where the nonconformist and artist types—the beatniks—would go and they played jazz and chess and so on. Angie was a waitress there and she was a very attractive girl. She had a long braid, high cheekbones, and very pretty eyes. I thought she looked like an Indian and later I called her my Indian princess.

At first we didn't pay much attention to each other. I think Alex had his eye on her more than I did. But Alex and I started going to the coffee house regularly and Angie and I became interested in each other. Then we exchanged telephone numbers and I started to go and visit her.

My new interest was not a particularly popular one with my family, or with Beverly's. My sister Putie was not very happy about it, as she recalled much later.

I'll never forget him saying he met an Indian princess—his Indian princess, who was later his wife, Angie. I was feeling sad inside because I always thought Beverly was supposed to be his wife, and the Indian princess, or anybody else,

was not supposed to be in the way. But those
were just my thoughts....

Hers seemed to be the general opinion at home. Beverly
was 16 when I told her that I was seeing someone from the
coffee house. She was terribly hurt. She had never before in
our relationship felt threatened by any other girl, but Angie
was an older woman and Beverly felt she just couldn't compete.

Soon after our initial meeting, Angie's mother died. I
wanted to help console her through her grief.

She really took it hard and we spent a lot of time together
when she was mourning. I don't think the original attraction
was sexual. Here was this young lady who was crying a lot
and seemed to be depressed; so I would take her out and we
would do things together and we became closer and closer.
As a result, of course, I was attracted to her; but also she felt
better when she was with me. She didn't focus so much on
the death of her mother. We started seeing each other a lot.

I wasn't looking at breaking up with Beverly. I was still
very much in love with her. I began to lead a double life,
going out with Angie and Beverly at the same time.

I separated myself more and more from the church. My
friends were no longer there and I was much more interested
in going to parties at the weekend than I was in going to
church. This put me beyond the reach of the only real source
of moral guidance which might have helped me to straighten
out my life.

I thought I had the best of everything: an older, more
sophisticated young woman to satisfy one side of me—Angie
was three years older than me—plus the younger, loyal
Beverly with the bright smile and wonderful personality
whom I thought I would eventually marry. Not that marriage
was really on my mind. I had a whole life ahead of me and I
wasn't planning to settle down yet. In my immaturity I didn't

see what this double life would do to Beverly or Angie. It was the cool thing to do and I was thinking of myself.

Although she and I continued to see each other, Beverly would avoid meeting Angie.

By its very nature, this arrangement could not go on indefinitely. One day it came to a dramatic end. I was sitting in the living room at home talking to Beverly and my mother when the phone rang. I got up to answer it and it was Angie.

"I'm going to have a baby," she said.

I don't know what I said, but I was in shock when I put down the phone. I walked back into the room and I must have looked startled. I told them what Angie had said.

Beverly didn't have anything to say at the time. But this was a terrible time for her, as she explained much later.

> I could have died. I was just so totally upset. I can remember vividly when he called us to tell us that his father said that he had to get married. I was downstairs in the kitchen and I handed the phone to my mother and I can remember going upstairs and just crying, crying, and crying.
>
> After that I remember the talk between my mother and Mrs. Booker because they shared a love for Vaughan and they both hurt for him. I recall the two women talking about it and then just hoping that things would work out okay. I knew that he was such a decent guy that he would probably stay in it regardless of what happened.

Later, we would all discover that there never was a baby. Beverly feels certain that Angie was pretending to be pregnant just to get me to marry her. My mother won't commit herself.

One of Angie's sisters claims that this story about Angie being pregnant was something that Angie and I invented so that I could dodge the draft. This was also inferred by Ivan Czap, Assistant District Attorney, at my trial in 1970. He was cross-examining Dr. Alikakos, a psychiatrist who was giving evidence about me.

Q: Doctor, the information received from him [the defendant] was that which he volunteered to you; there was no, let us say, cross-examination that was made of any of the items that he volunteered to you?

A: Yes, that is correct, as any psychiatric examination is an evaluation of the individual and not an effort to determine the outside significances apart from the interview.

Q: Did you make any determination to determine whether in truth there was any truth to his statement that he married this woman because she said she was pregnant?

A: No, I did not.

Q: Did he not tell you that he was subject to the draft and that he married her at the age of 18 so as not to get in the draft?

A: He did not tell me this.

Q: Did he not tell you that he was not in the service and was not called up?

A: I knew he had not been in the service.

Q: Did he not tell you that he was not in the service because he was married and had a family?

A: I don't recall his saying that.

The questions beg the answers and Mr. Czap clearly wants the court to believe that I married Angie in order to dodge the draft. The prosecution never backed this up with any evidence, however.

Angie's sister, Geraldine, told a reporter later, "I never had the impression that that [her being pregnant] is why they got married. We planned the wedding. If she was supposed to be pregnant, I didn't know it, and I'm sure she would have told me."

Nobody else who was involved seems to doubt that Angie's announcement of her pregnancy was the direct cause of the our matrimony.

Looking back on it, there wasn't any draft situation for me to dodge and even if there had been, I would have been quite happy to go into the service anyway. If I had merely wanted to dodge the draft, I could have married Beverly. It just wasn't an issue.

But to this day I don't believe that Angie was just pretending to be pregnant. I am sure that she genuinely thought she was. And I did too.

I remember the phone call. She said, "I'm going to have a baby," and it was as if the wind had been knocked out of me. In those days a child born out of wedlock was an "illegitimate" child. It was something that you just didn't do. Abortion wasn't even considered an option at that time. My parents had always told me that if I got a girl pregnant, I would have to marry her. But here I was, just 18, still finishing up high school at nights while I worked at the pharmacy during the day. Marriage was the last thing on my agenda at that point.

But the catch here is that at 18, with the sort of home life which I had where I would want to be away from the house as much as possible, this could be an opportunity to get away from home. In a way there was a certain excitement and a challenge to it as well as a feeling of relief. I really can't say that this was all negative as it was also an opportunity.

I don't think I was in love with Angie. I was still in love with Beverly and it was a terrible internal struggle. I do believe that Angie really thought she was pregnant. She went to the doctor and was being treated for pregnancy. She was on medication and she had morning sickness and she looked pregnant.

We didn't find out until later after we were married, when the nine months came and went with no baby and the doctor said there had never been a baby. Until that time we both thought that there was a child on the way and we had no reason to believe otherwise. She was large, she looked pregnant and she felt pregnant. She did want to have a child and I've read about what they call "psychological pregnancies" where women go through all the symptoms including enlargement.

But I wasn't ready for marriage. I was still a child. Although I tried to give the appearance of being a suave, sophisticated guy, I was still immersed in my insecurities. I didn't have an inkling of who I was. I was 18. I was still Giggle. I didn't know how to face problems or my own feelings.

As I look back on the whole thing there were so many mixed messages I was getting, even from my own parents—it was really confusing. Because of my lack of sophistication and maturity I tended to take everything at face value, as children do. If the girl's pregnant, you have to get married, even if you're 18. Angie didn't object to getting married. I think she was happy.

Ready or not, just a couple of months after the announcement that she was pregnant, March 18th, 1961 saw Angie and me standing before the altar at Angie's Baptist church, she in a white wedding gown and me in a blue suit, both saying "I do" to vows that would later make liars out of both of us.

But for a time, life was rosy for the newlyweds. Beverly had gone off to college and I didn't hear from her again for many years, although we are still good friends to this day.

For a month or two we lived with Angie's brother, Leon, in South Philadelphia. Then we moved into an apartment in West Philadelphia, paying $44 a month in rent. I was still going to Temple Prep in the evenings to finish up my high school education, and was working at the pharmacy during the day.

My mother and Angie attended my graduation from Temple Prep. I moved on from my job at the pharmacy to get a merchandising job with P. Lorillard, the tobacco company. Along with that came a salary of $100 a month, a company car and an expense account. This was my first taste of corporate America, and it tasted good. I was on the way to great success, or so I felt.

Angie's discovery that she was not pregnant came as something of a relief to me. I certainly do not recall consciously resenting the fact that the reason for our hasty marriage turned out to have been a false one. Later on, when the marriage was in trouble, I began to see it differently and to feel that I had been trapped into marrying.

But for the first three years married life was blissful. We had a lot of fun. I bought a little Izetta, the kind of car that opens up in the front—it used to get 50 miles to the gallon. I bought a large novelty key and stuck it on top so it looked like a toy. We would go out to places like New York.

We were partying and running from place to place. I used to hang out with Angie's brother Leon. As a matter of fact I spent a lot of time with her family. We did a lot of things together. Leon owned some land in New Jersey and we used to go out there. We used to watch baseball together and drink a lot of beer.

Then Angie really did get pregnant and I took on a second job, back at the pharmacy with "Doc" Clark, to supplement the income from Lorillard. I also decided to go to college and enrolled at St. Joseph's in Philadelphia.

Working a full time job, studying three evenings a week and then working at the pharmacy on those nights when there were no classes, I was out of the house much of the time. Angie wanted me at home. She knew where I was so she didn't think that I might be out with someone else; she just wanted me home with her.

From my point of view, I was the head of the family so I would decide what I would do and what we would do. This was the macho way. There was no discussion—no real attempt to reconcile diverging views.

I was the man of the house and this was what I was going to do. I didn't even consider Angie's feelings really. I was on a mission. My attitude was that this was how I was going to fulfill my goals. The way things went then, or at least the way I thought they went, was you didn't negotiate with your wife; you told your wife what you were going to do. That was the way real men did it.

And I needed to be a real man which I thought involved being in control and avoiding uncomfortable situations. There had been so much violence in my own childhood that I shied away from arguments and when they got too heated, my solution was just to walk out. So if there were arguments I would walk away rather than resolve them—a chronic failing I can admit to freely in looking back on the relationship. These things are far easier to see, however, in retrospect.

On the 25th of January, 1964, Kimberly Booker was born. Of course life became a lot more serious then. We moved downstairs into a larger, 2-bedroom apartment, still at 4441 Chestnut Street. Our rent went up from $44 a month to $47.

"When the pressure came down and it came time to be a real father and a real husband, to go to work every day, and life wasn't that exciting, carefree type of life any more, he couldn't deal with it." That is how Angie's sister, Geraldine Williams, saw it, as she told a reporter in an interview much later. "He rejected it. He ran."

The next and final period of the our lives together, from the birth of Kim to the death of Angie, seems to be the least clear. Different people tell different stories. The one voice that might be able to really help clarify the events which led, step by step, gradually downhill to eventual total catastrophe, is not here anymore. It was silenced forever in that very catastrophe.

I remember a gradual decay in my own life, not just the marriage.

After Kim was born we had an added responsibility. I did not want my wife to work. Why? Because I grew up that way. The husband worked and the wife stayed home and took care of the family.

We could have lived a basic life with what I was making at Lorillard—$100 a week was a lot of money in 1964. I was even able to go out and buy a brand new Mustang. The job at the pharmacy added an extra $50 per week. Then I went to work selling insurance for Prudential and I was making $217 a week and taking home $196. We also moved to a duplex and the rent almost doubled to $75 a month. We wanted to buy a house and I also needed money to pay for my college tuition fees.

Angie didn't want me to be away from home so much. It upset her. I remember one night I had a report to write—it was a business brief that I had to put together for business law—and when I came home she was so angry with my being out that she threw all my books down the stairs. I was in night school and wouldn't get home until 10:30 or 11:00 at night. There would be incidents once or twice a week.

My response was to come home later and later. I would find something to do that kept me out of the house. I loved to shoot pool and I would go out to a local tavern and shoot pool and drink beer. It wasn't to get back at her. It was just my way of escaping. I didn't have to confront it or deal with it. Again, it was my immaturity.

Kim was my heart. My pride and joy. As she got older I remember I would come home and she would be there saying, "Daddy, Daddy," and that was just too much for me. I became more responsible and started coming home, but then the arguments would start again. It was the same thing over and over. I wasn't going out with other women at that time so that didn't enter into it. I never came home smelling like perfume. If anything it was cigarette smoke from the bars. I used to shoot pool for a beer. Sometimes I'd win and someone would buy the beers and I would get bombed from drinking them all. It was fun.

It was certainly much easier dealing with that than going home and listening to a nagging wife. I'd come home drunk—not staggering, but certainly impaired—a couple of times a week. I still had to go to college. I did my assignments and I worked. Then it got to a point where I would drink and be hung over and I would be late for work. I had been the type who, if I was supposed to be there at 8:15, would be there at 8:00. Now the drinking was taking its toll. I began coming in to work hung over.

When the opportunity came for me to go and work for Prudential, selling insurance, I didn't hesitate. They were paying twice what I was earning at Lorillard and there was the chance to make even more in commissions.

I was with Prudential for about a year, in '65 and '66. Selling insurance, especially the family plans I was working on, really requires night work. I spent a lot of evenings out working. Almost every evening I had to set up appointments. But it paid off because even in my first couple of months I was receiving all kinds of awards for production.

During this time Angie's accusations of my being out with other women started with some frequency. Previously, when I was studying and working at the drug store in the evenings, my nights were accounted for and there was no problem. Even though she hadn't liked my being away from home, she had no reason to accuse me of being out with other women because she knew she could always call the drug store or call the school.

When I started working for the insurance company, however,

I didn't give her a list of all my clients and where I would be at what time so there was a much greater frequency of my being out and unaccounted for. And I was also staying out more often, even after work.

At first I had this really strong moral attitude: I wasn't going to cheat on my wife. But I suppose I got sick of being accused so I said, "Hell, I am going to do it."

There were a couple of times when I did have sex with other women. There was no one that I saw regularly. They were one night stands. Angie never knew about these incidents. There was no steady person in my life. It was when I would be staying at a hotel away from home for work reasons that I got involved. There were no more than three or four times in our entire relationship.

I also came to distrust Angie. There was one time, for example, when she took our car one night and didn't come home all night. I had to go to work the next morning for the Prudential and she wasn't back. I was alone with Kim. I didn't even want to know where she had been. I called her parents and she wasn't there. I never did find out where she went that night.

Careerwise, I then made a serious mistake. I left Prudential where I was earning good money and went to work for an organization called Sales Consultants who turned out to be, basically, headhunters. There was a promise of more money but it was an empty promise. After a while I realized my mistake and asked Prudential if I could come back. Uncharacteristically, probably because of my previous success with them, they agreed. But I now had a serious failure—Sales Consultants—to live with and during my second stint with Prudential I didn't perform nearly as well as I had done previously.

I started drinking more. I wasn't making appointments. I wasn't meeting my goals. It was as if I was a whole different person the second time I worked for Prudential.

Also by this time I had accumulated substantial debts from the time I was working with Sales Consultants and not making enough money there. I couldn't pay our bills because there were no commissions coming in against the money I was drawing. And no money coming into the house created additional problems. The relationship with Angie became more strained.

Even in terms of my appearance I was going downhill. I wouldn't shave as closely. I felt things crumbling around me. I just didn't know how to handle failure after all that time of being up. I was 24 or 25 and I was beginning to feel a sense of failure for the first time and I didn't know what to do about it.

The sexual side of our relationship also dwindled so I was shocked when Angie told me she was pregnant again. I almost passed out. We didn't have a lot of money and we hadn't been to bed that much. We were living under the same roof and sleeping in the same bed, but we weren't living closely together.

The fights were fairly frequent. Unlike me, Angie drank very little, but sometimes she would get angry and jump on me and once or twice I slapped her. I hated physical violence but I would suppress my feelings and this built up inside. I would just ignore her, which only made things worse. I didn't see her with other men, but I didn't trust her either. Sometimes the fights would contain the "I'm going to find me a real man" type of dialogue. Angie really knew how to push my buttons, and one of these buttons was my own insecurity. We had stopped going out and doing things together and there was no real affection between us anymore.

For a short while when Vaughan, Jr., was born the relationship improved. I had a son and this was something to feel good about. But this did not last long because nothing had been resolved between us.

In 1967 I recall things were so bad that Angie tried to take her own life. She swallowed a large number of pills and had to go to hospital to get her stomach pumped.

Then I was fired from Prudential for poor performance.

After leaving the company, I began working for a fledgling business called Lavender House, making and selling hair products for African-Americans. It involved traveling to Chester every day. I saw it as a way of getting myself back on my feet. If it went well, I could have a position in the business because I had helped it get off the ground.

I was drinking almost every night, usually beer and wine, and this was getting worse. I'd be out shooting pool and I might start at 7:00 P.M. How long does it take to drink a beer while shooting pool, waiting in turn? When I'd win a game I'd get two beers instead of one. This would continue until 11:00, 12:00, 1:00 in the morning. So that would be more than 10 beers a night. I would come home impaired and I would be more verbally aggressive and I'd argue more. I'd try and come home late so that Angie would be asleep and I wouldn't have to argue with her. I would usually end up going to sleep on the sofa.

My sister Delphine saw another side of the relationship. She used to spend time with Angie, call her on the phone, have her over with the kids and listen to her.

> I would say it was a typical young husband and wife syndrome—the time of trying to get used to each other. They were young and didn't really know how to deal with relationships as far as marriage is concerned. If things don't go your way you get mad, you leave the house—husbands or wives—and Angie loved him so much, she really did. She loved him so much she couldn't function because they hassled a lot and he would leave the house and this would make her unable to function.
>
> She wasn't the greatest housekeeper in those

days and when you're young you don't care about washing the dishes and all this kind of stuff if you're unhappy. So it didn't help when he would come home from work and maybe dinner wasn't cooked even though she was home all day—because she wasn't working at the time— and he had to help get dinner or whatever.

He would bring her over to my place to wash clothes and then he would be gone a long time. I mean, how long does it take to wash clothes? But he would come back at maybe two or three o'clock in the morning and it was that kind of thing that just got on her nerves. It was a matter of, "Where is he? Why isn't he home with me?"

At the time he was selling insurance and then he would say he would go swimming some- where—Temple's pool or somewhere—but who has a pool open at two or three o'clock in the morning?

Then he would drink and that didn't help the cause. I think that was a big factor because he would have his moments of drinking and when people drink they're not always nice.

Whenever we were there they were always laughing and joking but when people would leave them I don't know how he was.

I would talk to Angie at times, woman to woman, and she would complain about his not being home with her, but I really can't say how he treated her.

Then there is the voice of Geraldine Williams, Angie's sis- ter, with her view of the relationship expressed in an inter- view in 1993.

They were not together [at the time of the murder]. He had left and was living with someone. She was really having a hard time making ends meet, with the babies. She had just gotten a job at Strawbridge & Clothier in Philadelphia.

He was very abusive to her. He threatened her with that bow and arrow, the same one he killed her with, before that. I think he threw a knife at her at one time. We tried to get her to leave, but she loved him.

Her father had loaned them money for the car and Vaughan forfeited on the loan.

They'd go through periods where you couldn't separate them and then periods where they were having problems.

As far as I know he was living with another woman.

I know he didn't want the second child. He didn't pay much attention to Tawney [Tawney was the nickname given to Vaughan, Jr. when he went to live with Angie's sister, Alice].

Even if she was seeing someone else, they were separated. If that was the case it seems to me, I'm her sister, I think I would have known if she was seeing someone.

The way I saw it she wanted to have this other baby to bring them closer together.

Angie's niece Brenda was spending quite a lot of time with her aunt during the period before the murder. She also spoke to reporter Jim Naughton.

When I was there somebody would always call looking for him and they would hang up on me when I answered the phone.

When he left she had no way of supporting herself. She was trying to get her life together. She
had resigned herself to the fact that they were separated.

She would never want to leave him but he was
abusive to her. He had threatened her with that
bow and arrow so many times. Somebody said he
had burned her with matches.

I used to stay over while she worked. I didn't
live with her, I just took care of the kids for her
while she worked. I don't know what happened
but she got real depressed and she couldn't work
anymore. She told me I could have her job
because she couldn't make it and she couldn't
work anymore, so she stayed home with the kids.

The times I had gone out with other women were in the
past and I was certainly not living with someone else at the
time. As for threatening Angie with the bow and arrow,
throwing a knife at her, burning her with matches, these
things are fiction, the products of angry minds—justifiably
angry, since I took Angie away from them forever—but fiction nevertheless. I don't know where the idea that we were
separated came from.

Finally there is the trial itself. Dr. Louis Alikakos was a
psychiatrist who had examined me on two occasions and was
brought as a witness for the defense at the trial.

Under Mr. Czap's cross-examination of Dr. Alikakos, further "facts" emerged, but none of this was backed up by any
evidence—just implication.

Q: What specifically did he seek approbation for from his
   wife and did not find?

A: As the breadwinner of the home.

Q: Was he indeed the full and only breadwinner? Sir, did

you know whether she was employed on other occasions beside the two or three months before the death?

A: I don't know that for a certainty.

Q: How much was his income except what he told you with respect to the Prudential Insurance Company?

A: What his income was at what time?

Q: At any time except for that period of time when he said he was making over $200 a week?

A: He made $60 per week draw on his next job, which was at the personnel agency, Sales Consultants, in 1966. He then returned to Prudential for a year and his wife again struggled with him. So I am not sure when you indicated before that he was fired whether it was his first period of employment with Prudential that he was fired or whether it was his second period of employment with Prudential.

Q: Doctor, specifically, did he not tell you or did he tell you that he had borrowed a considerable sum of money from the Household Finance a few months or within a year or so of the killing?

A: No, he did not tell me that.

Q: Did he or did he not tell you that that loan was made possible because of the action of his wife's relatives in cosigning for him?

A: He did not, but I did not ask him for that kind of information, either.

Q: And you did not then determine how low the income was which he had during those years when he might have been borrowing money from the Household Finance?

A: I have that during that time that he told me that his average income was $100 a week while he was working for the Lavender House.

Q: Did he or did he not tell you whether or not he had a car?

A: I did not ask him whether he had a car.

Q: Did he or did he not tell you what his hobbies were and whether or not they were expensive?

A: He told me he was drinking a fair amount.

Q: Was he drinking in Philadelphia or out of Philadelphia? That is, he did not limit his drinking just to the City of Philadelphia?

A: Yes.

The cross-examination, while it doesn't introduce any real evidence, does raise questions about the Booker household which are legitimate.

Later in the trial, when I was in the witness box being cross-examined by Mr. Czap, further information concerning our family life emerged:

Q: I am going to ask you a few more questions with respect to your family finances.

You said that you had discussions about economic problems with your wife, or so you stated in your statement to the detective. Is it true that your wife also worked a number of times during the course of your married life?

A: She worked a couple of times, yes.

Q: And the last place she worked was at Strawbridge and Clothier's?

A: That is correct.

Q: And she began working there in August of 1967?

A: I think that is correct.

Q: Do you know whether she worked full-time or part-time?

A: She was working part-time.

Q: With a salary in August of $26.63, would that be approximately correct, for at least one of the weeks that she was working there—as gross pay?

A: I don't recall what her pay was, to be honest with you.

Q: You know she worked there until the weekend before she died?

A: Yes.

Q: Were you actually living at home at the time or were you living in Chester?

A: No, I was living at home.

Q: Where were your clothes?

A: At my house.

Q: All of them?

A: All that I had, yes.

Q: Did you not during some of your married life with Annabelle Booker also live in Chester where he [your employer] lived?

A: No.

Q: So there were a number of occasions when you would not come home overnight?

A: Right.

Q: Wasn't that part of your problem with your wife that you would not come home every night?

A: I guess you could say this would make sense.

Q: Wasn't another problem the fact that you would drink outside and you would be drinking alone, at least not with her, and not come home?

A: This is true.

Q: I take it you were aware then that she did work for some garage up around 40th and Walnut or 40th and Market where she was a bookkeeper at a gas station?

A: Yes.

Q: Were you aware also that she worked for a while for Fox Weiss at 12th and Chestnut in April, 1967?

A: Yes, she worked there for a little while.

Q: Were you aware also that for quite a while she was selling dresses and other women's garments?

A: From the home, yes.

Q: Is it also true that in 1965 you had domestic problems, that would be about four years after your marriage, and she applied to the Family Service of Philadelphia and you received word from them?

A: When was this, please?

Q: In 1965, sometime in the summer or early fall of 1965?

A: I don't remember that.

Judge Nix asked for clarification:

Q: Forget the date for a moment. Do you recall your wife going to and seeking the help of the Family Service and their contacting you?

A: I think we did discuss this matter at one time, yes, but I never remember hearing anything from them.

The questions by Mr. Czap resumed.

Q: Are you aware that the Family Service of Philadelphia makes a charge for its services?

A: No, I wasn't aware of it.

Q: I show you a letter dated August 10, 1965, marked Commonwealth's Exhibit Number 13—

Q: Does that recall to your mind the problem you had with your wife at the time?

A: Yes.

Q: Was it concerning some woman?

A: No.

JUDGE NIX: Concerning what?

MR. CZAP: Concerning some woman.

A: No.

MR. DELLA PORTA: I object, your Honor.

MR. CZAP: What was the problem.

A: I don't remember.

JUDGE NIX: Just a moment. What is the objection?

MR. DELLA PORTA: I don't think it has any relevance to what happened in 1965, whether it was a relation with some woman or having someone to see at the Family Service.

JUDGE NIX: You introduced a great deal of testimony by this young man that he was an innocent spouse, that he had been disappointed in marriage in that his wife had failed to meet her marital obligations. Overruled. Proceed.

A: I would like to answer the question. I don't remember exactly what we were having difficulties about.

Q: I think you had better keep your voice up.

A: Right. I don't remember exactly what it was.

I don't think it was another woman, but whatever it was I remember we sat down and we discussed my wife's going to some Family Service. I gave her the money for the fee. As a matter of fact, whatever problem we had at that time, we were able to settle it among ourselves and we decided that we didn't need Family Service.

Q: So that you yourself did not go to the Family Service?

A: No. My wife and I discussed it, though, and we felt that at the time we didn't need it then, that we could solve our own problems.

Q: As a matter of fact you declined to go. Thereafter she asked you to go and after you received notice you decided to try to adjust it between yourselves?

A: We discussed it. We discussed this matter and we decided together that it was not necessary that we involve anyone else.

Q: Do you recall receiving notes from your wife concerning your attention to other women?

A: I remember receiving letters from my wife concerning what she thought were my attentions to other women.

Q: I'm going to show you a letter in handwriting, the top of Page 1 so numbered. It starts out, "Vaughan," V-a-u-g-h-a-n and winds up with Page12 with the signature Angie, A-n-g-i-e.

A: Yes.

Judge Lagakos then proceeded to question me further about my drinking and about women.

Q: Mr. Booker, while counsel are examining the letter, let me ask you: You testified that you drank sometimes with people in the evening and your wife was not in the group or the party. Now, approximately how many times in 1967 up to October did this take place? About how many times were you out drinking in that year and your wife was not present?

A: Quite a few times, Your Honor.

Q: I beg your pardon?

A: There were quite a few times.

Q: Well, please give me some indication of approximately how many times. How many weekends or evenings during the weekend did this happen in 1967, 30, 40, 20? How many?

A: Well, maybe sometimes a couple of times during the week and on the weekends I would go to maybe the neighborhood bar, shoot pool and drink. My wife would not be there.

Q: Now, approximately how many times on these occasions would there be women present, other than your wife, with whom you were drinking?

A: You mean personally women with me?

Q: With you or the group with which you were that evening?

A: Well, in most of the places where I drank women were allowed to drink there also, but I never went to a place where I actually took someone and was sitting down drinking with them instead of my wife.

Q: Did you ever during that year of the previous year leave with women—leave that place that you were at with women? Try to think well.

A: There could have been times when I left, because we were leaving together, or something like that, but that would be it.

Q: On about how many occasions was it that you left because you knew the women well?

A: There weren't many occasions like that.

Q: About how many in 1967?

A: Oh, maybe one or two, because the neighborhood bar isn't too far from where I live. If they were going home and I was going that way I would just walk down the street on my way home.

Q: Did you take them home?

A: No.

Q: To their home?

A: No.

Q: You just walked down the street after you left the bar with them?

A: Because I was on my way home, yes.

Q: Mr. Booker, did you have an occasion to be with women, other than your wife, during the evenings?

A: I have drank with other women before, yes.

Q: By arrangement? By arrangement did you meet women at the bar, other than your wife, knowing that the woman would be there and she would know you would be there that particular evening?

A: I can't think of any such pre-scheduled appointments, no.

Q: Was there not indeed a car accident which you were involved in, where there was another lady passenger?

A: I remember now, yes.

Q: Well, this lady who is driving in her car when the accident happened, how did you meet her in Chester? You

testified that you were in the car, there was an accident—you were in her car, is that right?

A: Yes.

Q: How did it happen that you met her?

A: It was purely coincidental. I was in this bar drinking.
They had a pool table. I was shooting pool and I sat
down. We started talking. I found out she was from
Phillie and I told her I was from Philadelphia and she
offered to give me a lift back home to Philadelphia. I
have never seen the woman before in my life. I didn't
know her.

Q: It would appear to me that you frequented tap rooms
and neighborhood bars during the week and at the
weekends with a degree of regularity, is that correct?

A: Yes, unfortunately at that time I did.

Q: But you never took your wife—

A: Yes, I did.

Q: —to any such place?.

A: Yes, I have.

Q: In 1967?

A: In 1967, yes.

Q: Well, percentagewise how many times—what percentage of the times that you were out drinking at these
places was your wife with you?

A: I would say it would be a small percentage of the time,
Your Honor.

Q: How small?

A: Five percent. Not that small. Maybe at the rate I was
going drinking and going down I would say that if we
want to use it on a hundred per cent basis, I would say
maybe 25 percent.

Q: Your Honor, the Commonwealth suggests that it (the twelve-page letter which the lawyers had been reading) is a letter from his wife Angie written to the defendant, undated, apparently in 1967, at the time when she says that Vaughan Jr. was just learning to walk and had just walked halfway across the floor apparently the day she wrote the letter, referring to certain marital difficulties, referring also to his interest in other women.

Is it true that your wife in the last few months of your married life complained about your staying out at night?

A: Yes, she did.

Judge Nix interrupted to ask:

Q: Excuse me just a moment. Was there any basis to that complaint?

A: To me staying out, yes.

Mr. Czap picked up the line of questioning:

Q: Were you indeed separated from your wife on several days, at least, in 1967?

A: I wouldn't say for several days, no. Maybe a day or two.

Q: Is it true that your wife complained because after you would have normal relations with her you would then not return the next day but stayed out overnight the next day?

A: This may have occurred on one or two occasions, but it was not routine.

Q: Is it true that she complained about your attentions to other women during 1967?

A: It is true that she thought that I was giving my attentions to other women.

Q: Is it true that you told her that you had brought other women to the apartment?

A: No.

Q: Are you the father of a child by a woman other than your wife?

A: No.

Q: Did you spend money in the evenings that you would be out without her?

A: Yes, I did.

Q: Was that not a great drain on your modest financial resources?

A: Yes, it was.

Q: Was that not the subject of a considerable amount of discussion between you and your wife in 1967?

A: In 1967, yes. Prior to that this was not a problem.

Q: Is it not true that you did not cut down on your going out and drinking in 1967?

Q: That is true.

Q: Is it not true that from at least 1962 that you have been borrowing money from—particularly from Household Consumer Discount Company using the credit of her father, Sandy Banks?

A: That is true. I made the payments on my Triumph TR3, which is an automobile, and I paid the loan back in half the time.

Q: Is it also true that the last loan that was made was one which you did not pay back?

A: Yes. This was during the period of decline and I wasn't very responsible with any of my debts at that time.

Q: And that loan was for a few thousand dollars—over $2,000?

A: I don't think so. I don't think they would extend a loan over a certain amount....

Debts, fights, staying out, drinking, accusations about other women, a car being repossessed, losing a job, financial problems. This was a far cry from the earlier successes I had experienced. Certainly not the way I had envisioned my life turning out when I had looked to the future in my younger days.

The scene was set for the worst act I would commit in my entire life. What would it take to push our marriage over the edge?

...he has shed blood, and he shall be cut off from the people.

(Leviticus 17:4)

There is no generally accepted account of the murder. The only part of it that everyone involved—police, judges, family, medical examiner, priests, psychiatrists, and I—all seem to agree about, is that on the morning of Monday, October 23, 1967, I, Vaughan Booker, fired five arrows into Angie's 5'6", 107-pound body, and killed her. Some facts surrounding the murder are, to this day, vague, even to me.

One of the most important aspects of the entire crime, one which certainly helps me understand my uncharacteristic behavior that morning, was never mentioned in my statement to the police or at the trial, even though the information was known to my defense counsel and to me. In fact they advised me not to bring it up as it might do more harm than good.

Here is the "trial" account of the murder. Mr. Czap, Assistant District Attorney, in summing up in his somewhat clumsy if flamboyant style, expresses the Commonwealth's suspicions about the facts of the case:

May it please the Court, this is a classic case of a first degree murder. It is an intentional killing with premeditation. It's willful and deliberate. It is profitless for anyone to stand before the Court and say, "I did not intend to do this," when the facts are to the contrary, no more than "I don't intend to make a noise when I intend to put my hand down hard on the door or on the board."

His knowledge of the bow and arrow is just as definite and positive as his knowledge—that is the defendant's knowledge—of the history of marital disputes and the basis of them from 1965, at least when the Family Service of Philadelphia was involved, until possibly September, 1967, when he was found in a car with another woman late at night or early in the morning. It may or may not be true, but certainly it has not been proven that that was a casual meeting at a casual time for an appropriate purpose. It is just equally possible that it was not a casual meeting for a different purpose which was thwarted by his being stopped by the police. And what explanation does a husband make when he comes home at four o'clock in the morning to the first question, quite properly, "Where were you and who were you with?" Carmen may or may not be Carmen. He may really be Carmella and an entirely different person and an entirely different sex. Carmen may actually be Carmen, but he was absolutely used as a dodge. If I were to come home at four o'clock and desired my wife not to accuse me again of being out with a woman Saturday night and I had spent all Saturday night out and I am coming home so late after Sunday night it's already four o'clock in the morning, I would much rather be seen driving down with a man at four o'clock in the morning than either alone or with a woman. It's just as consistent since Carmen was well hid that this man spent Saturday night with someone else and may or may not have spent part of Saturday with Carmen and may, indeed, only have met Carmen 3:30 or quarter of four to be driven from 52nd and Vine, from the Republican Club to the 5700 block of the street that he lived on.

In any event, he himself has indicated there was an argument. He himself has indicated that there were family disputes and difficulties and some of those were economic. To almost every one of the difficulties he had to admit that he contributed more than did his wife. He is a good-looking fellow, but so was his wife good-looking. He may have tried, he may have sought approbation. I think he got approbation for precisely everything he did.

Then follows Mr. Czap's rehash of the murder, going over in considerable detail the weapon used and describing his view of how each arrow must have struck Angie's body, comparing the shooting to a hunting expedition where one might be killing a deer or a moose or a bear.

He went into how I must have carefully chosen the barbed-tip hunting arrows rather than the target arrows, taken great pains to methodically string the bow and other indications that the murder was a deliberate, premeditated affair, rather than an act of passion or a temporary "irresistible impulse" which was the term the psychiatrists had used:

I believe that she did thrash about. He said that she was in pain and agony. And I believe that the second arrow was the one that he really tried to dispense her with by shooting her out of the pain and agony by striking her right at the heart and did, but at this point she must have leaned over, or whatever it was, and the arrow went downward and missed the heart and went through the cavity. I believe that she must still have talked. She must still have said something and at that point he took the third steel-tipped arrow right through the neck, which would have silenced her forever and kept her from asking any more questions that he didn't want to answer. Right through the jugular.

Then there was the matter of the alleged attempt to strangle my son:

I have in mind to remind Your Honors that with respect to the child there should be no problem whatsoever. Lorenzo Booker is the grandfather of the child, was the one that received the boy and his testimony by stipulation is of record, that he knew that Vaughan told the officer that he had tried to strangle the boy and then his next statement is, "I checked the boy—" and I'm quoting, "I checked the boy and he was perfectly normal."

Judge Nix asked him, "What do you think is the significance of that coupled with the writing on the wall?"

That this was the great hoax which we have seen in other cases. History is full of the attempt to throw off from the scent by saying this man is absolutely insane, look what he has done, look what he tried to do to this child, isn't it horrible. Lieutenant Malcolm Kachigian, whose testimony is before the Court by stipulation, he said he checked the front bedroom and found both the son and daughter alive and apparently in good health. And then finally after two days the testimony of Mrs. Arnold said the child did not need, as far as she could determine, any care and did not have any injuries. With respect to irresistible impulse and diminished responsibility, Your Honor, I don't think they have been made out. But even if they had been made out it would still not prevent—there are other cases which is clearly the law and probably will remain so for a long while it still does not mean that it's murder less than first degree murder.

I ask Your Honors only as I would ask a jury to put yourselves on that bed in that bedroom and don't flinch at what you are thinking what is going to happen after the first arrow hit you.

The Commonwealth's contention is that this is a very clear case of first degree murder.

At the trial, my testimony paralleled my statement to the police. But the trial was three years after the murder and my memory on certain aspects of the crime was vague.

I told the Court I had left my house on Saturday following a slight argument with my wife. I went to a bar in Philadelphia and met up with two friends one named Carmen and the other unnamed, both men. We went to Carmen's house, somewhere in northeast Philadelphia, and drank. I stayed the night at Carmen's house and the next day we watched the ball game on TV and drank and went out to various clubs and drank some more.

I could not recall Carmen's last name. Nor could I state

where Carmen lived any more closely than, "It was some-where in the northeast. I don't know exactly where."

At the trial I recall Carmen driving me home in the early hours of Monday morning. I said I was drunk enough to have to concentrate to get up the stairs.

> And I went home at this point. I went into the house. My wife was awake. She asked me where I had been. I told her. An argument started because she accused me of being out with anoth-er woman. I don't know how long the argument went on. She kept accusing me about another woman. I don't know if I could go on.

When I found I couldn't continue, Judge Nix called a five-minute recess so I could have a drink of water. When court resumed Judge Nix asked me:

Q: You told us, young man, that after you returned home your wife started arguing with you and accusing you of being out with another woman. Continue from that point.

A: It's difficult to remember, because it was like a flash. I don't know what you would call it. And I no longer seemed to be like myself. It's as if I had become two people.

Q: What do you mean you had become two people?

A: It's like I was watching the other Vaughan Booker stand up there and shoot those arrows, as if I wasn't doing it myself.

Mr. Atkins then picked up the line of questioning:

Q: Vaughan, what is the next thing that you remember?

A: I don't know. I don't know whether I went to my chil-dren's bedroom and tried strangling my son. I don't know if I left the house. I don't know what happened.

I'll be perfectly honest, I don't know.

Q: Do you specifically remember anything? What is the next thing that you remember specifically?

A: I remember going to my mother's house.

I couldn't even remember firing five arrows (I remembered firing three), where they hit, writing anything on the wall in the children's room, who Carmen was or where he lived. I stated categorically that I had never had any prior intention of killing Angie and didn't remember telling the detectives who questioned me that it was something I had planned to do for a long time. I testified that I had never hunted with the bow and arrow even though I had thought about it. I couldn't stand the idea of inflicting pain on animals. I still can't to this day.

There were many questions about archery, a subject in which the judges seemed to share an almost morbid curiosity. For example, Judge Lagakos wanted to know:

Q: Let me ask you, Mr. Booker: What is the largest and the heaviest game that could be killed if the metal-tipped arrow struck with the necessary impact and force required to produce its greatest degree of effectiveness if the arrow struck a vital part of the animal's body, namely the heart? What is the largest game that could be killed?

A: An elephant. It has been done.

They established that I was an expert in the theory and practice of archery, if that was their intent.

But information about the murder itself was vague and incomplete, even concerning my feelings at the time:

Q: You must have had a very strong feeling within you to do what you did, Mr. Booker, to kill your wife, isn't that right?

A: I would imagine I did at the time, Your Honor.

Q: What was that feeling that led you to go to your home and do this? What was the feeling you said you must have had in you?

A: I don't know, Your Honor?

Q: What?

A: I don't know.

Q: You just got through saying that you must have had a very strong feeling. First of all, tell me what kind of feeling was this very strong feeling that you must have had that led you to do what you did?

A: This I don't know. This question I cannot answer, Your Honor. I wish I could answer it. I think this is something that more or less a professional person could help me with. But I don't know what the feeling was at the time.

Q: Do you remember walking up the stairs to your home? Can you remember that?

A: Yes, I can remember.

Q: What kind of a feeling did you have at that time in regard to your wife?

A: I don't think I was even thinking about my wife. It's hard to remember what I was actually thinking, but I am sure when I went into the house I didn't have any feelings whatsoever. I think my main objective at that time was to get up the steps.

Q: What do you mean by that?

A: I was pretty high.

Q: Did you love your wife at that time?

A: Yes, I did, and I still do, Your Honor, if it means anything.

Q: In spite of the arguments?

A: Yes. I don't think there was anything abnormal about the arguments. Despite the bad things that happened in our life, we did have some good times. We had a happy life, part of it. It wasn't completely miserable for both of us.

Q: And yet you selected the most lethal arrows in that quiver of over 20 arrows with the barbed tip and you used both of them, didn't you?

A: Your Honor, I cannot say that I selected these arrows.

Q: You didn't select them. All right.

Of the elusive Carmen, no trace was found. Mr. Czap called Detective Joseph Schimpf back as witness for the Commonwealth:

Q: With respect to a certain individual called Carmen, did you receive as much information from Mr. Booker about him as was given in court today, or less?

A: Less.

Q: Were you able to locate a person named Carmen?

A: No, sir.

Q: You have not located him to this date?

A: No, sir.

No one ever asked, "Did you ever try to find him?" We don't know if any effort was made.

Throughout the entire trial, I was withholding an important piece of information. I also withheld it from the detectives who questioned me. In fact, the first time I ever disclosed it at all was in talking to The Reverend Fred Powers, who was the Episcopal priest who really took an interest in me when I was at the Philadelphia Detention Center and at Holmesburg prison and later at Graterford penitentiary. This information was known to my defense counsel, when I went to trial.

I told Father Powers, for the first time, what had happened on the morning of October 23, 1967. I told him what I had been too ashamed to admit to anyone before, and what I was reluctant to say because it would only do more damage to Angie after I had already done the worst damage that could be done. This is also the way I recall the incident, 27 years later. Tears still come to my eyes when I remember the details of that tragic night and what I did to my wife and my family.

I was home all day Saturday. On Sunday I went out. I went to various clubs, which were open on Sunday, to shoot pool and drink.

I was coming home in the early hours of the morning, pretty intoxicated. On approaching my home I saw a man coming down the steps, apparently leaving our house. I went upstairs and found Angie awake, sitting on the edge of the bed, smoking a cigarette. I asked her about the man.

"Who was the dude I saw leaving?"

"What are you talking about?"

"You know what I mean. Who was he?"

"Your son's father."

It was as if I had been hit over the head with a baseball bat. You've heard the saying "see red." Well I saw red. Every possible hidden or dark emotion that I had came to the surface. I remember the flash, the anger.

I don't remember where my bow was. I had a 3-year-old child in the house so I wouldn't have left the bow and arrows lying around. I had a closet in my bedroom and they may have been in there or they could have been in the closet in the living room.

I remember stringing the bow, because it was a recurve bow and you have to lock it behind your leg to string it. An expert archer can do it in a second. I must have taken the quiver into the bedroom.

Angie was sitting on the edge of the bed smoking a cigarette in a very self-assured, cocky way, sort of goading. This is difficult for me to explain, even after so many years, because I don't want it to look like I think it was her fault.... Nothing she did could possibly justify my actions. I was jealous and angry. I held the bow in a threatening way. She said something like, "What are you going to do with that?" indicating the bow. She wasn't at all concerned that she was in jeopardy because she knew I would never do something like that. I had never beaten her up or shown that I was capable of real violence, although I had slapped her before.

I had an arrow in it now. She said something about this other person being more of a man than I was. I think that's what really did it. She challenged me. I felt emasculated. If she had cut my testicles off I probably would have felt more of a man than I did then. I was so angry. I really didn't have a thought in my mind that I was going to kill her.

I had the arrow pulled back. When you have let an arrow go you can't pull it back.

You know how an arrow sounds when it goes into a target. I remember that sound when the first arrow hit her. I'm almost certain the first one went into her neck. She didn't scream. She had a blank look. She went backward and it was like she was gagging and there was blood flowing out.

Then I didn't feel angry any more. I felt compassion. I wanted so much to take that arrow back. I wanted to hold her. The rest was pretty much panic. I didn't know what else to do but to take her out of her misery so I kept shooting her until I thought she was dead. I remember just feeling so empty and hopeless. I don't know if it was necessarily anger after the first shot. I don't know how long it took. It isn't much for an archer to hit a target and I was close. At the trial they made it look like I had carefully selected the arrows. I didn't select them. It was just another arrow.

I think I remember putting the bow down and leaving the bedroom and going to the children's bedroom which was right down the hall. At that time I intended to kill my children and myself. I have an image of going into my son's room.

My son was in his crib. Both children were asleep. They say I made it up, but this really happened. I wasn't angry with my son, I wasn't trying to kill him, I didn't know what to do. I just panicked. I picked him up and started to strangle him. She had told me my son wasn't mine so I was going to take this child...Then I remember letting go of him, almost as if my senses were coming back to me. I didn't know if he had stopped breathing or not—I didn't want to take the chance, so I did artificial respiration. I remember he opened his eyes: that's how I knew he was alive.

I thought I was going to take my own life. I hadn't gone as far as planning how I would. I do remember I didn't touch my daughter. Remember my daughter was my heart. I can still remember the love that I had for my children.

The next thing I knew I called the police. I didn't try to run. I didn't try to say some man had come into my house and killed my wife. The way I was brought up made me say: I did a terrible thing and I should pay for it. That's how I felt.

That's what I remember. There are other things I do not. I have never been able to put a face or a description to the man I saw leaving the house as I went in.

I'm sure he must have been black. I don't see why a white person would be in that area. I don't think my wife would have been involved with a white person. I don't know. I don't have a picture. I have for 27 years been trying to picture this person because after she told me, one of my first inclinations was to go and find this man. I was drunk enough to be feeling kind of sick. I didn't hear a door close. I saw him walk down the street. I know he came off those steps, walking.

People have questioned this story. I don't have any doubts now but there were times when I really had to ask myself if there really was another person because there's no image. Sometimes I still try to see that face.

People said, "It may not exist because you can't tell us who it was." So certainly it created doubt in my own mind when I had people saying things like that to me—psychiatrists. I told the psychiatrist later and he was trying to tell me I had made it up. But my question is: Why did I feel so relieved about telling this [to Father Powers] if I made it up? Why should this be a burden lifted from my shoulders?

For a couple of years I was tortured by conjuring up images of a man sleeping with my wife, being the father of my son. But after I told Father Powers I didn't see those images anymore.

After I got to know him he asked me to tell him everything and I did. Things began to really change in my life after that.

There are some obvious questions that have to be asked. If there was another man and Angie used this to taunt me before I killed her, then I had very definite grounds to claim that there was legal provocation and have the murder reduced to voluntary manslaughter. There is absolutely no mention of another man in the statement I made to the detectives immediately after the crime.

The defense attorneys knew my story and yet never brought it up at the trial. This evidence was suppressed. No one made any attempt to locate this other man, even though it was their right and duty to do so. Didn't they believe my story?

I know why I didn't mention it at the time. I was too ashamed and embarrassed to talk about the possibility of another man sleeping with my wife. I had that same emasculated feeling. All I wanted to do was make myself look as bad as possible and I think that comes through in the statement.

I definitely wasn't going to say it to my mother or my father. Definitely not to them. I never would have said anything to them.

It was too difficult to bring up. There was the shame that I felt, the embarrassment, the macho image: You are less than a man if you can't keep your own wife from cheating on you.

And the other factor was that that would have been piling up damage on top of damage after her death. I didn't care what happened to me. There was no sense in me trying to build up a defense. And I didn't want to do further damage to Angie.

At the trial, it was the attorneys who told me not to bring it up. They thought it would be more damaging than not. The first person I told about it was Father Powers. I didn't tell anybody because I had already done enough damage. This would be putting a knife in and twisting it. I had already told them that I did it. And for my in-laws. I didn't want to hurt them further. Angie was not there to defend herself and I didn't want to accuse her.

I don't remember clearly but I think the lawyers told me not to bring it up at the trial because it would hurt me. I think they said that because it wasn't in the confession that the judges wouldn't believe me anyhow. They did tell me it was no defense.

I never expected the conviction to go above second degree murder anyway and I believed that this would not have been a good defense.

As to the real paternity of Vaughan, Jr., I came to accept him more and more as my son later on, until it was no longer an issue to me. Nobody else seemed to ever doubt that I was the father. My mother recalls the subject coming up but she was incredulous. She felt Tawney was the spitting image of me and looked exactly like I did when I was little.

Delphine thinks Angie said it because she was angry—to get back at me:

> I would believe that it was because they were probably hassling and you say things you don't really mean at the time, just because you're angry. It comes out and people take it for what it's worth and some people know that it's just something to say to keep the argument going.

> I don't really think she might have been see-
> ing someone else, but then again, I didn't know
> everything they did. She and I talked and I never
> heard her speak of anyone else. She could have
> been seeing somebody and I would never have
> known and I didn't know anything. When I read
> that Giggle claimed there was somebody else or
> something, I was so shocked I didn't know what
> to do. Because I didn't know there was ever a
> question that there was somebody else in her life.

Carmen remains somewhat of an enigma. I remember little
about him or about what I was doing immediately before the
murder. I do remember going out on Sunday and going to
bars and drinking. I remembers being quite intoxicated. I
never took any drugs, either before the murder or since, so
that was not a factor. I don't remember how I got home that
morning, whether I drove myself or whether, as stated to the
police and the court, I was dropped off by someone called
Carmen. I cannot put a face to Carmen.

Perhaps these details are not that important when taken in
context of the whole incident, the magnitude of the crime and
the fact that I admitted to the murder and did not try to build
any kind of defense out of the mysterious man I saw leaving
my house that night. The crime was murder. I committed it,
admitted that I committed it, and took the consequences. But
the truth is always important. Nobody likes an unsolved mystery.

When Angie was dead, I went to my parents' house across
the street to tell them what I had done and ask them to call
the police.

The reaction to the murder from my friends and family was
what one might expect under the circumstances. Delphine
recalls:

I got a call and it was, "Oh my God!" I just couldn't believe it. And then I was a nervous wreck. I mean that shock...not my brother. I just couldn't believe this person could have...whatever happened could have gone to the point where he killed someone. I just couldn't believe it. Not him. He was good, you know. I didn't think he had that kind of feeling inside him.

It was truly a shock to me when I found out and it was something that at the time manifested itself inside me: I was afraid. I was afraid of him, and this was my brother that I loved dearly. But I was only scared because he took a life. Your mind is roaming and you wonder what happened. How could this happen? It's craziness, you know. You just can't believe it.

I say I was afraid of him and that was just a feeling I had, but maybe I'm not expressing it right. Maybe it wasn't that I was afraid of him so much as I was angry at him for doing this and putting us in this position.

You get pushed or pressured or whatever and I guess you don't know what you'll do at the time. I've never been in a position like that so I have no idea, but it's about control. I just can't see myself getting that mad with anybody to want to take their life.

And it put such a strain on the whole family. I think it just devastated everyone.

My mother recalls the morning that she and my father had to deal with the immediate situation.

Your mind gets boggled. I remember when his father came down and said, "Why did he have to

kill her, and why did he have to come here?"
Well, where else was there for him to go?

I was in a state of shock where I couldn't talk.
It took me 5 minutes to say one word. And I was
like that for 6 weeks or more. I would stutter
instead of talking. I haven't cried since that happened. Now that sounds stupid but I haven't cried
since it happened. I haven't cried in 20-some
years. I went to the ophthalmologist and he said,
"Well, your body just hasn't adjusted yet."

My father thinks that's what killed my husband so early—the shock. You see he woke out
of a deep sleep when Vaughan came to tell us.
And then Vaughan told me what had happened
and I said, "I'll go and get my coat and see what
I can do." He said, "Don't bother." And he called
the police and just sat there and waited.

My husband was never a nervous person.
Never a person that got upset. This just changed
his personality too. For the longest time he
wouldn't go to see Vaughan at Graterford
[prison].

I felt like Putie felt. I couldn't believe that this
had happened to someone who was so gentle to
animals. And he was always one that wasn't a
violent person. He never wanted to see anything
killed.

Beverly Gray, now Beverly Bell, was overseas at the time.
She received the newspaper clippings from her family.

The first thing I said is that I can't imagine what
would drive him to do that because I couldn't
fathom him doing anything like that unless he
lost his mind.

Later he told me what had happened. He said that he was coming home from being out at about 4 o'clock in the morning and as he was approaching his apartment he saw someone leaving and he went in the house. He asked Angie who it was and she said that it was the baby's father—they had just had a new son—and he said he just snapped.

I felt sorry that it occurred, of course, but my heart went out because I felt that it just seemed like all of this could have been avoided so many years ago, if he hadn't gotten married, and his father hadn't made him get married. I'm sure through the years they learned to love each other but I don't think in the beginning it was love and I just think that it was hard to have to go through all of that.

Apart from Angie herself, the hardest hit were the members of her family. Geraldine Williams remembers the day all too clearly:

I was getting ready for work and got a call from my sister who had heard from the wife of a cop that maybe...I called the morgue. And then I heard it on the radio. I probably heard it all along because the radio was on and the news would come on but it never registered. Then I heard it and I never stopped hearing it after that.

I always wanted to believe that she was asleep and did not know what was happening. For my own peace of mind I wanted to believe that she was asleep.

She was not afraid of him. She should have been.

This was my best friend. Now there is an emptiness.

To me it still hurts. As I get older I really miss her.

Brenda Lowery said, "I wanted him killed. I'll be honest with you. I wanted him dead."

But Geraldine's comment was, "I didn't. I thought it would be too easy. I have never actually expressed to him what he did to me."

Kim and Vaughan, Jr. were taken to Angie's sister Alice and her husband Billy's home where they would spend their childhood.

I was taken to a police headquarters where the detectives questioned me and prepared a statement—one that at least they were satisfied with.

Nothing would bring Angie back. Her life was over. Others had to continue.

CHAPTER FIVE

"...to give light to those who sit in darkness and in the shadow of death..."

(Luke 1:79)

The detectives had what they wanted: a confession which could easily be used to argue first degree murder, although I didn't know that then. Their job done, they left me alone until it was time to load me onto the bus that would take me from the Roundhouse (Philadelphia's central police headquarters) to the Philadelphia Detention Center.

They put me in C or D block, which was high security, because they said I had threatened to commit suicide. This block was more carefully monitored than the others. I was in a cell on my own, solid steel all around with a window through which you could look in or out and I was watched constantly by a guard.

Everything in the jail was automatic: they'd push a button and the doors would open, *clank*. On one of the walls was a solid metal bed, welded on. On this bed was a thin mattress. The toilet was right there in the cell.

I only left the cell to eat and for some recreation. At first that was an hour a day. The thing to do was to get a job on the block. If you could come out to sweep or mop the floors it gave you some freedom; or you could watch TV, play chess or other games.

It was months before I got a job.

For some time I had no visitors. Then my mother and father came to see me.

My mother's concern—and a valid one—was how the family was going to look, after I had done something like this. My father was crushed. I remember he was sad when he came to see me. He asked me how I was doing—how they were treating me. He didn't say how he felt, but I could tell he was devastated.

There were outlets for me. After a while I was able to play chess and cards and I did a lot of reading, although the library at the Detention Center was very poor.

And I asked God for forgiveness. It was not in a particularly personal way. It was more along the lines of: "Is there a God out there?" I didn't even know who God was anymore.

I was at the Detention Center for about a year before I was moved to Holmesburg Prison in northeast Philadelphia. Holmesburg was a much older facility, a prison where men went who were serving up to two years. It was two and a half years after the murder before I was brought to trial.

While I was at Holmesburg a man entered into my life who was to play a very significant role in helping shape my future. The Reverend Frederick F. Powers, Jr., later testified at my trial. He was the most articulate speaker of anyone in court (including the judges, defense counsel and prosecutor). Perhaps it was his Harvard education showing through. He was a very wise man. His testimony in response to questions put to him by Mr. Atkins provides an insight into my journey during my years of incarceration prior to the trial in February 1970.

Q: Father Powers, what is your background and in what capacity did you first meet Mr. Booker?

A: I am the Episcopal chaplain at the Philadelphia prisons. I'm an ordained minister of the Episcopal Church. My responsibility is to supervise the programs at the Three County Correctional Institutions for Adults. I have been there nine years. I have graduate degrees in theology, education and clinical pastoral training at the State Hospital at Byberry.

I met Mr. Booker in the course of my duties at Holmesburg Prison, and on that first occasion he approached me to assist me at the Communion service. I don't know whether you want me to go into the details, but I have seen in him several stages of development in his character over the last two years which I would like to mention.

Q: Please do.

A: In the first case he asked me if he could serve at the Communion service because he had been an acolyte of the Episcopal Church in the past. As we prepared for the service he asked me to pray for a person he called Annabelle. Subsequently after the service I asked him who this was and he told me who it was. He was in an obvious state of conflict of values. He asked me to pray for this girl on the one hand. On the other hand the circumstances, of course, were in violent conflict with his concern for her at this point. He broke down. He seemed to be on the verge of complete disorientation. So I did not pursue that matter with him, nor did I bring it up again.

He was able to express himself in a rather artificial way at that time. He attempted to engage in small talk. However, his smiles were obviously forced and his reactions seemed to be rather artificial. That was the first stage in which I came to know him.

As we consulted and as I conducted my interviewing with him and as he became more active in the prison program, his attention turned to subjects such as psychology, sociology and theology. He borrowed a number

of my books. At that time he was certainly unsophisti-
cated in any of these areas, and yet he was able to learn
a great deal on the basis of his reading and our discussions. He was obviously a person of high intelligence
and he was able to do many jobs. In the prison, for
instance, I used him as a chaplain clerk, the school
instructor used him as an inmate instructor. He was
used also to lead inmate groups. He became the chairman of a group that I supervised of inmates who elect
their own leaders, and he was instrumental in forming
an inmates vocational training program which was the
closest thing that we have to inmate self-government in
the county prisons.

However, as weeks went by I became concerned that
he had no concern himself for his own legal defense.
He didn't seem to be in touch with the realities of his
own legal position. I also noticed his preoccupation
with such concerns as rehabilitation in the prison, the
development of our own religious program, and very
little concern with himself in his own defense. So I and
others urged him to give attention to this matter and to
come down to earth. He seemed to be out of touch with
reality.

Whereupon in the next phase of his development he
turned to the question of his defense, and unfortunately
he consulted with inmate lawyers and he was concerned with whether his constitutional rights had been
violated. He became suspicious of his own attorneys.
He told me he didn't trust them. Ultimately they left his
case after that episode. Again he seemed to change. He
began to settle down and to be able to reflect more easily. He seemed to resign himself to his fate. In short, he
became more human in his relationships. He caught the
attention of several of the volunteers who worked with
me in the prison program, because of his personal qual-

ities, his intelligence, his ability to relate socially, and in terms of his character.

And the value structure that I see in this young man he seemed to reflect, well, the structure of values that had been taught to him by the middle class society in which he grew up, including his parents, his teachers, and his clergyman whom I knew. We were impressed by the whole pattern of his life in terms of achievements. He obviously had been a person who had a very high need to achieve—to achieve well. He had a high regard for the quality of his work, and in terms of my supervision of him in the prison he did not live up to this standard of achievement. He was obviously disappointed in himself and depressed. This he clearly learned from his parents, the teachers and his pastors. And I am sure it's no accident that he has such a high need for achievement. I feel—I was very concerned about this, because I felt that he was trying too hard to live up to a very difficult standard, and in my opinion this is the flaw in his character. Not that he has not tried to reflect the idealism of persons in the community that are highly respected, but that he perhaps has learned too well to value their standards, has tried too hard to maintain those high standards of policy.

I see in him during the two years I have known him a development and a growth in his character, a change in the value structure of his personality. And I would feel that he has great prospects for complete maturity as a whole person who can make, indeed, still a great contribution to his society.

Looking back on that time period 25 years later, I see more clearly than ever just how important Father Powers was to my return to life.

You must understand that a lot of my involvement in the

church was because there was this person reaching out to me, Father Powers, and particularly at a time of need. When I was feeling terrible about myself, here was someone saying, "God loves you." That meant a lot to me.

But Father Powers's testimony did not end there. He continued his story to the end, with none of the usual questions, objections and interruptions that other witnesses were subjected to when counsel or judge felt that they might be straying from the path, omitting important information or being unclear in their report.

> I've gone to the point of introducing him to the bishop of the Diocese, Bishop Robert L. DeWitt, who has seriously corresponded with me about the possibility of this young man participating in the church, his ministry. So there is no question about how I evaluate his character in terms of its dynamics and future possibilities.
>
> My own feeling about his own faults is that there are levels of his personalities with which I do not deal, because I deal at the rational level. There are levels and conscious levels of his personality, the dynamics of which would be very susceptible to treatment by psychoanalytical oriented psychiatry. He has the intelligence for it. He has the ability to express his feelings sufficient for this type of treatment. Unfortunately, I know that this kind of treatment is not available in any of our penal institutions, and this is the tragedy.

Mr. Atkins continued the questioning:

Q: Father, could you tell the Court approximately how many times you met with Vaughan?

A: I have seen him at least three times a week for two or three hours at a time in the course of his work and also in the course of interviewing him in regard to the pastoral counseling that I do. He has been, as I said, the leader of the inmate group, so I have supervised him on that basis as well, although he has participated in the therapy group supervised and led by Reverend David Myers, who testified here earlier. So my association with him was rather frequent during the week and it amounted to several hours of interaction with Mr. Booker practically every week.

Q: And this has been throughout the approximately two years that you have known him?

A: Yes.

Q: Doctor, are you familiar with this pamphlet?

A: Yes, I am.

Q: Which bears the words, IVET[P], the Inmate Vocational Education Training Program. Are you familiar with Mr. Booker's participation as chairman and in other capacities with the Inmate Vocational Education Training Program?

A: Yes I am. I am very familiar with it.

Q: Could you tell the Court what Mr. Booker's participation was in this particular program?

A: Well, as in the other program I mentioned he acted as chairman and was responsible for the direction of the group, according to the parliamentary procedures that we teach. These two particular groups—the group you mentioned does not exist at the present time, because many of the inmate leaders were transferred to other institutions or necessarily released from prison on parole or other reasons. The staffing, therefore, became a problem. So it does no longer exist. However, during Mr. Booker's association with it he exercised a creative leadership role in the development of this unique program which made use of the inmate talents in the inmate population. Individuals with vocational skills were sought out. These inmates taught other inmates the skills that they had command of. A minimal amount of supervision was provided this group. They were given considerable freedom to develop their own program. They had a curriculum development committee. They developed their own methods of classroom evaluation. In one case an inmate who was teaching plumbing skills determined that the members of his class could not read a ruler, and so instead of going on with the teaching of the plumbing skills that inmate reorganized his class program to teach the basic mathematics of reading a ruler. This is the kind of sophistication that you would expect from a graduate student in education. This is the kind of thing Mr. Booker was promoting.

Q: In what area did Mr. Booker participate and teach?

A: I believe he was teaching mathematics and possibly blueprint reading or business mathematics, as I recall.

Mr. Atkins had no further questions. Even the flamboyant Mr. Czap in his bow-tie seemed to be impressed with Father Powers' testimony. His cross-examination was uncharacteristically perfunctory.

Father Powers's evidence gave a great deal of information about my life at Holmesburg and the gradual changes I went through. There were others at the trial who also gave their view of my life at the time. One of these was The Reverend David Myers, referred to by Father Powers in his testimony. Father Myers was, at the time, a chaplain in the Methodist Chaplaincy Service. Most of his time was spent in the Philadelphia Prison System. Mr. Atkins questioned Father Myers about his association with me.

Q: In your capacity with the Philadelphia Prison System,

did you have the opportunity to meet the defendant, Vaughan Booker?

A: Yes, I met him two years ago when I began my work at Holmesburg. He was in a counseling group that I held once a week until he was transferred to the Detention Center. [He must have been confused about locations here because I went from the Detention Center to Holmesburg, not the other way around.] Then I think I have spoken with him since then about once a week.

I feel that I suppose in the last several months that Vaughan seems to have opened up much more to me. He talks about many more personal things, and he talks hopefully about his plans for the future and his attempt to carve a much more meaningful life for himself.

Q: There is just one statement I wanted to question you further about, and that is in this letter you say, "Of all the inmates that I know, I would rate Mr. Booker as having the greatest potential for service to his fellow man." Is there anything you could add to that to make it more specific?

A: Yes. From my perspective, I think that Vaughan looks at this present time—when he looks at a particular situation he seems to have a balanced look at it. I think he's very concerned for his people, and—but I think he understands the complexity of society, and I think that he doesn't seem to go off in a tangent and he would apply his logic to a situation.

Q: In the two years or more that you have known Mr. Booker, has he shown any significant change?

A: Yes, I feel—perhaps it was just getting to know—but I feel at first the conversation would always be away from Vaughan, but recently it has been much more personal. He seems to be much more open, much more relaxed person.

On cross-examination Judge Nix wanted to know:

Q: Do you feel that you have helped Mr. Booker in the two years that you have had him under your discussions or under your group?

A: I'm not sure I have helped him, but I feel that I detected in him a growth. I'm not sure what role I played in that.

Not all of my time in the Detention Center and Holmesburg prison was taken up with good works: there are many aspects of prison life that one doesn't really think about unless one is forced to participate in it. People's ideas about life inside a prison are, in most cases, formed by television dramatizations and the press's questionable interpretations of the facts. This was new to me and I have clear recollections of what life behind bars was really like at these two institutions from 1967 to 1970.

I remember the gates at the Philadelphia Detention Center opening as we approached in the bus and I remember the dogs. It was unlike any experience I had ever had before.

When I got to Holmesburg the first thing we had to do was put on uniforms. Everybody wore green jumpsuits that looked like military uniform.

Everything was regimented. You were supposed to do everything at the sound of a whistle. You got up in the morning and they blew a whistle and you went to breakfast; they blew a whistle and you came back. The same thing happened at lunch, dinner, recreation time, et cetera.

At Holmesburg and the Detention Center there were no regular jobs like there were later at the penitentiary. So if you could get some kind of a job, it was a real privilege. Otherwise you would stay locked up almost all of the time.

I saw a lot of homosexuality, brutality, drugs and all the rest of it going on that prisons are notorious for, but I also found that you could choose the life you want to live. A lot of it has to do with the way you carry yourself and the way you treat others. Of course you have to understand that when you go in there it's the sort of place where everyone is going to test you and you have to hold your ground. I never had a fight. But I did see a lot of fights, stabbings, guys being hit with baseball bats and other violence.

I was facing a life sentence and my attitude was, first of all, I had no interest in being a homosexual or getting involved with homosexuals, and if I ever did, that would be my choice. No one else was going to make that choice for me.

So I made it known what my position was. I said, "I came in here one way and I'm going to leave that way. And if it means I'm going to have to hurt you, then I will." A lot of them believed me because they thought I was crazy. Anybody who could shoot somebody with a bow and arrow can't be exactly right.

I was really very quiet and I didn't choose to hang around large groups of people. I kept pretty much to myself. I didn't do a lot of jail house things other people were doing. For example, they have drugs in jail. All some people do is run around trying to find drugs: illegal and prescription. You have people who are supposed to take something to help them sleep so instead of swallowing their medicine they will put it under their tongue and they are really expert at this. They will save them and sell them to other inmates or will take them all themselves to try to get high or they will try to inject them.

I know a man who lost his hand because he was trying to inject drugs from capsules—prescription medication. It was some type of sedative and he tried to inject it and blocked an artery.

Some inmates would get drugs through the guards. Because I wasn't involved I didn't know who was doing what and I didn't want to know. If you didn't know, you couldn't tell. I wasn't involved.

But what I did do a couple of times with some other inmates was to make wine. We used to take fruit, like plums, and put bread in the juice and stash it somewhere and wait for it to ferment and then drink it. I only did that a couple of times. You had to strain it to get rid of the cockroaches and that turned me off wine making. So I got healthy. I stopped smoking. I stopped eating meat. I started working out and playing basketball and handball.

I remember we had a food strike at Holmesburg. The food was terrible. They used to have what they called beef and pork stew and it looked like garbage. It was high in fat content and obviously unhealthy. You could buy an egg and cheese sandwich for a pack of cigarettes, and that was more healthy than the stuff they had on the line. There were a number of Muslim brothers who were concerned about pork being in the beef and pork stew. They were supposed to pick the pork out. So we got together and we quietly organized a food strike which instilled fear in the administration because they didn't find out until after the fact.

What we would do was to get in line, put the food on our trays and go back to our tables, but we just didn't eat any of it. The exception would be the older inmates or the diabetics or people who really needed to eat.

Eventually word got back to the officials. They wanted to know who the ringleaders were and my name came up. So they came one night after we had showered—it must have been about 11:30 at night—and took about five of us, herded us into a van, took us back to the Detention Center and put us in solitary.

Immediately after this, there was a negotiated settlement between the prison officials and some of the inmates, a dietitian was brought in, and the diet was changed.

It was in this unlikely environment that my own personal redemption began. It was not a single, earth-shattering event. Rather it was a gradual change, like an awakening from a coma and beginning to find out where I was and who I was.

I felt a need to go back to church. There was a chapel at

the Detention Center and services were available. At first I
didn't go to really get involved—I just felt a need. There's a
part of the Episcopal services which is a confessional and
they were using the old prayer book then and I just felt the
need to gain some understanding of God. That was what I
needed to talk about in church. The chapel was the place
where things happened.

There was an intake process. I joined a group called the
Fellowship of St. Dismas (Dismas is the name of one of the
criminals crucified at the same time as Jesus, to whom Jesus
said, while he was dying on the cross, "Truly I tell you, today
you will be with me in Paradise").

Because I had gone to school and was an Episcopalian and
also because I was a good reader, the Episcopal chaplain took
a little more interest in me. After some time I was elected
president of the fellowship. This meant a great deal to me
because after my fall it appeared that something was happening which meant I was moving up again. I was involved in the
church and active and here was this group, so it was like life
was coming back.

But I was not yet dealing with the consequences of my situation. I wasn't even thinking about that, and it concerned
Father Powers, the Episcopalian chaplain who would later
testify on my behalf at my trial.

My duties included making sure that I identified every
Episcopal inmate coming into the facility. Men who were
interested would get passes to come to our meetings. I provided them with membership cards and sometimes I would
lead entire services when Father Powers wasn't there. We had
morning prayers on Sundays.

I began to see a new beauty in the written word. Father
Powers used to bring me books on philosophy and theology.
He was the first one to get me really reading the Bible as a
real story and talking about the relationship between humani-
ty and God. Not a fairy tale. Not Adam and Eve and talking

serpents, but something that really has to do with our relationship to each other and our relationship to God. And I began to read from that perspective. This is how I came across the story of Moses and the Egyptian in Exodus 2:11-15 which I read many times because it was such a surprise to me.

> *One day, after Moses had grown up, he went out to his people and saw their forced labor. He saw an Egyptian beating a Hebrew, one of his kinsfolk.*
>
> *He looked this way and that, and seeing no one he killed the Egyptian and hid him in the sand.*
>
> *When he went out the next day, he saw two Hebrews fighting; and he said to the one who was in the wrong, "Why do you strike your fellow Hebrew?"*
>
> *He answered, "Who made you a ruler and judge over us? Do you mean to kill me as you killed the Egyptian?" Then Moses was afraid and thought, "Surely the thing is known."*
>
> *When Pharaoh heard of it, he sought to kill Moses. But Moses fled from Pharaoh.*

I began to see the prison as my wilderness experience. There was a great deal of temptation to sin all around me and I needed to find myself and establish my relationship with God. I actually began internalizing many, many stories of people whom God had chosen and began to understand it all in a different way.

In my talks with Father Powers I told him I would like to be a priest but I knew that I couldn't because of what I had done. I remember the conversation even now:

I said, "You know I wanted to be a priest at one time."

"Well, what's stopping you now?" he asked.

"What do you mean what's stopping me now? Look at me. Here I am in prison on a murder charge. How can I possibly be a priest? I'm unworthy."

"You need to do some serious Scripture reading," was his reply.

He gave me Scriptures to read about people who were unworthy but became worthy in God's sight. So I started to read the entire Bible, not necessarily from Genesis to Revelation in that order, but I began to read with a commentary and with an understanding of what it is.

I also started to see that I was not the only one who had been of little faith; not the only one who has committed a sin; that my life could be turned around.

I gained an understanding of subjects like repentance and forgiveness: that this was something you worked for, not something you got even if you didn't deserve it. You have to become consciously aware of attitudes before you can start to change. You have to become aware of the fact that you don't see things that way anymore, that you don't harbor anger the way you used to or whatever it may be.

I began to really get involved in reshaping my own life and the way I saw myself: the whole idea of being such a bad person and committing such a bad deed. Although I had been a Christian all of my life, I never really understood forgiveness as I now began to understand it. I had never been involved in something so serious, so I hadn't grasped the concept of forgiveness from that perspective. Forgiveness always meant you may have said something or done something wrong to somebody and they say, "I forgive you," and that was it. Of course it's a lot more than that. It has to do with being able to live with yourself after doing certain things and that doesn't happen right away.

I began to feel different. I was less egotistical. It was a more secure, peaceful feeling. I was ready to let God back into my life. I had reached a point where, even though I was locked up, I felt free. I could walk among my peers and feel comfortable about things I was saying. I could say things with authority without being the tough guy, and I earned respect among the inmates.

Many people in prison turn to "religion" as a way out. Prisoners are notorious for their miraculous conversions to the faith. But if one follows the religious careers of these "born agains" after they have achieved their more immediate aims, one often finds that the whole thing was just a ruse to try and get out of jail sooner. At my trial, Mr. Czap's suspicion that this was what I was up to is reflected in his cross-questioning of Sidney Repplier, Director of the Philadelphia Foundation, who testified on my behalf. Mr. Repplier was brought as a witness by the defense and questioned first by Mr. Atkins:

Q: Mr. Repplier, could you tell the court what you know and what you observed concerning Mr. Booker and his participation in any of the programs in which you participated in?

A: I don't know what I can add to what Father Powers has already very graphically said in detail. I would just like to say that I think at least two factors stand out in my mind regarding Vaughan Booker: One, as Father Powers described, his participation in which I think is a very unusual program, the IVETP. I know Vaughan was very active in the business management part of the program that he directed.

I think the other facet of his personality that struck me was—we have talked on occasion about what he would like to do when he gets out, working with young people. We have gone into this in some detail. I work for a charitable foundation so this is more than a passing interest to me. He has told me that he's had an exposure to these young people. He has seen where they have gone wrong. He knows from personal experience what it's like to do time. He has, I think, a very well thought-out program of what he would like to accomplish when and if he had the opportunity to implement it. I think these two things are what struck me about Mr. Booker's personality in my relationship with him.

Mr. Czap followed this line of questioning:

Q: Is Mr. Booker's interest in these things deep and sincere or just spasmodic and sporadic?

A: I would say they were deep, Mr. Czap. When we first went to the prisons we were given an orientation session and I think it was Superintendent Hendricks who told us we were going to be conned, we could expect it. And indeed we have been so. I think we have a thoroughly detailed or at least a ready knowledge that we are going to be conned and we look for it. I would say that in my relationship with Mr. Booker his feelings were detailed, his feelings were deep, and I was completely convinced of his sincerity of what he said and what he did.

Yet another voice testifying on my behalf at the trial was that of Barbara Harris, then a community relations consultant working for Sun Oil Company, later to become the Right Reverend Barbara Harris, the first woman to be ordained a Bishop in the Episcopal Church, now Suffragan Bishop of Massachusetts.

Mr. Atkins asked her, "And from your opportunity of observing him, have you made any judgment as to his character?"

She replied, "I would say that I was tremendously impressed with what seemed to be Mr. Booker's qualities of leadership and interest in the programs of which he was a part."

Then came the cross-examination by Mr. Czap:

Q: Do you feel that he's sincere in his interest?

A: I was impressed by his sincerity in my monthly encounters with him.

Q: Did you find him brilliant or at least highly intelligent?

A: Yes, I was impressed with his intelligence.

Q: Would you use the term brilliant also?

A: I might be in error, but I would use the term brilliant.

At the trial, no one presented any evidence to show that I had done anything other than make myself useful to other inmates and start to take active steps toward my own redemption and rehabilitation.

That in itself is not conclusive evidence of anything, however. For this trial was riddled with the travesties, miscarriages, and general prejudices for which the judicial systems of the world are notorious.

CHAPTER SIX

...O LORD, in your justice preserve my life.

(Psalm 119:149)

If my case is typical, then it is small wonder that there are so many off-color jokes about lawyers, that the nation's jails are bursting at the seams, that a large number of dangerous criminals are roaming around loose, that the honesty of law enforcement agencies is so often called into question, and that the national crime rate continues to achieve new highs.

It does not take a legal expert to spot the trail of blunders (accidental or deliberate) involved in the handling of the case of *Commonwealth* vs. *Booker.* Not all of these can be ascribed to the legal professionals, however. I added my own self-destructive decisions into the general melee of stupidities and wrong moves which characterized the entire proceedings from beginning to end.

Hindsight reveals, however, that despite the errors and injustices which occurred at almost each step of my tortuous path through the judicial minefield, I came out at the other end relatively unscathed, having received the punishment I felt I deserved, and a lot wiser for the whole experience. Who knows if I would have been ready to come out sooner, or what would have happened if I had?

The average man in the street, acquainted with all the facts, would probably come to the conclusion that I got off quite lightly, considering the crime. But he might also realize that I had worked hard to earn the forgiveness and renewed trust of a society against whose laws I had transgressed so violently.

Others, including some members of Angie's family, but also complete strangers, hearing the facts, would no doubt feel that nothing short of my death could really make up for the damage I did and that the ten years I served were completely inadequate punishment.

Some people have ascribed this relatively short term of imprisonment to luck. Others to timing. But it was as if Someone were watching over my progress. The facts seem to reinforce the saying that, "God helps those who help themselves."

None of this excuses the incompetence or worse that marked almost every step of my path through the police, judicial, and penal systems.

It is important, first of all, to understand the legal concepts of the different degrees of murder, manslaughter, and so on. In criminal law, *murder* means intentionally causing the death (homicide) of any person, and it is distinguished from *manslaughter,* which means unintentional killing. In most states, criminal codes distinguish between at least two degrees of murder. In general, murder in the first degree involves a deliberate, premeditated design to cause the death of someone; murder in the second degree involves the intent to cause death, but without premeditation and deliberation. At the time of my trial, Pennsylvania law recognized the two degrees of murder as explained here. The penalty for first degree murder was either death or life in prison. The penalty for second degree was considerably less. Manslaughter carried an even lighter sentence.

With this in mind, it is worth examining the "due process of the law" as it pertains to my case, not because I feel hard done by, but because it sheds some light on the legal system of our country. At the time, I was fully prepared to be locked up for life or even sentenced to death, although I was led to believe that the maximum I would get would be a 20-year sentence.

First there is the matter of the statement presented by the police, supposedly a direct transcription of the confession made by me immediately after the crime. There is no need to repeat it here as it is printed in full in the first chapter.

But just imagine, for a moment, that a mere three hours ago you, the reader, fired five arrows into your spouse, by far the most shocking and violent action you have ever done in your life. Three hours later you're still in shock, realizing what you have really done and what your future now holds in store for you. Can you imagine yourself saying these words to the detectives examining you? (Spelling mistakes are as they were in the original.)

> ...I then proceeded to my children's bedroom with the vain attempt of first destroying my son, my daughter and then myself. I then at this time proceeded to choke my son, found that he was loosing his breath and his life at the same time, and then proceeded to administer mouth to mouth resuscitation to revive him. I succeeded in reviving him, put him in my daughter's bed, transferred my daughter to my son's bed. She woke up and said, basically, "What am I doing in my brother's bed?" I transferred my son back to his bed, my daughter back to her bed, she asked me, "Where's my mommy?" and I said, "She went away." I then went to the front room to find a pencil to go back and write on my children's wall exactly what I had done. And after not having the ability to think, I proceeded to my mother's house....

Maybe police officers "proceed" hither and thither in stilted, official English. But this is supposed to be a direct transcript of my statement to them. It couldn't be. I don't even talk this way. This is perhaps harmless enough, but one then has to ask to what degree the entire statement can be trusted. Remember that the literal words of this statement were the primary evidence used by the judges to determine the degree of my guilt, and then my sentence. Not so harmless is the following small piece of dialogue, surreptitiously slipped in:

Q: What reason did you have for doing this?

A: Well it was something I thought about doing for a long time....

Now that apparently innocuous string of 12 words, "Well it was something I thought about doing for a long time," were it true, would be enough, all on its own, to guarantee a verdict of first degree murder, because it proves that the crime was premeditated, "with malice aforethought," the requisite for a first degree murder conviction.

The police knew that. At the time I did not. When reminded that I had "said" this, both at the trial and when I finally saw the statement for the first time, 27 years later, I could not understand why those words were there. Never for a moment had I ever considered killing Angie prior to that morning.

The prosecutor also failed to provide any evidence that I had deliberately planned this murder. The fact that a bow and arrow was used tends, if anything, to show that this was an act done on the spur of the moment. With intent to kill, yes, but premeditated, planned, worked out, no.

What actually happened at the police examination and questioning is very different from what finally appeared on the paper which was supposed to be my "confession."

One played the good cop and the other the tough one. They said I made a statement, but what they basically did was take advantage of the fact that when you're in the state of mind like I was, you would say "yes" to anything they asked. They basically set the scenario with leading questions.

"Well, this is something you had thought about doing for a long time, right?"

"I don't know, I guess I might have, I don't know."

And we'd go back and forth and eventually the clerk would type:

Q: What reason did you have for doing this?

A: Well it was something I thought about doing for a long time....

And that would become my confession. It was like this throughout.

I signed without even reading what they had written. I had done a terrible thing and I didn't care what they did to me.

Yet it was that short string of 12 words that constituted by far the strongest part of the Assistant District Attorney's case for a first degree murder verdict. I never said those words, because it simply isn't true. In another case, this type of "confession" might have condemned an innocent person to death. As it was, I was undoubtedly guilty of a terrible crime and the long-term effects of the detectives' "poetic license" was minimal.

The questioning and the resulting statement provide some insight into the methods used by our trusted officers of the law, or at least the ones involved in this case. It certainly opened my eyes.

In August 1969, between the arrest and the trial, a hearing was held to determine whether or not this statement should be suppressed as evidence. The motion was heard by Justice Meade and denied. It should have been suppressed as it could hardly be called a voluntary statement made by someone who really knew what he was saying or doing. It would have been far fairer if the court had heard the case "from scratch" when

I was no longer in a state of shock and not caring what I said or did. It would also have helped if the trial had been closer (in time) to the crime, as all memories would have been fresher.

Why the trial did not take place until two and half years after the murder is another mystery. That's a long time, and certainly, in the case of an innocent defendant, could most effectively ruin someone's entire life. In this case, the defendant was not innocent. But if this is the typical time that elapses between arrest and trial, then the notion of swift justice is a farce.

"In all criminal prosecutions, the accused shall enjoy the right to a speedy and public trial, by an impartial jury of the State and district wherein the crime shall have been committed, which district shall have been previously ascertained by law, and to be informed of the nature and cause of the accusation; to be confronted with the witnesses against him; to have compulsory process for obtaining witnesses in his favor, and to have the Assistance of Counsel for his defense."

So says the Sixth Amendment to the American Constitution. Apparently the word "speedy" is open to fairly loose interpretation!

During this time period leading up to the trial, I saw little of my court-assigned legal counsel. For a long time I didn't care.

The first two attorneys appointed, Abraham J. Brem Levy, Esquire, and Anthony Minisi, Esquire, managed to arrange a plea bargain with the District Attorney. I turned it down.

This proposed plea bargain was later explained to the Honorable Ethan Allen Doty, in June 1971, when I was granted a Post-Conviction Hearing. At that hearing I was represented by David Kairys, an attorney with whom I had become well acquainted while in prison, and who remains my lawyer to this day, though he is now a law professor at Temple University in Philadelphia. He worked a great deal with civil rights law and has recently published a book on the state of freedom, equality and democracy in America, entitled *With Liberty and Justice for Some.*

David Kairys argued at the hearing that my plea of guilty was not entered voluntarily, knowingly, or with understanding of its legal consequences and that I had been denied my right to effective assistance of counsel. He brought up the subject of the plea-bargain agreement.

Q: What led up to Mr. Brem Levy and his co-counsel, your first set of counsel, withdrawing from the case?

A: They wanted me to plead guilty and I refused.

Q: Had they obtained any kind of a plea bargain or any kind of an arrangement with the District Attorney's Office?

A: Yes.

Q: What was the arrangement?

A: Seven to fourteen years for a guilty plea.

Q: That was going to be a guilty plea to what degree?

A: I think they were going to certify it as second degree, but it would be a plea to a general charge of murder.

Q: And you refused to plead guilty at that time?

A: Right.

Q: As a result of that, your counsel at that time was replaced by two other court appointed officials?

A: Right.

Q: Why did you refuse to accept that deal?

A: I wanted a jury trial.

Q: What were the issues, or what was the issue or issues that you wished to focus on at your trial?

A: Insanity.

Q: And yet with the new counsel, with the new set of

counsel, you did wind up pleading guilty; is that correct?

A. Yes.

Q: Why did you plead guilty?

A: Because I thought that I could use the defense of insanity, although I think Mr. Atkins called it diminished responsibility, but it would still be an insanity defense from what I understood.

Q. Please explain to the Court, when you say diminished responsibility, what did Mr. Atkins tell you was going to happen at this trial?

A: Well, I was under the impression that insanity, diminished responsibility, would automatically reduce the degree from first degree. In other words, there was no possibility of a first degree conviction.

Looking back on it, there were other reasons for my not accepting that plea-bargain agreement, a bargain which, in hindsight, would have been quite a beneficial one.

Something wasn't right about it. I got the idea that I had to stand up and perjure myself in order to accept it. They had a statement of what happened and they wanted me to sign it but it wasn't the truth. It was their version of what had happened. I would have had to deny that there was any plea bargain. But I would have to live with myself. They told me that if I pleaded guilty and signed this statement, the worst I could get would be second degree murder, 10 to 20 years. I had no idea I could get life or even death for a guilty plea.

Later on I was told that I should have pleaded not guilty on the grounds of insanity. But a study of the trial records shows that it is highly unlikely that a not guilty plea on the grounds of insanity would have been effective, certainly with the judges assigned to my case. Perhaps a jury would have seen it differently. In Pennsylvania the law was quite clear on this point. Called the "M'Naughton Rule," insanity is a complete defense to criminal responsibility if at the time the criminal acts took place the person committing those acts had such a disease of the mind that he did not know the nature and quality of his act or did not know that the acts he was committing were wrong.

All the evidence showed that I knew what I was doing and knew that it was wrong and there was no psychiatric or other evidence to the contrary. It is unlikely, had I gone before a jury and pleaded not guilty on the basis of insanity, that any verdict other than guilty of murder would have been returned, whether first or second degree. But then the vagaries of the justice system are many and anything could have happened.

The three judges at my trial were not particularly impressed with any of the psychiatric evidence presented. This was not surprising since the psychiatrists and psychologists were not very convincing. Nor did they appear to be clear themselves on what they were trying to say. One comment by Judge Nix in response to Mr. Atkins' summing up, seems to clarify the position of the Court as regards an insanity defense and the related testimony:

> MR. ATKINS: He didn't try to make up any reason that would explain it. But we do know that even today, according to the competency examination, he still has mental problems and that these have existed for some time. They have gotten better and they have gotten worse.
>
> JUDGE NIX: I dare say that 80 percent of the people in our community, Mr. Atkins, upon examination would have some mental problems. I also have my doubts about many of the examiners.

All might have gone better if I had ignored all advice as far as my defense was concerned and simply done what I felt was right. But there were pressures.

I didn't know anything about the criminal justice system. I was completely ignorant. I didn't know what the options were. What happens is you begin to talk to people, other inmates in prison who are familiar with the system. And everybody is willing to give you advice: how you can get this if you do that.

Well, obviously, looking back on it, if they were that knowledgeable they wouldn't be in there telling me about it. It's similar to the time when one of the inmates was bragging that he was a bank robber. And I said, "No you're not a bank robber, you're a convict like me. Bank robbers are out robbing banks; you are in here doing time."

I was listening to a lot of men who were saying, "Don't take any deals and don't plead guilty." Everyone was giving advice based on his own experience.

It was confusing. I turned down the plea bargain agreement and asked the two attorneys to remove themselves from the case. Two new attorneys were appointed to my defense: Mr. Armand Della Porta, previously an Assistant District Attorney, and Mr. Richard Atkins. They came up with a plan to have me plead guilty to murder generally and it would then be up to the Commonwealth to prove that it was first degree murder. They said they would bring forth all sorts of psychiatric evidence to prove that I had "diminished responsibility" at the time of the crime due to my mental condition. This would confirm a second degree verdict and I would get 10 to 20 years. It sounded fine.

The only problem, as they would find out during the trial, was that this "diminished responsibility" defense was valid in California and some other states perhaps, but had been consistently ignored by Pennsylvania courts who only recognized the M'Naughton rule of insanity as a defense and took no other evidence of mental state into consideration when determining the degree of guilt. So the strategy was destined to fail before anyone ever took the stand. In reaching their verdict, the judges paid no attention whatsoever to this evidence and grew increasingly impatient as the defense counsel tried to bring on more witnesses to prove my "diminished responsibility."

Moreover, these attorneys advised me not to use the only real defense available to me, that of legal provocation. That is a valid defense which, if proven, would have resulted in a verdict of voluntary manslaughter with a significantly reduced sentence. Their reasons for this legally suicidal move were explained later by Mr. Atkins at thc Post-Conviction Hearing during questioning by Mr. Kairys:

Q: Mr. Booker just testified before you, and he discussed his story concerning a man coming out of the house when he came home that night. Are you familiar with that story?

A: Yes, I am.

Q: Who told you that story?

A: Mr. Booker did.

Q: Was any investigation ever done concerning the identity of this man Mr. Booker said was leaving the house?

A: No, none at all.

Later cross-examination was conducted by Mr. McKissock:

Q: Mr. Atkins, did the defendant cooperate with you during the preparation of the defense?

A: Yes, he did.

Q: During the time that you prepared your trial strategy, you knew about the allegation that there was a man coming from the house, and that his wife had a lover; did you know about that story?

A: At some point I knew about it. I didn't always know about it, but I did know about it and discussed it, at least discussed it briefly, I believe, with Vaughan, and I think with Father Powers.

Q: How did you assess the story?

A: I assessed it as that it was quite possible that it had happened, but that it might be very damaging to him to attack his wife in this manner. I felt that, for several reasons, one, that it wasn't brought out at the beginning at the time of his statement, that it was brought up at a later time, although it was actually brought up way before trial; that the Court might not believe it, and second, they might feel he was attacking his wife's virtue, et cetera, and that that was inappropriate.

Q: This was based on your judgment and experience, you thought it was inappropriate to continue on with that story?

A: Yes. I thought it would, that there would be less sympathy for him, and I wasn't completely convinced whether or not I felt it was true, and I felt that under the circumstances that the Court might not believe it. They might hold it against him.

Later on in the Post-Conviction Hearing, in answering questions put to him by Mr. Kairys, Father Powers further explained why the defense strategy of diminished responsibility rather than legal provocation was used.

Q: Did the lawyers tell you the reason for not telling the story, for Vaughan withholding this account that he had given you?

A: They did in effect—I remember, because he had a better defense in terms of the psychiatric testimony. The story, whether it was true or not, would raise a lot of questions that would complicate his defense. He had a better defense on the basis of the various psychiatric testimony that would be brought into the testimony.

Q: Was this testimony about Vaughan's mental condition? Was this to be used to reduce the degree of offense?

A: Definitely. That was the whole point. He was going to, definitely, he was going to plead guilty to the general charge, and his only strategy then was to defend himself on the basis of reducing the degree.

At the hearing, Mr. McKissock, in his cross-examination of Father Powers, tried to show that I had invented the story of the man leaving the house as a means of defense at the trial. But Father Powers didn't see it that way:

A: I do not associate that with his strategy for his defense. I think that came earlier.

McKissock also cross-examined me about this story:

Q: On direct examination you testified, first of all, that on the morning of the occurrence you saw a person coming out of your house?

A: Right.

Q: And that you then went in, and the reason you killed your wife was because you had an argument with her, at which time she stated to you that there was another man who fathered one of her children; is that correct?

A: Right.

Q: And you told this to a number of people; is that correct?

A: Yes.

Q: Whom did you first relate that to?

A: I don't remember. It's been a long time, almost four years.

Q: But you did happen to relate it to the police on the day you were taken down to the Police Administration

Building; did you?

A: No, I don't think I did.

Q: It was only sometime thereafter that you decided to tell some people the story?

A: Well, first of all, at the time—

Q: I'm just asking you a question. Would you please answer it?

A: I am going to answer your question. At the time the crime was committed, I was in such a state. Enough damage had been done. I had taken my wife's life. I wasn't going—

Q: I instruct the defendant to answer my question.

A: I wasn't going to try to degrade her lower, you know, like, what more could I do at a time like that. Plus, I was a proud individual. I am not going to go around telling people my wife had a lover. I don't think any man would do that.

Q: But at some later date you decided to tell some people your wife had a lover; is that correct? You did in fact tell them this?

A: Yes. It was weighing heavily upon me. I think it was Father Powers I told first, I think. I am not sure.

   Your Honor, there is something else. I'm sorry. I was also told by Mr. Atkins that there were pictures of my wife, the deceased, that if brought before a jury, they probably wouldn't understand as the Judges would, and would probably find me guilty of first degree murder, because of the pictures and the weapon that was used.

One other point came up in the hearing which was an apparent unwillingness on my part to receive a jury trial before a particular judge, Judge Leo Weinrott, who had a reputation as a tough judge who might persuade the jury to hand down a first degree verdict and then sentence me to death. Mr. Atkins recalls that this was a factor in choosing to have a trial with three judges rather than a jury trial. And it was.

Another serious blunder on the part of the defense counsel was when the judges at the trial asked if my lawyers wanted to again raise the point of the voluntariness and validity of the statement (my "confession" to the police after the crime). They advised me not to challenge it but allow it to be entered as evidence. The statement was probably the most important single factor which led the judges to return their verdict of first degree murder. There was evidence from at least two different psychologists or psychiatrists that I was not competent to make that statement.

Of course much of all this is either speculation or hindsight. Reading through the trial records, and with the benefit of additional information which only surfaced later, one can see that the defense was ill-conceived and woefully ineffective. Perhaps my court-appointed attorneys did their best on my behalf, or perhaps that was all they had time for.

The court records do not give a real picture of the trial. They are cut and dried pieces of paper covered with lifeless symbols, devoid of passion or even emotion. Not so the trial itself. My mother remembers it differently.

> What you see on TV is not what happens in a courtroom. They put me on the stand. I never answered one question correctly because they were throwing questions at me so fast I guess I answered the fourth or fifth question and never got around to the first three of four questions. When they sentenced him I don't think I thought anything, I was so numb.

My own recollections of the trial are of an emotionally overwhelming experience. It was all so very formal and a little scary. The judges, one black and two white, were up there in their robes and it seemed they were speaking this foreign language, this legal terminology of which I had no knowledge. I didn't really understand what was going on.

Mr. Czap, the Assistant D.A., was this very flamboyant man with a beard and mustache, wearing a bow-tie. He had a reputation for flair. I remember my lawyer saying to me before the trial that Assistant District Attorney Ivan Czap was interested in Byzantine art, and that maybe I should familiarize myself with Byzantine art.

I can see it now: He was going to question me about Byzantine art and I was supposed to respond to him in the stand! That really stands out in my mind. If these are the points on which verdicts and sentences hang, it's a sorry reflection on the nation's legal and judicial system. It is indeed fortunate, I believe, that higher forces were at work than the legal system, fraught with human error and prejudice as it is.

During the trial they used to wake us up each morning at the break of day and we would have to go to breakfast and then go back to shave and change into a suit for court. Then we went to the City Hall by prison bus. There were special cells where we would have to wait for hours from the time we got there until late at night.

As far as the guards were concerned, it was always us against them. We were prisoners and they were people.

Most of the important aspects of the trial have been covered. The prosecutor spent hours entertaining the judges with his recently acquired knowledge of the ins and outs of archery, bows, arrows, strings, the use of the bow and arrow in hunting small and large game and other irrelevancies. He had certainly done his homework. Ostensibly his purpose was to show the degree of premeditation of the act. In fact all this was simply designed to amplify the gruesome nature of the murder and the uniqueness of the weapon in the judges' minds.

In fact, Angie would have been just as dead, and probably

suffered the same pain, if I had shot her with a gun. Ivan
Czap knew this and he played on it throughout the trial.

The prosecutor and the judges also shared their little jokes.
For example, Mr. Czap asked: "Did you ever take her to the
Devon Club?"

JUDGE NIX: Take her to what?

THE WITNESS: I beg your pardon?

MR. CZAP: The Republican Club on 42nd Street or to the
    Devon—

JUDGE NIX: You are not making this a partisan matter,
    Mr. Czap? You are not trying to make this a partisan
    matter, are you?

MR. CZAP: I didn't choose the place, sir.

And later on the prosecutor quoted poetry and Judge Nix
found this quite impressive:

> I would remind—I don't think his name was
> Omar Kayyam. I think his name might have been
> Jallilud Dai Rumi, I have forgotten because it's a
> number of years, as Your Honor knows:
>
>> "The moving finger writes
>> and having writ moves on,
>> nor all your piety nor wit
>> shall lure it back;
>> to cancel half a line
>> nor all your tears wash out
>> a word of it."
>
> I do believe this defendant is showing a true
> sense of guilt, but I believe—

JUDGE NIX: That is from the *Rubaiyat*?

MR. CZAP: It is from the *Rubaiyat*.

Fine for a cocktail party. Perfectly acceptable at a social gathering perhaps. But at a trial where a man's entire future rests in the hands of these witty people? It's enough to make the taxpayer question seriously what his hard-earned tax dollars are paying for with such a justice system. Apparently this is just a game these people act out. They don their robes and go on the stage and perform.

At the time, I was simply bewildered. The prosecutor had his own way of making his presentation so he took what he considered to be all the facts and put it together and that's his story: "This is what really happened, folks."

I remember him saying things about me that had me thinking, "This can't be me." He was saying how I had thought about this over the years and then after murdering Angie I had made it look like I was insane. It wasn't a ploy. It was my actual emotional response to the event. If I had planned it, I would have done it very differently, I'm sure. You can't plan something so ill-advised. When I was listening to him it was like hearing a fairy tale and he was making up a story and presenting it to the judges.

The judges all seemed very stern and angry. They were hanging on Czap's every word.

Yet they were clearly unimpressed with the defense, as well they might have been. Had there been a conspiracy between defense and prosecution to raise the degree of guilt to first degree murder, they could hardly have done a more feeble job of their defense.

The one avenue they had open to them, realistically, was to have the statement I made to the police suppressed when the judges gave them that opportunity, and then to bring up my account of the murder, including the man I saw leaving the house and my wife's statement that I was not the father of

Vaughan, Jr. They would have had to have followed this up earlier and produced what evidence there might have been.

Had they investigated this account and come up with some evidence to support it, I would conceivably have been found guilty of voluntary manslaughter. There is no logical reason to explain why they did not at least attempt to verify this story. Mr. Atkins admitted that absolutely nothing was done to follow up on it.

Perhaps they simply didn't believe what I was telling them. Yet, taking into account all the other evidence available, this is the only explanation of my actions that morning that makes any sense. It doesn't justify the action in any way, but it does explain it. They should have followed up on this. But perhaps they didn't have time.

Even earlier than that, perhaps I should have accepted the plea bargain, taken the 7 to 14 years and got busy with redeeming myself for my act. In a justice system such as this, expediency rather than truth seems to be the guiding factor, since so little attention is paid to the truth anyway.

The judges listened to the arguments of the defense and the prosecution, were obviously in agreement with Mr. Czap's conclusions, and openly scoffed at the defense counsel's attempts to backpedal at the last minute and claim legal provocation. The psychiatrists and psychologists testifying were obviously uncertain of their facts and made fools out of themselves, invalidating their own testimonies.

And so, on Friday the 13th of February, 1970, at 4:02 in the afternoon, the court retired "for the purpose of deliberating and arriving at the degree of guilt." They reappeared at 4:37. Perhaps it was significant that it was Judge Nix, the only black man on the panel, who read the bill of indictment. This would help avoid any accusations of racial prejudice.

Let me have the bill of indictment. Mr. Vaughan P. L. Booker, in this bill of indictment, December

> Sessions, 1967, No. 1639, in which you entered a
> plea of guilty to murder generally, this court finds
> you guilty of murder in the first degree.

The other two judges concurred, making it a unanimous decision. They then heard testimony with reference to the penalty. The choices open to them were death, or life—life in prison that is. I listened to the testimony of Father Powers, Sidney Repplier, Barbara Harris—"so many very respected persons of the community in high positions who think so highly of him that they have taken time out from their very busy schedules to be here in his behalf," as Mr. Atkins put it to the judges.

In a way one could say I owe my life to these people, particularly Father Powers who clearly impressed the court. But it is fairly apparent from the trial records that any bloodthirsty desires on the part of Mr. Czap had been assuaged by the first degree finding and the judges themselves seemed already to have decided the sentence. Father Powers was, however, very persuasive in his testimony as to the importance of preserving my life. Who knows what effect this may have had?

I remember that brief period of time when my life was in the balance—the balance which was held in the rather shaky hands of the justice system where it could be tipped either way without much difficulty.

I had gone into the trial expecting to get 10 years, second degree. I was told not to worry because it wouldn't rise above second degree, 10 to 20 years. When I heard the sentence I was relieved, in a way, because it was over. Had they given me the death penalty, I wouldn't have been upset about it. I could have dealt with it. I was still feeling that way.

I had been crying uncontrollably through much of the trial. I remember seeing my family there and Angie's family and it was terrible. I hadn't seen my children in three years. I was heartbroken. I didn't know what was going on with them and

I felt awful. But now at least I knew that it was over.

The end of the trial was rather anticlimactic. It was also a bit more human than the rest of it.

JUDGE NIX: Anything further, gentlemen?

MR. ATKINS: No, Your Honor.

JUDGE NIX: Mr. Booker, is there anything you would like to say to this Court before the Court recesses for deliberation as to punishment?

THE DEFENDANT: Your Honor, there is nothing I would like to say, except I would like to extend to my in-laws apologies, which is all I can do. I feel I have been given justice by this Court. I have been found guilty of said crime. I think I've gotten to the point of maturity now where I can reflect back on things that have happened years ago and try to just make a better life for myself today and tomorrow.

JUDGE NIX: All right. We now again tell Counsel not to leave the confines of the room. We do not anticipate being out that long.

(The 3-judge panel retired at 5:15 P.M. and returned at 5:23 P.M.)

JUDGE NIX: Bring the defendant to the bar of the court.

Mr. Booker, after due deliberation the Court after considering the testimony that has been offered in mitigation, the facts of the case, and all of the other factors that have been brought out during the course of this hearing, it was unanimously decided that the punishment to be imposed is that you be sentenced to the

Eastern State Penitentiary at Graterford for a period of your natural life.

I may say that this Court with heavy heart had to first find an adjudication of guilty of murder in the first degree, and of course, impose the sentence. You were a young man who had all the promise. God had endowed you with many, many gifts that many youngsters don't have, and it's unfortunate that this incident, these few hours, marred what was otherwise an excellent life. Certainly we cannot in our limited facilities understand the working of the Divine. I am sure, however, that there is some reason that this happened, and I hope that you profit by it. I feel extremely sorry for your parents and I know the disappointment in their feelings. Equally I offer my regrets and the regrets of the members of this court to the family of the victim. It was a useless, senseless death.

I trust, young man, that you will never forget the seriousness of what you have done. I also hope that you have been impressed by the fact that these persons, like the Father and the others who have come here, have taken of their time to say a good word for you. I think it demonstrates that when you give of yourself to others that when the need arises there will be someone who will give of themself for you. I trust that wherever you will be assigned you will take advantage of the opportunities of that institution, and that when you are considered for parole that you will have profited by the experience.

Whether or not I heard what Judge Nix said to me, I seem to have taken his advice to heart.

As to the workings of the Divine, I have my own explanation of the events. I liken my story to that of Jonah, best known for his well-advertised residency in the belly of a whale, the prophet who didn't heed God's word but decided to strike out on his own, with dire consequences.

I feel I was called to the priesthood when I was quite young but I didn't listen and I turned away from my church, ignoring my calling. I went through the storm and ended up at Graterford prison (Jonah's prison was the belly of a sea monster—who can tell which was the worse punishment! Mine lasted longer, for sure.). But my faith was renewed and I was received back by God.

This explanation, at least, takes the matter of justice out of the hands of prosecutors and defense counsels, witnesses and judges, forgives them to some degree for their ineptitude, and puts the events of my life in a more understandable light.

For despite all the vagaries of the justice system, I served a sentence no shorter or longer than I felt I deserved. I took the opportunity and all of that time to change my life. I had murdered Angie and nothing in the world could diminish the severity of that crime or excuse it in any way. After all, there is divorce available. I accepted my punishment and looked on it as an opportunity. I was still alive.

But now, the belly of my sea monster, Graterford Penitentiary, awaited me with locked gates, mean dogs, and unsympathetic guards.

CHAPTER SEVEN

"...I was in prison and you visited me."

(Matthew 25:36)

The waiting was over. The decision was made. It wasn't exactly my idea of going home, but Graterford State Correctional Institution would be my home for many years to come.

I went back to Holmesburg and packed up my few belongings. There were some other men from the Detention Center who were also going to Graterford. In the years I had been in the system I had come to know a lot of people, so the prospect of going to the penitentiary was not an overly ominous or frightening one. It was a matter of seeing friends again when you went to the pen. In a way I was looking forward to it. I had heard about this wonderful food, because they had a farm and were self-contained. There was even fresh milk.

The inmates knew I was involved in academic and religious programs and I had the respect of a lot of them. People probably have the impression that the tough guys get the respect in jail. The place was full of tough guys. With the tough guys it's always a matter of who is tougher. Everybody wants to be the fastest gun in the West. A lot of men came in like that. But times were changing. The real respect seemed to be more for thinking people.

There were about 25 of us on the bus, handcuffed in pairs. We were conversing on the way, watching the countryside go by through the bus's heavily meshed windows. Although we talked a lot, one thing I didn't discuss was my case and I didn't want to know about other people's cases. I had heard stories about people who would work their way into someone else's confidence, find things out about them and then would call or write the District Attorney and snitch in an attempt to get themselves a reduction in sentence.

Graterford is way out in the country about 30 miles northwest of Philadelphia. It was a long ride but a beautiful one and we began to think it would never end. People would see the prison bus go by and some would wave while others would boo.

Holmesburg had resembled a medieval castle with a dungeon. By comparison, Graterford looked rather modern although it was built in the 1930s. It had a huge wall around the outside with massive main gates and guard towers at each corner.

When we first went in, we were assigned to the diagnostic and classification center which I think was E Block. We had to wear blue uniforms instead of the tan uniforms everyone else was wearing. We were given psychological and academic tests to see where we would be placed.

My number was H90-95 and that's what the guards would call me. But that's just a mind game. You can call me H90-95 but I know my name is Vaughan Booker and that's just a code for my name, so I didn't feel dehumanized.

We spent two or three months being classified. You have to remember that this is an institution with up to 400 men to a block and 5 blocks, so it could hold 2,000 men. These were criminals of all types: murderers, rapists, armed robbers, drug dealers, forgers, you name it.

I was classified as a lifer. This was a maximum security

institution so there were a large number of lifers there. Part of the purpose of the classification process was to determine where you would work, because everyone at Graterford worked. It was like a self-contained estate. Everything was done by the inmates, and the guards were there to oversee their activities. The inmates worked in the boiler rooms to ensure the place was hot; they butchered the food; they did all the work, under the supervision of the people hired by the state. Everyone had a job.

If you had a mental illness you didn't really belong at that institution and would be sent to Fairview, which was for the criminally insane.

I did well on the tests. On the academic one I scored a 12.6 and I think the highest you could get was a 12.9. On the psychological, which was an IQ test, I believe I scored 125. This helped get me a job, later on, in the school as a clerk.

I started to settle in. This was where I was going to be for the rest of my life—a life sentence in Pennsylvania was supposed to average about 18 1/2 years. I regarded it as an opportunity. We were moved to one of the regular blocks. Each man had a cell, about 6' by 9' with walls, and a door that had a grille you could see through. I changed to the regular uniform which was supposed to be tan but rapidly faded to a sort of dirty rose color.

To begin with, like everyone else, I went to work in the kitchen. Each block had its own dining area but there was one large, central kitchen for the whole prison. The food was delivered to the blocks by cart. I used to cook. All new arrivals went to work in the kitchen first. I think they wanted everyone to do the kitchen detail to let us know that we were all convicts. No one escapes this.

We would get up early in the morning, 5:30 I think it was. Breakfast was at 6:00 or 6:30. Then we'd come back and go to work, probably at about 8:00. At 11:15 we'd go back to the block for a head count—count the cattle to make sure none are missing—then lunch, then back to work until about 3:30. Then there was a 3:30 head count. Usually everyone was there for the head count and it would take 15 minutes unless there was a miscount. There were times when they would have to shut the whole jail down until they found someone who was unaccounted for. Every once in a while someone would really be missing: he'd gone out on the garbage truck or something like that. But that was the end of the work day. Then we'd have a shower and get ready for dinner and recreation. If it was winter time the residents would watch TV or play chess. There was even a group of men who would get together and gamble, even though that was completely illegal. Recreation would go on until about 9:30 and then they would close the cell block for the night. You could go in your cell.

Actually when I first went there the lights would be out at 9:00 but when Mr. Johnson became the superintendent he would leave the lights on all night because he knew people wanted to read.

Some jobs gave you time in the morning to go out in the yard, which was a huge recreation area, big enough to hold a football field and a full track. There were twenty handball courts. In the summer there was a yard period in the evening as well. They would have baseball games, sometimes three games going at the same time, and you could play volleyball. Sometimes they would have talent shows outside, because there was a lot of talent in that place: people who could play various musical instruments and so on.

They used to blow a whistle again for every meal, but now I used to respond negatively to the whistle. I had read about Pavlov and his dogs by this time and I thought, "Hey, they're conditioning us." So I checked it out—I wouldn't go so far as to look into the men's mouths to see if they were salivating— but the fact is they would be hungry when the whistle blew. The whistle would blow and the reaction would be, "Oh man, am I hungry."

So I stopped going to regular meals when they blew the whistle. I would pay the swag man a pack of cigarettes for a sandwich. The swag man is the man who sold the sandwiches. You pay him a pack of cigarettes and he drops a sandwich in your cell—jail house life.

But discipline was tight. We were given a booklet with the rules and everything had to be done within the rules. There were lines on the prison floor and you had to walk the lines. If you got out of line you could be written up and put in solitary confinement. You weren't allowed to roll up the sleeves of your uniform shirt. You couldn't be late for work. All these rules were enforced.

I realized that if I was going to survive this experience and benefit from it, I needed to establish a personal regimen and then maintain it.

I had an academic program, a spiritual program, and a physical program. I used to lift weights just about every day. I played handball and another inmate and I even worked our way up to winning the championship. I set my own curriculum based on my priorities. I had a television but I only watched some sports. Most of the time I used to lend it to my friends. Usually I was reading—reading with a purpose. I did like to play chess and that would make a nice break in my rigorous program. Otherwise I would just be lost in what I was doing.

I followed that same routine for years. Even to this day I am usually up at 5:30 or 6:00 in the morning, giving me time for prayer or meditation or just to reflect and get my thoughts clear.

After my stint in the kitchens which lasted a few months, I went to work as a clerk in the school. Here I was administering the same tests that I had received when I first arrived. Later I went to work in the dental lab. For this job I had to study dental technology: how to do survey and design, how to fit up dentures and make partials; how to do metal work. I became proficient at making plates and supplying false teeth. The lab at Graterford would do the dental work for all of the state institutions.

During this time, my connection with the Church in no way diminished. The Fellowship of St. Dismas continued to meet regularly, and I stayed in close contact with Father Powers. There were meetings at 8 o'clock every Wednesday—Wednesday was our Sunday—and we would have Eucharist. There was a service on Sunday as well, but that was a general Protestant service. The chapel at Graterford is a huge auditorium, capable of seating many hundreds of people. It has a revolving altar in order to accommodate different faiths. On one side is a Protestant altar with just a plain cross, then when you push it around it has a crucifix on another side, which is the Catholic altar; if you turn it around another way it has the star of David and can be used in Jewish services.

When Father Powers moved on to another ministry, his place was taken by Reverend Dick Swartout. He has many memories of religious life at Graterford. He also remembers me very well, not surprisingly since he is one of the individuals most responsible for my progress in the Church, all the way through to ordination as a priest after I left Graterford. We first met at Graterford in September of 1971 when he began attending the Wednesday meetings of the St. Dismas group. In a recent interview Father Swartout recalled his prison ministry and his relationship with me.

> I remember my first Eucharist. I looked in my briefcase and I had brought the bread and the wine but I hadn't brought a chalice. So I said, "Does anyone here have a cup?" Well at that time each inmate had a cup on his belt that he would take to the chow hall with him. It was his personal cup to use in the cell and the mess hall.

One of the fellows (this wasn't Vaughan) said, "Sure, you can use my cup. But wait a minute." And he ran outside and did something and came back in with a paper towel and he was shining his cup and that cup shone like silver.

I said, "What did you do? Where did you get the metal polish to clean your cup? It's so pretty."

"There's no metal polish in this institution," he replied. "I just used cigarette ashes."

The acid in the cigarette ashes really cleaned it up and made it sparkle. From that time on I never brought in a chalice: I used a different person's cup every service. It was very special.

We had the various inmates or residents read the Scripture readings in the Communion service. And then rather than have a sermon, we would have a rap session about those Scriptures. [That's not the music form, but *rap* as in "discussion or conversation."] The men would build their own sermon out of those discussions. It was my belief that if you are not living there, how can you talk about how to live there. These rap sessions would last about an hour or an hour and a half, which is longer than any sermon on the outside.

Vaughan was different from the run-of-the-mill population. You could tell right off the bat that he had a different agenda. He wasn't a street runner, you might say. He was just a guy who was like a number of other guys in there who did something and were incarcerated. He wasn't a school drop-out or on drugs early on or into some kind of drug related thing or playing a game within the institution.

Early on I had had a conversation with Fred Powers about Vaughan's desire to study for the

ministry in the Episcopal Church and I concurred
with Fred that that seemed like a good idea. Fred
told me that Vaughan stood out like a sore thumb
at Holmesburg, because here were all these jitter-
bugs running around the place and here's this
guy standing there with a nicely shaved afro,
with a kind of presence, but distraught—just like
you are seeing now with O. J. Simpson. You
know, he had some college education. Maybe
Father Anderson, the Rector of St. Thomas, had
called Fred Powers and asked him to look in on
Vaughan, I don't know. I would have colleagues
calling me from around town saying, "Hey, Dick,
one of my altar boys just got busted, would you
go and see him in the Detention Center." So that
may have happened.

Reverend Swartout and I both recall a distinctly anti-
rehabilitation attitude that pervaded the minds of some of the
officers in the employ of the Department of Corrections at the
time. Despite the name of the department they worked for,
they were of the old school which held that prisoners should
be locked up and that was it. Anyone trying to do something
to help them or make them better people was simply wasting
his or her time. This is much the attitude you see today, but
for a while when I was at Graterford, perhaps sparked off by
the Attica prison riots, there was a serious attempt on the part
of the institutions to change this attitude. But that came later.

Father Swartout remembers a couple of incidents that
exemplify this attitude.

One day I came into the institution and it was the
opening of the hunting season so the regular
guards weren't at the front gate. They had pulled
a guard down from one of the towers—his name

was Nichols—and he was at the front gate.

I opened my briefcase and I had a little bottle of wine there, the same bottle I had been bringing in to the prisons for years, for the Eucharist. Nichols decided it wasn't going into the institution and he took it out of my briefcase and put it on the stand.

I said, "I'll have to go in and talk to Mr. Wolfe about this."

"You do anything you damned well please, but that ain't going in this institution while I'm at this gate," was his reply.

I went in and talked to the assistant superintendent, Bob Wolfe, and Bob said, "Oh my gosh, call one of the lieutenants over." And he said, "Chaplain Swartout's sacramental wine is out at the front gate and Nichols won't allow him to bring it in. Will you take care of this?"

So the lieutenant got on the phone and said, "Nichols, give the Reverend his bottle," and hung up.

I walked back to the gate and I went over to one side of the corridor and put my briefcase down by a stand. Nichols approached from his stand on the opposite end of the gate and just as I got to the middle of the gate, he put his hand through the bars and threw my wine and said, "Here's your goddamned wine," and it smashed all over the floor.

So I stopped right there at the gate and I looked at him and said, "Mr. Nichols, please open this gate." He opened the gate and I went over to the telephone and dialed Bob Wolfe's office and said, "Bob, Nichols just busted my bottle out here, now what do we do?"

"Oh my God, Dick, you'd better go and get another one." So I hung up and walked over to the outside gate and said, "Mr. Nichols, please open this gate," and he did and off I went. I drove down to the liquor store in Collegeville and bought a little bottle of wine—I think it was sparkling burgundy—brought it back in a brown paper bag. My briefcase was still laying there, open when I came up to the gate. There was a brand new guard there and when I walked in he went straight over to the gate, opened it and let me in. I said, "Good morning," and he said, "Good morning," and I put the wine in my briefcase and away I went to the chapel.

Now what was happening at the time is that a lot of these officers didn't like the policies of Bob Johnson, the new superintendent at Graterford who was very liberal and open. The guards didn't like that.

Well, later on that morning, we were at the Eucharist, we'd had the rap session and I was getting ready to consecrate the bread and wine as our Lord's body and blood. I had about 25 inmates around the table in the chapel area, and right at that point a sergeant and two guards walked in the door. They came up to where we were and said, "Chaplain, this area has to be cleared immediately."

I said, "Sergeant, there must be some mistake. I'm in the middle of a Communion service here. You'd better check with the major. We're going to be done in about 10 minutes."

He turned around and went back down the corridor with the two guards who, during our conversation, had circled around behind the altar to make sure we didn't have any kind of activity going on back there.

So I started reading the prayer of consecration, which begins, "For on the night in which he was betrayed..." and here the three guards are walking away, "...he took bread and gave thanks and broke it..."

They came back in at the end of the of the prayer of consecration, while we were saying the Lord's Prayer and everybody was reciting it together. At the end of the prayer the sergeant said, "Chaplain, I've checked with the major and this area has to be cleared immediately."

I said, "Yes sir, Sergeant, we will clear it immediately." And I picked up the bread and Vaughan picked up the chalice with the wine in it and as the men came by I administered bread to one man and Vaughan administered the chalice and they all started walking single file down the corridor singing, "We shall overcome, we shall overcome...."

It was the most poignant moment in ministry that you could have. It was unprepared, but someone started it and the guards, who looked like you could have melted them, were chagrined, because in that moment they looked like fools messing around because something greater was happening.

It was in 1971 that Robert Johnson was appointed superintendent at Graterford, to the dismay of many of the "old school." In the first place, he was an outsider: He came from the parole department. Secondly he was black—in fact he was the first black superintendent in the state of Pennsylvania, which says something for race relations at the time. But Allyn Sielaff, State Bureau of Correction Commissioner, appointed him knowing full well that this might go against the grain.

I remember the time well, because life in the prison began to change.

This was the time of George Jackson and Angela Davis and there was a revolution occurring—a change in black awareness. We started reaffirming ourselves, wearing afros and calling ourselves black instead of Negro. This filtered its way into the prison system. And because this was during the Civil Rights era, you didn't always just have stereotype criminals in prison. There were also educated people, professors, and others who would be locked up because of their activism.

The old philosophy of lock them up and throw away the key was changing. The focus was different. When I arrived we were only allowed to use the earphones that were supplied and we could only listen in to whatever was on, but now we were allowed personal radios and TVs. We began to see volunteers and people from religious groups and social service groups coming into the prison and working with the inmates. The old guard was getting ready to change. The strict warden type where you had to walk the line was giving way to a new type where rehabilitation was considered important. You could feel the tension being relieved.

When I first arrived you couldn't even have anything up on the walls of your cells, but these regulations were relaxed with Bob Johnson. I dressed my cell up. I had pictures of family and girls I had been in touch with and some posters. I started collecting books and I had them stacked and lined up all along the whole wall. We had a foot locker and, of course, a bed. If I had to be there I might as well make it as nice as I could.

Bob Johnson used to have entertainers come to the prison: Patti La Belle, Billy Paul and people like that. It became a more humane experience. The guards were apparently being retrained to be more humane in their treatment of prisoners.

Robert Johnson, since retired, remembers well his time at Graterford and his contact with me.

> I was an egalitarian kind of individual. I wanted the country to be as good as it said it was, when I knew damn well it wasn't. I thought I would try and have some impact on the place.
>
> I accepted the job of superintendent of Graterford in 1971. I had never worked at a prison before, although I had done voluntary work with group therapy. This was unusual but it was planned that way. Commissioner Sielaff didn't want to use people who were already in the system because he wanted to bring about real reforms.
>
> He wanted to get somebody with potential and a willingness to take risks and make changes. People already within the system were not willing to take those risks, for the most part.
>
> The prison's capacity at the time was 2,000 but any time there were over 1,300 inmates it was a dangerous place to be.
>
> I started to bring the community into the prison. I started talking directly to the prisoners themselves. I would get on the PA system and talk to them all at the same time or I would talk to them in groups. I brought my family in and had them meet with and talk to groups of inmates.
>
> I had a system whereby the men could write me a letter and I would respond to it in writing. I'd go home at night and sit down and answer the letters. Sometimes I'd get 400 letters a day and respond to each one by hand.
>
> Talking to the inmates the way I did and responding to them like that, the old, hard-line staff thought of me as the inmates' superinten-

dent, rather than the superintendent at Graterford.

I wanted to do a good job and keep the staff as safe as possible and make those changes. I did everything I could to keep the inmates there who had been sentenced there. I refused to participate in any additional punishment beyond the incarceration. I insisted that people be spoken to in terms of their names rather than their numbers.

I got to know the inmates and groups of inmates. Graterford was a large place with a very diverse population. We had a group of radical white inmates, a group of radical blacks; there were Muslim groups, Christian groups, Jewish groups, homosexual groups, groups interested in law. I allowed the inmates to establish a law clinic with the help of some of the students of the Pennsylvania Law School. They could do their legal work if they decided to file post trial motions and that sort of thing.

Vaughan was one of those inmates who were middle class in their views. There are inmates who come from very poor socioeconomic educational situations and there are inmates that come from middle class or "wannabe" middle class situations. I came from a wannabe middle class sort of background so I related more to people with similar origins.

Vaughan was in one of those groups that we could talk to about the sort of changes we could make and get them involved in educational programs.

It was an exciting time to be working in the prison system in Pennsylvania because the emphasis was on reform. Robert

Johnson initiated the first furlough program at Graterford. Lifers were excluded, but certain inmates, based on an evaluation by the staff, were allowed to go on weekend furloughs. Opposed by law enforcement agencies and District Attorneys, particularly by Senator Arlen Specter, the furlough program achieved a 97% success rate and gained a lot of bad press.

Graterford under Robert Johnson was also the first prison to have an inmate marry while inside. The wedding was held within the cold, looming walls of that institution.

Mr. Johnson also gave his approval to residence outside the wall, of which more later. He even made an effort to send inmates out to work—they'd leave in the morning and come back at night.

> We were also the first to bring into the institution a female social worker who could walk freely through the prison. Her name was Anne Cleaver and she eventually became the superintendent of the female institution for the state.
>
> Before she came I spoke to some of the inmates and they said they would see that nothing happened to her. She was safer than I was in that institution.

On Monday May 21, 1973, the Philadelphia *Daily News* ran an article by Nels Nelson on Graterford, "A Changing Prison," with further insight into Robert Johnson and what he was accomplishing:

> Prisons are the attics of State bureaucracy.
>
> The superintendent's office at the State Correction Institution at Graterford is crammed with dark, old-fashioned furniture of World War II vintage.
>
> Finding the superintendent among these

bureaucratic discards can take some doing.

Robert L. Johnson, a flamboyant and controversial man of 48 who never ran a prison before his appointment in March 1971, avoids his office like a small boy avoids a cemetery.

He is strong on community relations and spends a lot of time on outside missionary work.

Johnson has an agile mind and a flair for the dramatic. He reminds one of a pony-sized Muhammad Ali. He is likely to begin an interview by saying: "I don't believe in prisons."

He'll amplify: "Society is kidding itself by thinking that prisons are going to solve problems. Only a small percentage of those arrested end up in penal institutions and you have a vast number of people still out there creating danger in the streets.

"The least we can do is to try to humanize places like this, so that when we send these men back to society they are not quite as angry or dangerous."

It is unlikely that many of Graterford's residents are as free in their praise of Johnson as Anthony ("Tough Tony") Scoleri, a murderer who lived for 14 years on "death row." Scoleri schooled himself in the law and until very recently directed the prison's law clinic.

"In prisons, people are treated like animals and then expected to act like human beings," Scoleri told a reporter. "Johnson treats us like human beings. I've found my vocation. It was Johnson who started the law clinic. He's the best."

Jack Lopinson is another inmate who was at Graterford when I was. Like me, he was there on a murder charge. He was sentenced to death for the contract double homicide of his wife and business partner. Unlike me, Jack is still there, although he is no longer on death row. In fact, he is living outside the walls in the trailer camp and is considered a real asset to the institution. He remembers the law clinic and comments on our time together as fellow inmates of Graterford in the '70s.

> I met Vaughan when we both enrolled in the Villanova Criminal Justice Program that Philadelphia University brought into Graterford under the tutelage of Dr. James McKenna (ironically he was nicknamed "Killer" McKenna, as he was very strict). It was an excellent program. So we were taking courses together and Vaughan and I just happened to hit it off. I have to admire him. He was different, and I mean that in a complimentary, not a negative way. He didn't try to compete with the mores of the prison; Vaughan did his own thing.
>
> I had to respect him for it because not too many of us were doing that and he was a good man. Vaughan was helping others even before he became a deacon at the church. If Vaughan saw someone he could help write a letter home or something, he would.
>
> He got involved in the inmate law clinic when it could be started here in 1971, which was the first inmate law clinic inside a prison in the United States. Vaughan was a member of the law clinic with us—he was one of the founding members.
>
> We used to work with the Clerk of the Court for Philadelphia and in the other counties and assisted other inmates in prosecuting their appeals.

A vast majority of men in prison can't afford private counsel so the court appoints Public Defenders. And they are swamped. Their case loads are horrendous. It's almost a physical impossibility for them to prepare a case adequately so most of their representation boils down to deal-making.

When all new inmates arrive here they are faced with a limited time in which to appeal. We would help them file their Notices of Appeal.

We never went to court to represent anyone— we knew we were amateurs and laymen. Educated laymen, but laymen.

But Vaughan even went beyond legal work and this is what I mean when I say he was a good man. In talking with some of the men he was helping file papers, the man might mention some personal problems that had nothing to do with the filing of legal papers. And Vaughan would sit and talk. He never tired of listening. He would write letters and would try to smooth troubled waters between the inmate and his family or loved ones. He was practicing his vocation before he entered it officially.

I came to know Vaughan very well. We became close. We found that we could talk to one another and we kind of let our guards down.

I once asked him why he was doing all these good things—because it was so unusual in a prison setting to find a guy like that—I said, "Vaughan, is it that you are doing this as an act of atonement? Are you trying out of remorse to atone for what you did?"

He said, "I'm not consciously doing that because of that. Maybe subconsciously I am, but no, I don't say, 'Well, what can I do today to help towards atoning for this?' I'm just doing what I can to help people." He said, "I'll never be able to atone for what I've done. No one can."

I agreed. I said, "You're right, all of the atonement in the world will not bring that person back to life." And I said, "But it does help to try and do something—as much as you can as long as you can in the parameters in which you are working."

He said, "No, Jack, I don't do it consciously. In fact I never thought about it till you mentioned it. Perhaps you're right, perhaps I am. But I can't just sit by and watch somebody not get help when I can help them." He said, "Don't get me wrong, I'm not trying to save the world. I'm not a goody-two-shoes or anything like that. If I can help a guy and the guy sincerely needs it and I can do it, and I have the time, and the guy will accept the help, I'll help him, because that's what life's all about."

He told me about his crime and how he came to get a first degree murder sentence. I would stake whatever life I have left on the fact that I do not believe Vaughan premeditated that murder. I'm not lessening the fact and Vaughan has never lessened the fact. If Vaughan had to do it over again I know he would much rather shoot himself than shoot her. No way could anyone in the world convince me that Vaughan coldly sat down, planned it, plotted it and executed it. I think it was a spontaneous thing that simply happened. Nobody could say it was planned. Who plans a murder with a bow and arrow? Come on.

When word came that Vaughan was going to

be accepted by the Episcopal Church and enter the program to become a deacon, it was unheard of and everyone thought it was great. As a mark of the respect the guys had for Vaughan, nobody put him down.

In other words, nobody said, "Yeah, well, he's one of these people who all of a sudden found religion and God and now he's going to use that as a cop out to get out of prison." That's usually the first thing that enters the cynical minds of most prisoners. "Yeah, he's as phony as a three-dollar bill." I never heard anybody say Vaughan was a phony. Because Vaughan didn't come out of nowhere with this. It just seemed a natural flow of events that Vaughan did: that the next step was that Vaughan was officially recognized or given the opportunity by the church to carry it further. This just seemed natural to Vaughan.

It wasn't like a guy came in and, quite often he becomes, for lack of a better term, born again. There are a lot of sincere born again men here. There are also a lot of phonies. You see the guy all of a sudden going to church and he is holier than thou. And he no sooner leaves the service than he becomes anything but holier than thou. You know, he turns it on and off like a light switch. The guys know it. It's pretty hard to con a con. Most inmates know who is sincere and who isn't and it's not what you say out of your mouth, it's what you do, the way you carry yourself, the way you act, the way you are thought of by others.

If convicts sat on a parole board, half of these guys wouldn't make parole. Then again, a lot of men who aren't making parole would make it.

Vaughan never played that game; Vaughan played it straight. This is what I think I most admire about him: there wasn't a phony bone in his body. Vaughan was a straight shooter. He didn't tell you what you wanted to hear. He told you what he honestly felt. In fact he was just sincerely good. He was almost too good to believe. At first I was very skeptical.

Jack married while he was in prison. I also knew his wife, Diana, quite well. She was the outside chairperson with the United Church of Christ task force in criminal justice. Like Jack (and many others), she was suspicious of me at first.

To be very honest, when I first met Vaughan I was very cautious. He, like Jack, did not fit the type of person that you would expect to find. And I was quite familiar with prisons. My mother had worked at Delaware County Prison in the office when I was growing up so it wasn't like the first time I had walked into a prison.

But you always have a pre-design of what you are going to find and Vaughan did not fit that image. He was very well educated, very well spoken. I was cautious. But it didn't take me long to realize that he was very sincere, very repentant.

What changed my mind was his sincerity. When you do a lot of work within prisons or you're around them a lot you find a lot of people that use the religious thing as a means to obtain an end, which is, of course, getting out.

Being a very skeptical person I was very cautious and suspicious in the beginning because I felt that this was what he was doing.

Everybody else that I have ever seen that is into the religious bag is strictly using it as a means to an end. I can tell that because I see them when they're not "on," so to speak. I see them cheating on their wives, causing trouble for someone, doing things that don't "fit" with what I would call a truly religious person. So I know them to be a phony. Over the years you can't help but see when they're honest with you when they're not "on"—when they're not performing for a certain group or individual who might be of help to them or something like that.

But I can honestly say that he's the only one that wasn't using it. I can't think of any others. The rest of them did not live the life they preached.

The more time I spent with him the more I realized he was sincere. That it was not a means to an end for him. It was a true vocation. It was something he was truly called to do.

One thinks of prison as a place where people go when they are outlawed by society and that all life for these people ceases when they are so outlawed. But it is only in the eyes of the society that has shut them out that they cease to exist. To the men and women inside prison, life goes on, and still holds, within those all-containing walls, most of the elements of life in the world outside.

It may be a different kind of society, but it is a society nevertheless: an environment in which people from all walks of life are thrown together to make what they can of their lives, getting any help they are able to from wherever it is available.

And this was the environment in which I took my first official steps on the path to becoming a man of God. These were just a few of the many people who helped me on the way.

CHAPTER EIGHT

... let them first be tested; then, if they prove themselves blameless, let them serve as deacons.

(1 Timothy 3:10)

Father Powers had planted the seeds in my mind when he asked me why I should not consider serving in the church, even though I was in prison for murder.

"You made a mistake, but God will forgive you if you are truly penitent," he had told me. "If God can forgive you, He can move His church and His children to forgive you." After that it was up to me.

Those seeds had fallen on fertile ground and now they started to sprout.

I read extensively, from *Principles of Christian Theology* by John MacQuarrie, *Siddartha* by Hermann Hesse, various books by C. S. Lewis, *Blood in my Eye* by George Jackson, *If They Come in the Morning* by Angela Davis, and of course the different versions of the Bible along with Bible commentaries. There were books on Greek philosophy, books on theology, the criminal justice system, utilitarianism, the difference between the justice systems of Great Britain and America.... The range of my reading was broad and I read with an appetite. Later on at when I was working in the chapel at Graterford I would find even more time to read. For now, I used the time that was available.

Then came the day in October 1971 when I felt ready to write to the Episcopal Diocese of Pennsylvania with an extra-ordinary request: that I, a resident of Graterford penitentiary serving a life sentence for murder, be accepted as a postulant in the church, to study for Holy Orders.

I had already spoken to the bishop, the Right Reverend Robert L. DeWitt, and had met with encouragement in this plan. So it was not without hope that I penned my request, the first of its nature ever to land on the bishop's desk.

Bishop DeWitt was by nature a progressive man. He had already demonstrated that he was not of a cautious, conservative mold. There was the incident with Girard College in Philadelphia, a segregated, all-white college located not far from where I grew up. In fact, I knew it well, because the only real brushes with racism I had had as a child were when going to Scouts past Girard College and being set upon by some of its students.

The bishop, mindful of the biblical precedent where the walls of Jericho fell to the Israelites, led a procession around the walls of Girard College, in protest of its overt racism.

Unlike with Jericho, the walls of Girard College did not fall flat so that the besieging army could pour in. However, not long afterwards the college was desegregated and the bishop's aims were achieved. You could say the walls fell down metaphorically and symbolically. His exploits certainly raised some eyebrows, both religious and secular.

I was very impressed with the fact that the bishop would come to Graterford and visit me, a convicted murderer, in my own cell, sit there on my bed and have long conversations with me.

Bishop DeWitt later recalled his early contacts with me and his sponsorship of the young lifer, and there is some pride in the fact that his trust and vision were vindicated.

Reverend Fred Powers was the Chaplain at Graterford—a very well trained man, very astute, insightful—and I had conversations with him about his ministry at Graterford. In the course of that I visited the prison several times. On one of those visits I met Vaughan Booker and I remember some conversations with Fred Powers about Vaughan: he said he seemed to be a very seriously concerned young man. One thing led to another and we finally got to talking about the possibility of seeing if he would care to be ordained to the ministry. I was relying upon the chaplain's knowledge of Vaughan far more than mine, which was really only very casual contact at that time.

Subsequent to that I personally visited Vaughan a good number of times out at Graterford prison because the bishop is supposed to have the final say on whether a person is approved for beginning studies leading to ordination.

I had lengthy conversations with him out there. We talked about his crime; we talked about his theological convictions; what the source of his faith was; what he believed and what he didn't believe; and whether he would be interested in considering ordination as a possibility for his future and if so where that would take him. Because at that point it was not clear at all that he would ever be released from prison. It was a life sentence, subject to subtractions for this reason or that. At that point it seemed perfectly possible that he might be there for the rest of his life.

But there was something to this idea of having a person in prison ordained where his ministry would be essentially to his fellow prisoners. It had something very legitimate and appealing to it in my eyes. So we talked about that and I continued to talk to Father Powers about it.

Vaughan struck me as a very able young man. He had a lot of vitality and energy and seemed to be putting things together pretty well in terms of his understanding of himself and the world, his prison sentence and everything else. He seemed increasingly to have his feet on the ground.

There were a lot of conversations within the diocese with priests and lay people and with official diocesan bodies like the Standing Committee which is the sort of council of advice to the bishop. They raised all sorts of questions about him and they discussed it at great length at two or three different meetings. My concern was increasingly out of feelings that this was a legitimate thing to do and a fair thing to do and that it would be unfair not to do it because Vaughan increasingly seemed to be interested and showed evidences of being called to the ministry.

There seemed to be no question about his ability and no question about the validity of his intentions. The question came to settle down more and more around what kind of a situation is it where we're taking somebody who is convicted of murder to be ordained in the ministry. That was the hard thing for the Standing Committee to swallow.

I remember one of the committee members commenting that on that basis Moses would have been forbidden the right to ordination in an Episcopal Church because, as the book of Exodus tells us, in a fit of rage he killed an

Egyptian who was oppressing his people.

I had made a point of having Vaughan interviewed by a psychiatrist in Philadelphia who was
the psychiatrist who interviewed all applicants
for the ministry in the diocese. This is an effort
that is true of most dioceses to use psychological
insights to determine if there is some applicant
who seems to be off base and does not seem to
know what he or she is doing or seems to have
ulterior motives. The psychiatrist gave a very
high report on Vaughan and that seemed to carry
a lot of weight with the Standing Committee.

If I was to become a postulant, then I wanted to do it right,
despite the rather unusual circumstances of my situation and
living conditions at the time.

We talked about how I saw my ministry unfolding. I didn't
see any freedom on the horizon at the time. My aspirations in
regard to the ministry were not related to anything that was
going on or might go on in the criminal justice system. They
are two separate issues. I thought I would go on and become
first a deacon and then a priest while still in prison.

I wasn't able to go to seminary. But my goal was, if I was
going to be a priest, that I should go to seminary to be trained
as a priest. Otherwise I wouldn't have completed the process.
I was very concerned about that. If I was going to be a professional then I wanted to receive all the required training—no
short cuts.

The letter I wrote to Bishop DeWitt covered by background, my involvement in the church, when I was chris-
tened, when I was confirmed, the church I went to, my crime
and my desire to become a candidate to study for the priesthood, and the situation I was in.

I received an acknowledgment to the letter which was neither approval nor refusal. Then I waited.

Finally, on the eve of Epiphany, January 5, 1972, Bishop DeWitt came to Graterford to the service at the chapel with the St. Dismas fellowship.

I thought he was just coming to preach there because it was Epiphany, but there was another reason for his presence. It was during that service, much to my surprise and joy, that Bishop DeWitt announced to our group of 25 or so and some outsiders the fact that I had been accepted as a postulant. I had no idea he was going to do that.

I just can't tell you how good I felt. It was a historic event.

The press got hold of this shortly afterwards and there was a press conference at the prison with Bishop DeWitt, Dick Swartout, and Superintendent Robert Johnson. There was a great hullabaloo that a convicted murderer was going to study to become a priest. It made it into all the papers. You can imagine that there were very varied responses to the bishop.

And while the bishop had accepted me, I still had hurdles to jump. Now that I had become a postulant, the process really began. In order to become a candidate, which was the next step, I had to go before the Standing Committee and the Commission on Ministry and also have two psychological examinations.

I was escorted to these committee meetings by Dick Swartout and it says something for Superintendent Johnson that he allowed me, a lifer who had only been there for a couple of years, to be escorted out of the prison.

These committees each consisted of 10 or 12 people, both lay and clergy, men and women of the Episcopal church. None of them were black. I could sense as much tension on their side as mine at the beginning of those meetings.

They asked me why I thought I should be considered for the priesthood; why I wanted to be a priest; how I could justify wanting to be a priest in the situation I was in; how I had atoned for my sin and other questions along those lines.

I would repeat the biblical stories which had impressed me so much and ask them, "What's so different about these biblical characters—Moses, David, etc.—and me?" I think in their heart of hearts they thought, "Well, he's got a point."

They began to realize that I wasn't a real ogre, that I was truly a repentant sinner, not a career criminal and that I wasn't going to go out and commit more crimes.

They began to believe me and I felt the tension relieve, but I had to work at it. I didn't come up with any slick answers. I was honest with them. As they got to know me they began to see me more as a postulant: one who could take the Holy Orders and eventually become a priest.

I remember one lady saying that this was the first time she had met a real sinner. I knew what she meant, but it betrayed the fact that her understanding of the Scriptures was much more theoretical than heartfelt, as if the Bible wasn't really connected to everyday life situations. I think she realized what she had said as soon the words were out of her mouth and she was embarrassed.

There was a lay person there who said to me, "You know, my religion was in my head and you have made me put it in my heart." He had to determine whether he truly believed in repentance and forgiveness. It was no longer a theoretical matter, and he had never had to deal with it in the way they had to deal with it with me, because here I was, a convicted felon, no question about my sin.

Eventually they gave their approval, although I don't think it was ever unanimous. My candidacy came through about six months later in 1972.

Now I could go ahead and take the steps necessary to become a deacon. Normally postulants attend a seminary for three years. There is a special Episcopal canon, however, stating that under special circumstances if you live in an isolated community, you could be ordained to be a minister in that community without going through seminary. In that sort of situation the education would take on more of a do-it-yourself character.

Bishop DeWitt had already planned this. He explains how my personal seminary was conducted.

> In Philadelphia we were blessed with an awful lot of clergy who were academically very adequate. We had a group of three African-American clergymen who were sympathetic with the project and who were glad to provide their expertise and their scholarship capacities as tutors for Vaughan.
>
> We put this committee at Vaughan's disposal and they met with him out there, had him write papers, read books, write reviews on the books and discussed things with him and so on. They conducted his educational program in prison and it was no problem.
>
> I think even if he had had to spend the rest of his life in prison, he could have been ordained a priest. He would have received a pretty solid theological education, both theoretical and practical, had he continued as an inmate. The Superintendent was very fond of Vaughan and very sympathetic with his intentions and his hopes and made it possible for him to be released for 24 hours to go out and do this and that so he would have been able to do the necessary field work.
>
> But it's a heavy, heavy business to face the rest of your life confined to being an inmate. I remember one time I was out at Graterford seeing Vaughan and we had finished whatever it was we were talking about. I was about to leave and I said, "You know, I'm quite impressed with Graterford. It seems to me it's a very well run institution and it's just an awfully nice institution; it seems to be adequate in every respect."

He said, "Yeah, I think that's right. Although it makes a lot of difference if you can go out that door when you want to," he added, referring to the fact that I was about to leave and could get out the door. He was an inmate and could not. It wasn't a bitter statement. It was just a sobering comment he made, which obviously stuck with me over the years.

Bishop DeWitt, to whom I owed so much, resigned in 1973. He was given a farewell party at the museum of the University of Pennsylvania, to which he invited both Superintendent Robert Johnson of Graterford prison and myself. What better escort for me, dressed in my civvies, than my own superintendent. It was an auspicious and most enjoyable experience. Bishop Ogilby was the Right Reverend DeWitt's successor, and it was he who would oversee my progress through the remainder of my program.

Now my training began in earnest. Twice a month, one of the three ministers assigned to me as tutors—Fathers Van Bird, Richard Winn and Paul Washington—would visit me at the prison to see that I received a thorough theological education and preparation so that I could become a deacon.

We would usually have discussions; they would give me reading assignments and then I would have to write papers. We would review theology and pastoral issues. They were my seminary.

We had a very good mentor-student relationship. I would ask questions to clarify my uncertainties, and ask them for more information when there were subjects I wanted to know more about.

I remember going out to speak at The Church of the Advocate in Philadelphia where The Reverend Paul Washington was the Rector. He published a little piece about me in the bulletin for that Sunday, September 17th, 1972.

Today we have as our preacher Mr. Vaughan
Booker. Mr. Booker is a postulant of the Diocese
of Pennsylvania, that is to say: he has been recognized by the Bishop and Standing Committee
as having the potential of becoming a Priest of
the Church. At present Mr. Booker is a resident
of the Graterford State Correctional Institution
serving a life sentence. He, as a postulant, is
receiving his theological instructions and is being
prepared for his vocation under three priests and
one lay person of our diocese: The Rev. Van
Bird, The Rev. Richard Winn, and myself, and
Barbara Harris of our church.

I have chosen to advertise the Advocate as
"THIS CHURCH LIVES THE GOSPEL." Mr.
Booker is a living testimony of what it means to
speak of a "LIVING GOSPEL." The Bishop and
Standing Committee and many throughout our
church are witnessing to the fact that our attitudes are not "conformed to this world" but that
we are transformed by "the renewing" of our
minds so as to understand the spirit of God's
Kingship in His Kingdom.

Today is Vaughan's birthday. At the "Kiss of
Peace" we may all take the time to make it
known that we are all happy on this beautiful day
which "THE LORD HATH MADE."

In addition to the assignment given to me by my priest-
mentors, I was taking secular courses provided by various
educational establishments. I was one of the first members of
the courses taught at the institution under Dr. James
McKenna of Villanova University's sociology department. I
also was able to study courses from Northampton County
Area Community College, Cheyney State College and

Montgomery County Community College. This continued until late 1974, by which time I had earned sufficient credits for an associate degree from Northampton.

I loved to study and here was my chance to make up for time lost when I was younger and other things in life (girls, sports, having fun, drinking, etc.) had begun to compete for my attention and resulted in a neglect of my studies.

On the strength of a 3.92 average (4.00 is straight-*A*'s) I was elected to Alpha Sigma Lambda, a national honor society for students in continuing education programs.

This was not an easy program that I had embarked on. It required levels of persistence and dedication which were hard to maintain, especially within Graterford. Kenny Tervalan, a fellow inmate who was serving a life sentence, remembers observing me in cell, getting on with my program.

> I have one picture of Vaughan in mind. He is sitting next to his bed with a lot of books around him, studying. The rest of the block was in bedlam, nothing organized, just an ocean of tumult, this chaos. And here is this guy sitting in the eye of the storm, concentrating on a goal. The contrast was so vivid in my mind. I said, "He is going to get out. And I am going to learn something that will get me out."

When I was accepted as a postulant, I left my job in the dental lab and became an assistant to the chaplain. This meant, in addition to being more able to follow my calling, that I had more time to devote to my studies.

There is a parallel thread to my progress in the church and in my acquisition of knowledge. Throughout this time period, and in fact ever since my trial came to an end in 1970, there had been various legal attempts to reduce my sentence. Although I didn't allow these to become a major part of my life or to consume a great deal of my personal attention, naturally they were important.

First there had been an automatic appeal to the Pennsylvania Supreme Court which follows all verdicts of first degree murder. The appeal to the Supreme Court would only have resulted in an examination of the trial records to see if there were any blatant miscarriages of justice. It would not hear any new evidence.

It was while this appeal was still pending that David Kairys became involved with my defense.

"His case, among all my legal cases, was one of just a handful that I really wanted to win even more than the others," recalls David.

We had met while I was still at Holmesburg. David was waiting to receive the results of his bar exam and was part of an experimental law clinic with the University of Pennsylvania which took him to the prisons to interview inmates. His memories of our conversations and of his impressions provide yet another view of my past.

> I remember Vaughan distinctly. He wore a prison uniform and he always had, at least at the beginning, a handkerchief around his neck—a loosely tied handkerchief sort of thing, bluish usually. He was very young, kind of well groomed. He was not a street person or a down and out person, certainly didn't look like he had any kind of drug involvement or anything like that.
>
> Vaughan was just one of the people there and we started to chat—just a friendly sort of chat. Then at some point he asked me if I knew any books about psychology and family dynamics. I gave him what I knew, which wasn't very much. I remember we talked several times and I just liked him as a person. I had no idea what he had

done, but he was obviously more educated than most of the people in there.

Then at some point he asked me if he could talk to me about his case. As I remember, the first thing he said was, "I killed my wife." He didn't tell me how right away. And the how is a big part of it. Murder, of course, really upsets people, but the how of this one was so strange that it added a freakish side to it that was a little more frightening. It's better the all-American way, you know, a .38 special.

Later on he told me about the bow and arrow and I remember my reaction to that was just to be horrified. I mean, I understood what had happened—he used the weapon that he was familiar with. There wasn't a .38 special in the house, there was a bow and arrows. That was the sport he was into. But it still has an extra gruesome feeling to it. And the reloading of that bow five times, I mean you mean to kill that person, there's no question.

He never from the beginning denied or attempted to deflect responsibility. And that stuck with me. In other words, if someone had done that and was making excuses, then I wouldn't have liked that person. But he didn't. He was trying to understand. He was saying, "I just don't know what happened. I know I did this and I'm confused about it. I'm confused about how families operate, what went wrong," and things like that. It sounded like he was trying to find some sort of intellectual way to understand it. Maybe he was searching for answers emotionally, too. I don't know.

Right away it was clear he felt totally responsible and totally awful. This was a horrible thing to him. It was a horrible thing that he had done. He knew he did it but he just couldn't imagine that he could ever have done this.

I wanted to know what had happened immediately preceding this, what brought it on, and he told me, though not in any way blaming his wife. It was something like this: He had been drinking, he was out late. When he came home he saw some guy leaving the building and that wasn't of much significance to him at the time. He got in and they got into this huge argument which they had been getting into a lot. He said the relationship was in a really bad state and they were on awful terms, really hostile. I don't recall him blaming her even for the argument, it was just sort of the two of them.

On this particular night he had gotten very upset and she had gotten very upset and he asked her, "Who was that guy?" At some point she said, "That guy is the father of our son." And that's what he says triggered him. But again, when he said that, what impressed me...he hadn't been coached by a lawyer or anything about this at all, and he didn't say it by way of excusing himself. He really wanted to know why he had done it, given she had said what she said, and whether it was true or not, he wanted to know why he would do such a thing in such a situation. He was appalled that he had.

So he told me that after killing her he had gone in and tried to strangle his son and it was during the course of that that he came somewhat to his senses.

So that was the story and, except for the bow

and arrow, it was, unfortunately for our culture, the stereotypical murder in the United States of America, and still is: a lover's quarrel that gets out of hand and somebody has an easily accessible weapon and does in the other one.

But he couldn't have imagined this happening to him, no matter what the argument was. So he wanted to understand where that rage comes from.

I felt he was seeking a rather intellectual path and that struck me—he didn't tell the story with a lot of emotion, but I couldn't tell if that was just his defenses or what. It wasn't until he revealed for the first time in this book what his childhood was really like that I began to understand many aspects of this whole affair, including his emotional tone. There were times when he got emotional, but he could tell the story without a lot of emotion and at the time that was a little unsettling. But on the other hand, I felt he was consistently accepting responsibility and I thought that was the main thing. He wasn't asking me, "Is there a legal strategy that is going to get me out of this or is there some way to explain it that it's not my fault?" He wasn't asking either of those questions at all and he never did. It was more, "Can I understand it?" and later on, "Can we minimize my time in jail?" but not, "Can I get out of going to jail or staying in jail?"

I did some research and I realized that this defense that they had tried to do was recognized in California, maybe some other states as well, but not in Pennsylvania. It was a new defense, that of "diminished responsibility," and his lawyers pursued a defense that didn't exist and that was, of course, the problem.

It's not that any defense would have gotten him off, but it could have lessened the degree and lessened the prison stay.

After the trial he thought, given all the Robin Hood stuff [the case had received much notoriety as the "Robin Hood Murder"] that he would spend the rest of his life in jail. He thought that was unfair, although he never thought he should escape punishment. He thought he should have been convicted of a lesser degree.

It was quite some time later that I asked David Kairys to take on my case. We had stayed in communication in the intervening time and I had participated in a book club David had set up within the prison system, where he would invite authors to come and talk to the inmates at the prisons.

The appeal to the state Supreme Court was already pending when David took on the case. He obviously felt quite strongly that justice had not been done or he would not have become involved.

While the appeal to the Pennsylvania Supreme Court was still awaiting attention, a petition was filed jointly by David Kairys and the District Attorney to have the case remanded (sent back to a lower court) and made part of a new hearing to look into my allegations that my guilty plea was invalid and that I had been denied my constitutional right of effective assistance of counsel. This is not to say that I felt I wasn't guilty of murder, but that I felt I wasn't guilty of first degree murder.

David Kairys also filed a petition seeking relief under what is called the Post-Conviction Hearing Act.

The remanded case and the Post-Conviction Hearing Act petition were consolidated into a single hearing conducted by Judge Ethan Allen Doty, Jr. on June 24th, 1971. The Judge

rejected both contentions—that the guilty plea was invalid
and that I had been denied effective help. This went to the
Pennsylvania Supreme Court in January 1972 and they
upheld Judge Doty's findings without even giving an opinion.

"It was quite galling," says David, "that it was such a substantial injustice and they didn't even explain themselves."

There were only two doors in the judicial system which
remained open. One was to try and bring the case before the
U.S. Supreme Court. The other was to go to a lower Federal
Court with a habeas corpus writ. A writ of habeas corpus is a
legal safeguard against individuals being unlawfully taken
into custody. This is the avenue David took and the Federal
Court refused to hold a hearing, simply relying on Judge Doty's
opinion that justice had been done by all the courts involved.

As a last resort, David and I took this to the Third Circuit
Court of Appeals, which is the Federal Court of Appeals
immediately below the U.S. Supreme Court for that part of
the country.

Here again the opinion of the court was that everything
that the lower courts had done was correct and in order and
they refused a hearing. However, they were split two to one in
their decision, with Judge C. J. Gibbons, a well known, brilliant judge, dissenting. The other two judges, Van Dusen and
Rosenn, agreed that the evidence of my "diminished responsibility" had been accepted by the judges at the original trial
and they simply glossed over the fact that this evidence had
only been considered in the sentencing, not in determining
the degree of guilt.

Judge Gibbons was not so willing to gloss over this. He
explained his point of view in the statement of his reasons for
dissent with the majority opinion.

> The record contains no statement by any one of
> the three judges, either while evidence was being
> taken, or during the closing arguments, or at the

time they announced their first-degree finding, that they ever considered the diminished responsibility evidence to be relevant in determining the degree of guilt.

The Pennsylvania courts which have considered the petitioner's case did not discover that the degree of guilt court [the three judges at the original trial] had considered the diminished responsibility defense. The district court did not discover that the degree of guilt court had considered the diminished responsibility defense. The state court record discloses that it was considered only to the degree that it was rejected as irrelevant. Thus, we are squarely presented with the issue whether the petitioner's guilty plea was induced by a misstatement by counsel that evidence of diminished responsibility would be taken into consideration in determining the degree of guilt...I would reverse and remand for such a hearing.

Judge Gibbon was outvoted and the hearing was never held. Forgotten was what seems to be the most major omission of the investigation: the fact that my claim that another man was involved was never pursued. Had evidence been produced to confirm this, a verdict of second degree murder or even voluntary manslaughter would have been assured. What Angie said to me on that fateful night could never be proved, but, if there was another man, he could have been found. There was also no statement by the medical examiner as to any evidence in the post mortem examination of sexual activity, and no one at the trial even asked him about it. That would have been an obvious avenue to have pursued.

It seemed that the argument was all centered around the minutiae of the legal procedure and no one just stood back and looked at the entire proceedings, all the facts, in order to detect the real breakdown of fair and just application of the law in this case.

Rightly or wrongly, there would be no hearing. All legal avenues available had been tried and I was still convicted of first degree murder and sentenced to life in prison. All possible doors of the justice system were closed in my face.

I was reconciled to spending the rest of my days in Graterford and in fact looked forward to my ministry within the penitentiary, but I couldn't help remembering that Jonah did eventually make it out of the inside of the sea monster to arrive safely on dry land and go to deliver the Lord's message to Nineveh.

There was one door, not a legal or judicial door, but still a door, that could be opened: the state Board of Pardons under the Governor Milton Shapp.

My first request to have the sentence reduced in 1973 was turned down. Prisoners can ask for a pardon, or sentence commutation, once a year.

With the help of David Kairys and a veritable army of supporters and friends, I appealed again the next year.

Appeals are made to the Board of Pardons which is directly responsible to the Governor. It is the Governor who must ratify, or not, the board's recommendation. Usually the Board of Pardons will consult with the judges at the original trial, the family of the victim, and the District Attorney's office to get their views on it.

The Reverend Dick Swartout was present when that appeal to the Board of Pardons, headed by the Lieutenant Governor, was made, and remembers the event.

> When Vaughan's case came up, Bishop DeWitt and Bishop Ogilby were both there with me to testify on his behalf to the Governor. I remember the Lieutenant Governor said, "I get the feeling

this inmate is being offered up on a silver platter here." And we tried to defuse that and tell him the bishops were just doing their job. One of the people there asked, "How many times do you folks do this, you bishops?"

As David Kairys says, "There was an unbelievable crowd there to testify. There was no precedent for this size of group in one of these actions."

I remember it was in April 1974 when I heard from the Board. I was at Camp Hill which is a juvenile institution near Harrisburg as part of a para-teacher program, a peer teaching program begun at Graterford by two women from North Hampton County Community College. They had put me through courses in remedial teaching and related subjects so that I could help in the program. I was just going to be there for six weeks but I ended up staying over a year because I was actually hired by the college to teach a class in Black History. So I lived at Camp Hill, all the time maintaining my "condo" at Graterford.

And it was while I was still at Camp Hill that I heard from the Board of Pardons that the sentence was commuted to 15 years to life, with the blessing of the Governor of Pennsylvania. The importance of this was that I could become eligible for a pre-release program in the future, something which lifers are not allowed to engage in in Pennsylvania. But I was no longer a lifer!

There was a stipulation, however, by Judge Lagakos, one of the three at the original trial, that I serve another three years before I could qualify for any pre-release program, to show that I really was serious about being a priest. Had it not been for this stipulation, I would have been eligible to enter such a program immediately.

This was definitely the thin end of the wedge that would eventually open the door a crack and finally give me my freedom. I knew that in another three years, in 1977, there was a chance that I would be allowed to enter a pre-release educational and work program and that in 1982 I would be eligible for parole.

My studies for the diaconate continued, spurred on now even more by the new reality that I might not be spending the rest of my days inside the belly of Graterford.

Finally, in 1975, my tutors were satisfied that I had met the standards of theological education required in order for me to be ordained a deacon. The next step was an oral examination in the areas of theology and the Scriptures conducted by the same people who had, three years before, accepted me as a candidate.

The examination went very well. The committee was satisfied and prepared their report for Bishop Ogilby. The Bishop gave his approval. I, Vaughan Booker, still resident H90-95 at Graterford Penitentiary, was to be ordained a deacon in the Episcopal Church.

The Reverend Dick Swartout was very excited. He took care of all the arrangements. The date for the ordination, to be held at Graterford chapel, was set for March 1st, 1975. I was in a state of mild ecstasy.

We had to have music and I was able to select my favorite hymns. What a wonderful opportunity. There were hymns that I had really liked when I was growing up in the church and I was able to choose them for the service. We had an organist come in to play.

On the day there must have been 250 people there: my mother and father, Beverly, people I hadn't seen for years, friends, supporters, all kinds of people. There were quite a few inmates, including all the members of the St. Dismas fellowship but also members of the Islamic community and members of the Jewish community including Jack Lopinson.

I was wearing an alb, which is the white vestment that reaches to the feet. Part of the service was that I was vested with the stole of a deacon. It was a magnificent event. It began with a procession with the crucifix all down the hall with the bishop in his cloak and miter.

We started in the hallway and progressed down the hall. My tutors were all there and Dick Swartout and other priests. There must have been a dozen in the procession, with the bishop bringing up the rear.

My feet didn't touch the ground! I floated right in to the chapel. This was an event where I was being affirmed.

The Reverend Dick Swartout also has fond memories of that service.

> I had arranged that the inmate coordinator of the fellowship of St. Dismas, his name was Charles Duffy, was to be one of the presenters of Vaughan to the bishop for ordination. His presenters were Fred Powers, my predecessor, Barbara Harris and Charles Duffy, the inmate. They were to be in the procession along with the inmate choir and the various participants in the service.
>
> Well, Charles Duffy wasn't there at 10:30 that morning, and here I was, lining up everyone for the procession and then I got to where Charlie was supposed to be. I said, "Where's Charlie Duffy?" And they said, "Well, we don't know, he's probably still out on the block."
>
> So I said, "This procession isn't going anyplace until Charlie Duffy is standing right there."
>
> So one of the institutional chaplains took off in one direction and another took off in another and a third headed down the main corridor to Charlie's cell block and I went back into the chapel and got up in front of everyone and said, "You folks can relax and have some more conversation because we've got a little snag: Charlie

Duffy, our inmate coordinator is not here to be in the procession and be a presenter, and it'll take us a few minutes to get him here. So just—we've had a little slowdown here."

And by the time I got to the back of the chapel, Charlie was there. The guard hadn't let him off the cell block. Even though he had a pass, the guard was doing something for prison reform—their style of prison reform, you know—just for a little harassment. So Charlie is there in the procession and we began. The procession took off, and the service went beautifully. Paul Washington's sermon was spectacular.

At the end of the service I had arranged with the institution to have a little reception in the back of the chapel. They set up tables and we had some juice and coffee and some cake provided by the institution. And during that, two inmates who had been on death row, came over to me and said, "Chaplain, can we talk with you for a minute?" So we went over into a corner of the corridor, and the two inmates, I think it was Jack Lopinson and "Tough" Tony Scoleri said, "Chaplain, you just put us old lifers in touch with some feelings we never thought we would ever get in touch with again, when you said you would hold up this whole damn thing for an inmate."

And I didn't know that it would have that effect. I was just doing my job. But they were so impressed at that point that I was going to stop the whole thing for an inmate.

The service was a memorable one. The Rev. Paul Washington's sermon was for me:

Why is this day different from every other day?
Because on March 1, 1975, God has seen fit to
break down a wall, which heretofore, Vaughan,
stood between you and the opportunity of that
fullness of life which He came in His Son, Jesus
Christ, to give to all of us.

Today God is demonstrating, not that He can
forgive, that even His church can increase in that
wisdom and stature where it can forgive even as
He forgives.

Today God is demonstrating again, that as He
long ago called Moses, whose hands were
responsible for the death of another – to be an
instrument of deliverance, a vessel of love, a
channel of grace and a source of life. Today we
will ordain you to be one of his special servants.

Why is this day different from every other
day?

Because today the church comes, not just to
minister to those who are in prison, but to ordain
a prisoner to minister; not just to visit but to
cause you to become an incarnation – as the
word becoming flesh, dwelling among us.

Because today the church is breaking out of its
own prison wherein it imprisoned itself and is
standing fast in that liberty wherein it imprisoned
itself and is standing fast in that liberty wherein
Christ has made it free.

Many will rejoice as the good news of this
witness is voiced abroad. I realize also however
that for some it will be confusing; for other, blas-
phemy. But for the most part those who stop to
ponder this action will probably end up saying
"and why shouldn't it happen?"

A question such as this places the burden on

those who are opposed to such an action to justify their opposition. The rightness, the oughtness are self evident if we believe in repentance, forgiveness, redemption and salvation.

And so my Brother, let me charge you: Listen carefully, prayerfully and intelligently that you may be convicted that it is God who speaks that which you hear.

You must speak, but speak lovingly and reconcilingly to heal and not to hurt.

You must act but make sure that your energies are advancing the kingdom, not setting it back, are serving the living God, not yourself, are life giving that the living dead in our world may arise to newness of life through the risen Lord.

This day is different, Vaughan, from every other day. You are a first born. Something very special is being given to you and from you shall much be expected, but remember these words, Come unto me all ye that labor and are heavy laden and I will refresh you. Take my yoke upon you and learn from me for I am meek and lowly of heart and you shall find rest for your soul. For my yoke is easy and my burden light.

And He said to Paul, "My grace is sufficient for thee, for my strength is made perfect in weakness." So gladly, Vaughan, glory in your infirmity that the power of Christ may rest upon you.

One line of Father Paul Washington's sermon stood out to me particularly clearly, and does even to this day: "Something very special is being given to you and from you shall much be expected." These were words I took particularly to heart.

The service culminated with the Bishop laying his hands on me, now fully vested, and proclaiming, "I ordain you deacon in the Church of God."

This was a momentous occasion for many. It was carried on all three national TV networks and was in all the press, and not all the responses were favorable by any means. The obvious question in the minds of many was, "What is the church doing, promoting a murderer in prison to the rank of deacon?" This was when *Newsweek* came up with their masterpiece headline: MURDERER IN THE CATHEDRAL.

Jack Lopinson described the ordination service to a reporter many years later in terms that revealed just what an important event that appointment as a deacon was to the inmates of Graterford penitentiary. "It was a very moving ceremony. Everyone was crying. Big, hardened, tough criminals, right?"

Beverly Gray Bell, remembers that we met again at that ordination ceremony for the first time since before I had gone to prison. In an interview, much later, she said:

> Would it sound strange if I said I never saw a different side of him? He was the same Vaughan that I'd known. When people say that this occurred, this incident with Angie and him, that was a part of him I didn't know. To me he always was the same Vaughan I met when I was 14 years old. So when I saw him at Graterford he was the same, sweet, warm person that I knew all of my young life.

My family was very proud of me, of course. In addition to my own happiness and accomplishment, I suppose I was reversing some of the bad fortune I had brought on everyone that morning in 1967 when I "lost it" and took Angie's life under such strange circumstances.

Not everyone felt the same way. Brenda Lowery, Angie's

niece, had a different reaction: "I saw his photo in *Jet* magazine and I just wanted to tear the book up," she said much later, remembering the incident.

There were mixed reactions in the press, within the clergy, and among lay people who came in contact with me and my story. Dick Swartout recalls that his in-laws, vacationing in Barbados, read about the ordination in the press down there, so this certainly made not only national but international news.

But at least for me, now an ordained deacon in the Episcopal church and therefore directly under the care of the bishop of the diocese, life would never be the same again.

CHAPTER NINE

...to those who repent he grants a return, and he encourages those who are losing hope.

(Sirach 17:24)

The people I was in close contact with, the inmates of Graterford, seemed to be overwhelmingly in my favor. They saw me living the kind of life which they felt a religious person should be leading, and they seemed to benefit from our conversations.

I had earned their trust: Before I ever applied to become a deacon, I had to pass the scrutiny of the St. Dismas group. This was reported in the *Philadelphia Inquirer* of June 21, 1977 in an article by Edgar Williams, staff writer:

> Sent to Graterford, Booker was introduced by Father Powers to the Fellowship of St. Dismas, a program of the institutional chaplaincy service of the Episcopal Community Services. It is an inmate organization, interdenominational and virtually impossible to fool.
>
> Thus when Booker in 1971 sought permission to prepare for the Episcopal priesthood, the

questions put to him by his peers in St. Dismas were at least as probing as those asked by the church authorities in their investigation.

"If he were a phony, the St. Dismas men would have exposed him," said Robert Wolfe, administrative assistant to the superintendent of Graterford. "He came through as tough an examination as a man could be given."

That was a long time before. Now that I was a deacon, the other residents started calling me "Rev." I really had a lot of friends. They were backing me. One incident I remember really demonstrates the way I was regarded, at least by some of them.

I had had a radio stolen. A couple of the inmates had an inkling that the culprit was "State Store" Sonny (they called him that because he used to rob state stores and one time he killed someone while robbing one).

So they came to me and said, "Look, Rev, if you want us to knock this guy off..."

I said, "My God, no, it's just a radio...."

So what they did, I found out later, was they went to Sonny and said, "Look, you either have the Rev's radio back by the time we come from the yard or we are going to take care of you."

I came back to my cell and my radio was there waiting for me. That was the end of that incident. It wasn't mentioned again.

The inmates elected me to represent them at Harrisburg (with the officials) because I was bilingual: I could speak their language but also spoke the system's language. So the same men who had earlier criticized me because I would cross my *t*'s and dot my *i*'s when I spoke now said, "Hey, Vaughan, you know these people..."

Prison can be a chaotic environment. There were always

odd, sometimes tragic, incidents happening around you. There was another incident I'll never forget. There was a man who was serving 20 years to life for a felony homicide. He had shot someone during a robbery. He was a young fellow and he was a boxer. Apparently he was trying to set up a homosexual relationship with someone in prison.

The other man told him, "Look, leave me alone," but this young man kept bothering him. One day they opened the doors and found the boxer in his cell, dead. He had been stabbed numerous times and hit with a hammer. The man who did it turned himself in. Essentially you didn't bother other residents if you were smart, because you didn't know what was going on inside their heads. There was lot of tension.

But on the whole these goings on did not involve me. There was really only one situation of that type where I was personally involved. This was some time later when I was getting ready to go into the pre-release program. There was a young man who had just been transferred from the psychiatric hospital because they had changed the mental health laws in Pennsylvania and all the offenders who had been sent to places for the criminally insane were transferred to Graterford. This particular inmate had a lot of problems. One of them was that he had fallen in love with his analyst.

They used to have movies on Saturday nights which I never went to because that was just another form of conditioning. So I was in my cell reading when this inmate opened my door and came in and began talking to me. You weren't supposed to go into someone else's cell, but he did so anyway. The door wasn't locked. He told me he had received a letter from his analyst who was saying, "Look, I'm not in love with you."

He was really distraught so I started to say—I suppose I should have been more sensitive—"This therapist, look, you've got it all wrong..." Well he got mad and took his ballpoint and tried to stab me. I was in tiptop physical shape and I took the pen from him and wrestled him to the outside and hailed a guard.

All the guard saw was a fight so we were both locked up. I explained what had happened, and there were other residents who had witnessed the incident who backed up what I said. There was a hearing and they realized I wasn't to blame so they let me out, but not before I had spent a week in isolation. That was the only incident of that type I ever had.

There was a time in the mid '70s when I was taking classes at Villanova. There was a particular inmate who had become a Muslim. He was a little slow academically and other residents used to make a lot of fun of him. But now that he was with the Muslims he had begun to feel a bit better about himself. Still the other inmates kept taunting him.

One day I was returning from classes with my arms full of books and I was in the hallway, and this man had been pushed too far and had stabbed one of his homeboys right above the heart. Just when I was coming through the door, the injured man came running through with blood pouring out everywhere, all over me and my books. They had to stop him or he would have bled to death. Fortunately they saved his life. This was part of prison life.

Men would come and talk to me about their situations. I remember one man was in for burglary and he told me, "Vaughan, I didn't do this one. I did a couple of other ones but I'm not guilty of this one."

There were also those who were addicted. There was no lack of all sorts of different drugs inside. They had heroine, cocaine, marijuana, all kinds of pills, black beauties, amphetamines. Some of the white bikers would be on LSD which could be transferred on the back of stamps and that sort of thing. The drugs that were popular inside were the ones that were also popular outside.

A lot of these inmates didn't have a plan for their lives. They were in prison and many of them were lacking even a basic high school diploma. The focus of my advice to them was, "You really need to have a plan for yourself. Go and get your GED."

I watched a lot of inmates change from just wandering around like lost souls, not knowing where they were going, to really feeling good about themselves because they realized that they had more going for them than they ever knew. They would get going on the college program and start to feel much better about themselves. So mainly my emphasis was on education. It did everything in the world to boost their self image.

There were some inmates who had religious concerns. Some would become Muslims or go back to Christianity and then revert to Islam again. They didn't know what they wanted to do. We would have discussions, but religion is a very personal thing. I can't tell someone what to believe. There are a lot of people who think it's their job to tell others what they should believe, but I feel the opposite. It's very personal and if it doesn't become very personal then it doesn't exist.

Belief doesn't have any basis in reality unless it is something that is very personal to the individual. We would talk a lot about personal relations and by that I don't mean just things like accepting Jesus as your personal savior. We would look at that. Well, what does it mean? It means something different to everybody. What it really means depends on who you ask.

It seemed that more people were steeped in the language of religion than the actual practice of religion. There was a lot of that. I met men there who could quote the Bible back and forth. But it wasn't consistent with the way they were living their lives.

There were some very talented people in there too: people of tremendous artistic ability, men who could go out and get a job for any illustration company outside. But for some reason the art was secondary and the life of crime held a greater appeal.

I used to see men, during my ten year period inside, come back again and again, as if they were recycling themselves. I just couldn't understand this. What was it? "Booker, I just couldn't get myself together." There was no support system. Later I would help set up support systems.

It was really hard for people who were drug addicts because they would go back to the same environment they had left. I used to call it suspended reality. What that meant was that everything in that environment had instant recall. They were going back to the same people in the same place, doing the same things, and they would end up coming back to prison.

To those that truly wanted to change, I would always recommend a change of environment. Go to a different place. But that's scary. Tough convicts were scared to go somewhere they didn't know. Their support systems were so much based on others rather than on the internal strength that they needed. They didn't think they could survive out there. Those that did make the break are largely still successful—they're still out there.

There was a lot of cross-religion going on, too. The Jewish people like Jack Lopinson would invite us to their seders and other religious events, and the Muslim group would have us to their Ramadan celebration. In our turn, we would invite the other groups to our St. Dismas meetings. I think we set the stage for how things should be done in the world outside, because it used to be if you were a Christian or you were a Muslim then never the two shall meet. But we used to read the Bible and read the Koran and find out we had more in common than we had differences.

I like to think I helped a lot of people, although I never looked at it from the point of view that I was dealing with a particular person because I wanted to help him. I interacted with a lot of different people because I was genuinely concerned about my brothers in the same way that I am genuinely concerned about people now. That's the reason for it, not because people may or may not be helped as a result of what

I say or do. I think it's possibly a little egotistical to think that because we may have had some influence over some person that it's going to be a positive one and we are going to help them change their lives. That's presumptuous.

But I tried, and it came down to a lot of human interaction, treating a person like he was a person. Nothing special. I didn't sit down and say, "I am going to counsel you." Sometimes I would be helped as much as they were.

Life for Deacon Vaughan Booker began to be quite different from how life for Vaughan Booker had been. Within the confines of prison, there were new freedoms. There were also new challenges and obstacles to overcome.

Beginning March 1st, 1975 I worked for the Institutional Chaplaincy Division of the Episcopal Community Services. This was the position assigned to me by Bishop Ogilby, because every deacon is under the care of his bishop. I was even paid $50 a week for this work. I had my own duties at Graterford under The Reverend Dick Swartout, helping minister to prisoners and their families, counseling emotionally disturbed youth in Group Homes and assisting with worship services throughout the Diocese of Pennsylvania.

Throughout the Diocese of Pennsylvania? Yes indeed. My work started to take me beyond the thick concrete walls of Graterford. I was in demand as a speaker and as a deacon, to talk to groups and to preach at churches around the diocese. During Lent in particular, when the theme at church was repentance, I was a particularly popular figure at Episcopal services in nearby churches.

Perhaps my own experience in the domain of sin and repentance was so much more extreme than that of the average parishioner that my story may have made it easier for others to take responsibility for their own wrongdoings, and repent. After all, if I could be forgiven for murdering someone, then why shouldn't George Smith be forgiven for the time he embezzled his employer out of a few hundred dollars, or Mary Jones for the time she went out with that nice man at work without telling Mr. Jones about it?

Of course I would be escorted on these forays into the world outside the pen, but this was no inconvenience. I enjoyed the company. My horizons broadened considerably and I greatly appreciated the new freedom. I used to go out with Tom Stachelek or one of the other counselors, sometimes with a professor at Pennsylvania State University. One of the guards used to take me out frequently. Sometimes I'd go out with Dick. It got to a point where I was going out almost every weekend.

This was during a time when the general correctional attitude towards lifers was changing. Lifers who were in jail for a single offense, who had no previous criminal record, were among the statistically safest risks in terms of recidivism or ever repeating the error of their ways. This was recognized. I don't believe there was ever any real concern in letting me go out on these speaking engagements and furloughs because I had proved myself already over time.

Tom Stachelek is now the Deputy Superintendent for Centralized Services at Graterford, but he remembers my career from the days when I was in D Block when Tom was the newly arrived counselor for that block.

> I had not worked in the criminal justice system before and Vaughan was, I thought, an unusual individual because he was very much interested in other inmates and he was also interested in helping the counseling staff to understand inmates and understand prisons and what they did and what they didn't do. I guess he was really, for me, almost a trainer and a mentor more than the other paid staff were. He helped me to understand the prison system and inmates.
>
> Vaughan introduced me to other residents. I

remember we used to eat fairly regularly on D Block where he was housed. I would go down and go through the chow line with him and eat with him and a couple of his friends. They would talk to me about the institution, about other inmates, about things that were happening, about things that I might not be able to see as a staff person that they could see as inmates. I remember those occasions where we would be in the inmate dining room on D Block discussing programs that Pennsylvania was instituting or thinking about instituting or curtailing. Really he showed me a lot about the system that would not have been obvious to a staff person.

Vaughan's religious activities and his strong religious convictions were, I guess, questioned by a lot of staff and some of the other inmates. A lot of them thought that they weren't for real and that he was just running a con game on them and on the staff and on the system if you will. But my recollection and my experience is that the majority of inmates trusted him and they believed him. They didn't see him as running a con.

My recollection is that while probably a lot of staff, especially correctional officer staff, were skeptical of his religious convictions and his efforts to help other people, I think the inmate population felt he was genuine. Inmates are a lot better at sorting out who's for real and who isn't than staff. So my recollection is that the vast majority of the inmate population respected him and really believed that he was sincere. He wasn't one of these gushy, preachy type people. He was a real man, but he was a gentleman. He had great credibility.

What may have happened to Vaughan after-hours when staff wasn't around, whether he ever had confrontations with other inmates or not, I don't know. I'm sure they questioned him and I'm sure they challenged him, but my recollection is that he moved about the institution as a respected inmate.

Through my personal experience—and I had almost daily contact with Vaughan, working with him and seeing him work with other inmates, advising each other—I did not think it was unrealistic that he should want to become a priest and I thought it was genuine.

There are very few inmates with whom you can have complete confidence in what they are saying and their intentions, and I have been in this business now for almost 23 years and I can honestly say that he was one of the few inmates that you could believe. He was a man who was sincere about his convictions, and his intentions were always positive. Again, this is looking back after all these years.

And I suppose the other thing that I remember about Vaughan was his sense of humor. He could see the lighter side of situations.

Vaughan went out on a lot of speaking engagements to various community groups and churches. He was invited as a guest preacher. I heard him speak. He is a fantastic speaker. I'm not just saying a fantastic preacher, but a fantastic speaker. He is an exceptional communicator. He has a lot of passion.

As a matter of fact, he keeps reminding me that I took him out to a church in my community and we had dinner at my house. He had come out

with me to go to a speaking engagement, and he
stopped at the house and he had dinner with my
wife and children.

We also talked about his crime. Of course, I
had the advantage of reading all the official
reports about it. My recollection of Vaughan and
I talking about his personal life was more of a concern for his children and what they thought of him,
and how he could ever be a father to them. Not so
much of why he did what he did, but how what he
did affected his children and what his relationship
in the future might be with them. At the time, as I
remember it, that was pretty much what his personal concerns for himself were: what would his
relationship be with his children. I don't really
ever remember talking specifically in any great
detail or in a personal way about the offense itself.

He expressed concerns about whether or not
his children could ever forgive him for what he
did; would they ever accept him back? Would he
ever be given the opportunity to be a father again?
I think after his release from prison and after my
regular contacts with him, that's when he began to
re-establish relationships with his children.

From the time that they were picked up by my father on
that bleak October morning and taken out of the house, carefully avoiding the room where their mother lay on a blood-
stained bed with five arrows in her body, Kim and Tawney
had been looked after by Angie's sister Alice Arnold and her
husband, Billy.

There they grew up, not knowing until they were quite a bit
older, what had happened to their real parents. How do you
tell a child of three that her father killed her mother and was
locked away forever?

It wasn't until several years later that I would again see my children, and even then the visits with them were brief.

I used to ask my mother about the children when she came to visit me. Looking back on it now, she might just have said things to try to comfort me. I think a lot of the time she didn't even know what was going on with the children. I had believed that my parents, and particularly my mother, were going to be the vehicle between my children and myself while I was in prison. For a while I thought my mother had the children and she never corrected this impression. She would bring me pictures. I gave her money for them which I suppose she passed on.

That changed when I began going out because when I went to places my children would be there. I think Dick Swartout coordinated that.

The first time I saw them, Kim must have been seven and Tawney four. I think it was at a church and I don't think they remembered me.

Obviously there wasn't a problem with Alice and Billy who raised them because every time Dick or someone else would ask for the children to come with me, they were always there. So when I would go out on speaking engagements on Sundays, the kids would be there to spend some time with me. Sometimes it would only be half an hour. I remember one time someone gave me an honorarium for speaking and I bought Kim a watch and Tawney a baseball. Kim wore that watch for years.

I know that one of the complaints about me that was leveled by members of Angie's family, however, was that I didn't do anything for my children.

Geraldine Williams, Angie's older sister, said to a reporter who spoke to her in 1993:

> If he had done something for those kids after tak-
> ing their mother away from them I might be able to

feel a little differently about him, but he never did anything.

I think I could maybe halfway forgive him if I felt that truly he was this good person. But I don't believe that.

If he had taken care of his kids, if he had been a father to them since he had taken their mother away, and went out of his way to do things for them and be there for them...

Linda Pickett, Geraldine's daughter agreed:

It was literally as if three lives were taken. I'm still a little resentful because out of all the entire family of four, he is the only one showing growth and he's moving on with his life.

It just does not appear that he has paid the price for almost ruining three lives and scarring so many others.

These comments were made much later and refer to the period of time which includes my release and my life after Graterford as well as the time I was in jail. Naturally there is more than one side to the story and I have to include the "other" side, even if I don't agree.

Not all of Angie's family expressed or felt this degree of animosity or resentment towards me. Alice and Billy, who were the ones who raised Kim and Tawney as their own, had at least a cordial relationship with me later on.

I remember we had a civil conversation and I was able to express my regrets to them. They are good Christian people and they responded well to me.

To this day the situation between certain parts of Angie's family and myself has not been fully resolved. There is a wound that is still festering. But there were other events concerning Kim and Tawney, including a major tragedy, yet to come. At the time that I was working as a deacon while still a resident at Graterford, my contact with the children was brief and sporadic, but I was reassured in the knowledge that they were being taken care of and loved by Alice and Billy.

I always remember a letter I received from Kim when she was 11 or 12:

> *Dear Daddy,*
>
> *I hope you get out of jail soon.*
> *I want you to be a priest.*
> *I love you.*
>
> > *Kim*

At Graterford, I had some status problems to overcome with the prison staff, particularly the guards. While still a candidate for the diaconate I had had a clash with one of the wardens who felt I was abusing my privileges.

I had had a conversation with this particular sergeant a couple of times about being in the chapel for head count. Everybody was supposed to be back on the block by a certain time—I think it was 11:30. But in this particular instance, The Reverend Williams even called and told him that I would be at the chapel for count and that's where I stayed.

The count had been cleared—when they are counting there is no movement within the institution; everything stops; most people are in their cells. You have to be in a specific area so that the count can be accurate.

I was there in the chapel, doing the work I had to do, and when I got back on the block the officer told me that I had a misconduct for insubordination.

"This goes for you and you are no exception to the rule," he snarled.

He wrote me up and I had to have a hearing. I was locked

in my cell until the hearing date which was two days later. When I had the hearing, it was thrown out because it was a trumped up charge.

But this was one of the old line guards who was no friend of rehabilitation. You were a convict and should be treated as a convict. You were a con.

Generally though, there were no problems. Most of the reaction was verbal because there was nothing they could do. I had the support of the superintendent and I had the support of the Episcopal Church. I imagine they would discuss my case among themselves and share their anger in that way. They couldn't really direct it towards me because I wasn't doing anything wrong.

Presumably they didn't like the fact that I had moved from the role of being an inmate, yet I was still an inmate. It was almost a conflicting role. You are taught to respect the clergy but I was still an inmate.

Even some of them were converted, however. Over a period of two years, they went from calling me Booker to Reverend Booker. I can only attribute that to the fact that I always respected them. I always called them by their titles and never gave them a hard time. I just did what I felt God had called me to do while I was in that environment. I didn't have a sense of my own importance and I didn't go around boasting. I tried to remain as humble as possible. One of the things you don't want to do, particularly in jail, is to try and lord it over others.

My position and experience gave me an ideal opportunity to act as a minister for the inmates at Graterford, as a story that appeared in *The Philadelphia Inquirer* of June 21, 1977 illustrates:

> On a recent Sunday morning, Vaughan Booker, a deacon of the Episcopal Church and candidate for the priesthood, delivered the sermon at the

Protestant service at Graterford State Correctional Institution.

After the service, a new inmate asked Booker if he would discuss a problem with him. Booker nodded, and the two moved to a quiet corner of the chapel.

"It's like this, Rev.," the new inmate began. Then he shook his head. "Aw, you just wouldn't understand. You don't know what it's like to be a con," he said.

"I think I do," Booker replied. He lifted his clerical robe, revealing his prison uniform.

The three year "trial period" mandated by the Honorable Gregory G. Lagakos went by quickly.

Ten years after my life had reached its lowest ebb and Angie's life had slipped away forever, 1977 was to be a year of triumph in more ways than one.

Among the blessings which seemed to rain down on me was a second chance at love: Portia came into my life.

CHAPTER TEN

...*perfect love casts out fear.*

(1 John 4:18)

It was May of 1977 (spring time!) and I was up for furlough. I had developed a friendship with Viola, the sister of one of the social workers who worked in the prison, and she came to pick me up. It was a Sunday and we went together to a church where I was to preach.

After the service we went to a shopping mall. On the way out of that mall, in the parking lot, something told me to turn around. I don't know why, but I did turn around, and there was this lady with her son, walking into the store that I had just come out of.

She had an afro puff and was wearing jeans, rolled up at the bottom, and a pair of clogs. She was a very pretty lady. Just for an instant our eyes met. I can best compare it to Maria and Tony in *West Side Story* when they first saw each other. Everything became misty and foggy and time slowed down, as if things were in slow motion. Then as quickly as it had begun, it was gone and we were both going our separate ways.

Two weeks later Vi and I went to a party at a condominium complex that had a clubhouse and a pool and so on. When I walked in I recognized Portia immediately. She was wearing a very slinky dress and high heels. I was on one side of the party and she was on the other, over by the food. I walked over and I remember thinking something but not saying anything and she turned around and said to me, "What did you say?"

I said, "Oh. What's that you're eating?" or something like that.

Then we started talking and it was the old line, "Haven't I seen you somewhere before?"

We talked and danced and exchanged numbers. She asked me where I lived and I said, "Graterford," assuming everyone knew what Graterford was; but she didn't. She thought I lived in the town of Graterford. I forget if it was then or later that I told her about my past.

In a recent interview Portia described in detail her recollections of our meeting and the beginnings of our relationship.

> At the time I was working with the Department of Public Welfare in Norristown and I certainly wasn't looking for a man, let alone a man who was behind bars.
>
> The first time we saw each other was at a shopping center in King of Prussia, Pennsylvania. I was with my son Manuel—Pepi we call him— who was about 10 at the time. Vaughan was coming out of the mall with another woman. He had a suit on and was wearing his collar. He was very handsome. The woman with him was wearing a yellow hat and she looked happy as a bird. I remember thinking, "My, what a good-looking man," and of course I noticed the collar. So I looked and then walked past and I turned around and looked back at him and he turned and looked at me and that was it, Pepi and I went on into the mall.
>
> Two weeks later I was at some affair at the clubhouse of some condominiums in Philadelphia.

I was sitting there in the lounge and Vaughan came through the door, this time without the collar. He was with a woman, and I recognized him right away.

Maybe 15 or 20 minutes later I walked to the area where the food and the band were and he was standing there talking to some women. There was a mirror that covered the whole wall. I walked past and he looked in the mirror and saw me our eyes met—and I knew then that he remembered me because it was that same look.

So I walked farther down and was talking to some friends. A few minutes later he walked past me and stood there, not saying anything, but just looking at the dance floor. We weren't that close but I knew that he knew exactly what he was doing because I felt it.

I walked to the food table and then my head started ringing. I heard this voice saying, "What's that you're eating?" He hadn't said anything to me, but I had some things on my plate, and when I heard that voice I looked over and he was looking at me.

"I'm sorry?" I said.

"Oh, what's that you're eating?" he replied.

So I went over to him and said, "Haven't I seen you before?"

"Yeah, you saw me two weeks ago at the shopping center. You had jeans on and your hair was pulled back and you were with a young fellow."

Well, when you think you know things and then they are confirmed like that, it's a bit scary.

I said, "And you had a collar on."

"Yes, I'm Episcopalian. We're allowed to marry."

I told him I was Episcopalian too and my parish priest at St. Augustine's was Richard Winn. Then I found out that he knew Richard well because he had been one of his tutors.

When he told me he lived at Graterford, to me that was just an area in Montgomery County. I didn't think of the prison.

I was beginning to get nervous. Too much was happening too fast. I was feeling vivacious and he was smiling at me and I really couldn't deal with it. So I said, "Well, it was nice talking to you and I'll see you," and I left.

Later I was dancing with someone who we found out later was a mutual friend and Vaughan came up and Larry said to him, "Oh, do you know Portia?" and Vaughan said, "Yes. I know Portia." I could tell Vaughan was responding to me but it was more than I wanted and it was really making me nervous.

Later he asked me to dance, so we danced. And then we talked. He told me everything about his past that night except the gory details, but I don't think it really sank in. I listened to what he was saying but it was an incredible story. First of all, I thought if you killed somebody you wouldn't ever be walking the streets. But not only was he out, on top of that he was a minister. It was just blowing my mind.

I was overwhelmed because it was just so much to deal with at one time. I told myself that this was just something that would come and go and I wouldn't have to deal with it. Maybe we would just have a telephone relationship. I didn't think I would get involved with him. It was all so unreal.

We were talking and dancing the whole time. The woman who came with him even interrupted us because she felt left out. When the night ended I gave him my number and he gave me his address. I remember it was Memorial Day weekend, a Saturday or a Sunday: May 1977.

He called me next morning and asked me what I was doing later that day. I said, "Nothing," so he said he would call me back and maybe we could do something.

He never did call back. I didn't hear from him for maybe two weeks. Don't ask me why, but I called Larry and asked him what was up.

"I haven't heard from Vaughan, Larry. What do you think about him?"

"He's really crazy about you, Portia."

So I sent Vaughan a card with a picture of Jimi Hendrix on it, saying, "I hope you haven't forgotten about me."

He got the card and sent me a big envelope of letters he had tried to send me. He drew me a picture. In his letter he asked me to call Chaplain Williams and he would call back.

We spoke a couple of times and he asked me to come up and see him at the prison. I don't know how I said yes to that. Working in the Welfare Department I had seen a lot of prisoners when they would come and get a small check on coming out of prison, so I had some contact with the human side of the Department of Corrections. Otherwise I probably would have been terrified. But I did go to see him in prison. I couldn't believe I was doing it.

I had to wait for hours and there were people in the waiting room and the children were crying.

Then I had to go behind bars and they put a metal detector on me and took my pocketbook before we could go down to a courtyard with picnic benches. I don't remember anything we said to each other. I just remember looking at each other.

It came time to leave and he walked me to the steps. I said good-bye and he pulled me back and gave me a little kiss on the lips. I didn't think I was ever going back there again. It was like, "I'm sorry. You're cute but I don't think I can deal with this." I knew there could not be a relationship like that where I had to go and visit him.

He called me the next day. Next weekend his brother-in-law went to pick him up and brought him over and we went to church. I forget where the church was but it was a long ordeal because he had to be there for two services—he was preaching. But that weekend was when our relationship really began to develop.

Two weeks later he was out! All of a sudden it just happened. I went to see him in prison. He came out to preach the next weekend. And then he was out. So I didn't have to deal with the prison. I don't think I could have.

What had happened is that the three years which Judge Lagakos had stipulated had run their course. The papers went back to him to approve my participation in a pre-release program, which must be approved, or at least not opposed, by the sentencing judge. True to his word, he did not oppose this and now it was up to the prison authorities.

Robert Johnson had already gone, but behind him he had left a legacy. It included a trailer camp outside the prison walls where inmates on pre-release programs or lifers who were considered safe bets were allowed to live. Jack

Lopinson described the camp in a recent interview. It's where he was still living in 1994.

> We live in the camp. We dress in grays rather than browns to designate that we're outside workers. The only time that we come into the institution itself is for special religious services. We are not allowed to leave the reservation. There are no fences, not even a cyclone fence, so the superintendent has to be very careful who he puts out here.
>
> The men could walk away any time they wanted to. There are checks and security measures but it's not like having to escape over a wall, as there are no walls. You are as close to a trustee as you could possibly be, in fact more of a trustee than you would be in other prisons.
>
> People consider men like me who have done almost 30 years, and say, "My God, why doesn't he just go?" But I wouldn't do that. Number one, I wouldn't do that to my family. And number two, I wouldn't do it because it would ruin the chances of other lifers who will follow. Every lifer out here in the camp knows that if he ever did anything wrong like that, all the remaining lifers would be pulled back inside and we just couldn't do that. We're too close to a realistic chance of getting out to ruin it.

That was what it was like when I was there too. I had been expecting this to happen but I didn't know the exact date. It seemed like more than coincidence that just two weeks after I met Portia, the approval came through.

It may sound strange, but there was some personal turmoil connected with moving from inside Graterford to the outside, to the trailer camp. I had been in this place all these years and there is a certain security you gain no matter where you are. You get used to it. Now I was going to a new place, a new environment. And there was a sense of sadness coming over me because I was going to leave my friends inside. It was like saying good-bye, and I had people coming over and shaking my hand and wishing me well—it was very emotional. I would still go back in to the prison every Wednesday to help conduct services, so to that degree I maintained my ties with the people inside.

Now I became eligible for furloughs every weekend and I could go out sometimes during the week as well. Whenever clergy conferences or other affairs came up, I would get permission to attend. I was always going out somewhere.

I lived in a trailer with three other men who were either on Educational Work-Release programs like myself and on their way out, or were lifers who worked outside, like Jack Lopinson. I had a bed and a place for a TV.

During the day I was working for the Episcopal Community Services, counseling troubled youths in Group Homes, working with inmates and their families, and assisting with services around the diocese. I had applied for and received a grant for $10,000 a year through the United Thank Offering and was able to lease a car. It was a little Datsun B210, five-speed stick, green, with racing stripes on it: great gas mileage and very dependable.

I was also taking a degree in history at Villanova University full time. I needed the qualification in order to continue on with the next step in the ministry which would be ordination to the priesthood.

My day would consist of leaving the camp at about 5:30 in the morning, going to study at Villanova, then off to work, then dinner and I had to be back at the camp by 8 P.M. every evening. I would see Portia in the morning or evening almost every day.

Portia remembers those days:

> We used to see each other a lot. He would stop
> by after work or before work, almost every single
> day. He was working in Philadelphia. My office
> was only a few blocks away from where I lived,
> so if he missed me at home he would come down
> the street to my office.
>
> That was also the beginning of nearly 15 years
> of going to church with him every Sunday and
> sitting through two services.
>
> Before him I was like a holiday churchgoer
> who went to church at Christmas and Easter and
> maybe if something special was going on such as
> a baptism or a wedding. When I met Vaughan I
> started going regularly because I went with him.

Portia had a tremendous effect on my life. It was very positive and very affirming, especially because it was my difficulties in the context of marriage and in the context of a woman
that had led to tragedy. There had been other women in my
life during this time period, but there was no real relationship.
I needed to know that I could enter into a healthy relationship
with a woman that I cared for and who cared for me.

It was a growing together. We did a lot of things together,
went everywhere together. We had a good time and we were
always doing things. If people saw me, they saw Portia and if
they saw Portia, they saw me. We really got to know each
other. I learned about sharing feelings and being honest. I just
felt so secure with her and I think she felt the same way with
me.

Portia discussed her feelings quite candidly in interviews
later. Anyone knowing our story and my history would probably say that she must have had more courage than anyone to
begin a relationship with a man who had killed his wife in a fit

of rage. After all, the people who accepted me to the ministry, who commuted my sentence, who released me from the depths of Graterford into the world outside, did not have to share their life, their home, their bed with me. They could all maintain a comfortable distance while they spoke about forgiveness, repentance, and rehabilitation. Portia was putting these concepts to a very personal test and her life might depend on the outcome of the test. And she admits she took a risk.

> I have friends who said, "Well, everyone believes that people can change," but it's really hard when you have to deal with it. People would ask me, "Aren't you afraid?"
>
> I certainly thought about it. What does it mean when a person goes off like that? What triggers it? What triggered it for him? I certainly wouldn't try that again, what had happened with Angie, although I'm sure he's past it.
>
> At the time I wondered if I really wanted to get into this relationship, and if I did get into it, could I ever get out?
>
> I suppose I romanticized it. I don't know if I was afraid, because I felt I would never put him in that position. I don't know if I ever really sat down and thought about the whole thing, but I suppose I felt that if a situation like that arose and I really wanted to get out of it, I could.
>
> Also I was in love with him. I couldn't really see past that. I did think that if I ever was in a position like Angie had been, I would certainly leave. How some women stay in certain situations, I don't know. I also wondered if that was the only thing that had caused it—the situation with Angie.
>
> But also I really needed to believe that a per-

son could change. I needed that for myself. It was very important for me to believe that. I needed to know that my own life could change, that God could forgive you and make a way for you.

I had seen the devil at work. I needed to believe in forgiveness and that you could change through believing and repentance.

You see I was born in a conflict of religion. My mother was religious but she didn't go to church. She had a crucifix and a rosary and she prayed three or four times a day. My father grew up in a religious family. His mother was a minister and an exorcist and he was into things like telepathy and mind control. I could never figure out if it was spiritual or not.

My father used to say, "You can control people like this and you can do this and that and these things are possible," and my mother used to say, "No, that's evil, don't do it."

I grew up praying a lot. Even when I was doing something destructive to myself I always asked God to protect me because I was conscious of the fact that I did not know what I was doing. I can remember doing such things and saying, "God, forgive me." You become a product of your environment and the things that happen to you, and you can become addicted to your own pain.

I had read the Bible but I didn't really believe that I could get over all the bad things of my past, the bad feelings about myself, and actually move on to a better life. Vaughan gave me proof that God does forgive. For me he was proof. It was like, "Can this really happen? Do you mean there is a place for me too?"

It was as if I really needed to believe in that. So in addition to his being very handsome and very charming, he gave me hope. Any fears that I had or that would come up were overwhelmed by that. It was important to me that I not doubt this to the point that it allowed evil to creep in, because it can come in and once you let it in it can really eat you up. Just like worrying about things can. I learned how not to worry about things because these demons would come in and eat away at you if you open the door, and faith is the only thing that will keep them off.

We went through a lot. We are human too. It wasn't easy. We had arguments but I'm not the type to argue. I just walk away from arguments. I don't push people because I'm secure in the fact that if I know something, no one can change it. I don't have to convince anyone.

Now I've never seen a picture of Angie but some people told me I looked like her. Maybe he told me that. I wondered sometimes, "What if he has a flashback?" if I look so much like her. I thought about that in the beginning. I wondered if he was trying to project this thing on to another person and I was the other person. That's the only thing that really bothered me. I asked him, "Do I look a lot like Angie?"

Looking back on it now, there are times when he has been angry with me and I have wondered what it would take to make him very angry. Certainly I wouldn't put him through the test, but I can't say I haven't wondered what really snapped him. I've never felt I had to walk on eggshells. Our arguments are not that type of argument. Usually we would argue about disciplinary things concerning the kids—I was too lenient and he wanted me to be more strict.

For me there was never any question of a repeat of my earlier experiences. I felt secure with myself and with Portia. I had also spent a great deal of time getting to know myself and I knew I would never let myself get even close to where I had been in 1967.

I have spent too much time getting to know myself since then to think that I could ever come anywhere near the point of violence against any of God's creatures again. I know myself so much better now. But the relationship with Portia helped confirm this.

This was an interesting time period. I would go to class and then to work for the Episcopal Community Services and I was often working inside prisons such as Holmesburg, the Detention Center and the House of Corrections, counseling prisoners much as Father Powers and Dick Swartout had done. There I was The Reverend Booker. Then I would go back to the trailer camp in the evening where I was still H90-95. But I was closer to being free than I had been in 10 years.

During this time period I also had the opportunity to get near to my father and close the breach that I had created in 1967. The circumstances, unfortunately, were that he was in hospital with lung cancer.

My dad was never really verbally communicative. It just wasn't his style. He was a very warm man, but quietly warm—quietly affectionate. And so when I was grown up we would do things together, he would come to different Boy Scout outings and things like that, but we never had a chance to do a lot of talking together until he went into the hospital.

I had been ordained a deacon now and I was attending Villanova University. I was close to graduation and I would visit him every day, and we would have long conversations. Sometimes I would shave him. We would talk openly and honestly and he talked to me about when I was growing up and why things were the way they were. He wanted so much for me to have a good life, to be whatever I wanted to be. He didn't say to me that he wanted me to be a doctor or a lawyer, but he wanted me to be something, and he was very happy with the progress that I had made.

He was just elated that I seemed to have overcome the tragedy of the crime I had committed. He often said that he wished it hadn't happened, but it had and there was nothing that could be done about that. He said, "You're strong—you have good genes," and he'd chuckle.

When the hospital can't do any more they send you home, and I knew that it wouldn't be long. They sent him home, and then he got really bad one night and he went back to the hospital and that's when he died. I remember it was cold: it must have been February. My tutor, Richard Winn, Rector at St. Augustine's, performed the ceremony and I preached the eulogy.

I was sad that he died, of course, but I was glad that we were completely reconciled before he did and that we managed to close that gap.

My father's death stands out in my mind in that period where I was gaining a little more freedom and gradually finding my feet again in the real world outside Graterford.

I wouldn't become eligible for parole until 1982 and it wasn't usual for anyone to get into a halfway house until they were within a year or so of getting out. However, in May or June of 1978, I was given special dispensation to move into a halfway house and was transferred from the trailer camp outside Graterford to a house on Broad Street in Philadelphia, just down the street from boxer Joe Frazier's gym. There I was to live until around October of 1982.

It was an old converted house where each resident either shared a room with a roommate or eventually had a room of his own. Since I was there a long time, I ended up with a room to myself, but that was something you had to work up to. There were monitors from the Commonwealth of Pennsylvania there 24 hours a day and there was also a Director of the program there. I suppose there were a total of 25 people in the program. I had chores to do at the house and I had to pay rent, not that it was a lot of money. And I was making good money at the time.

Rules at the halfway house were a little different from the trailer camp. I used to leave at about 6 o'clock in the morning and didn't have to be back until 11 o'clock at night. And I had the weekends off. More freedom.

In September 1978 I graduated from Villanova with a BA in history. Not long after that Portia and I became engaged. I think it was Mother's Day. I bought her a plant, and inside the plant I put a ring. On June 30th we were married. Portia remembers being amazed at the speed with which things moved, or perhaps her amazement was that we were married at all.

> I married him in 1979 at St. Augustine's church. Father Richard Winn who had been one of his tutors, performed the ceremony. I couldn't believe that I had married him.
>
> He still had to go back to the halfway house every night and was technically still in prison. If he did anything he could end up right back inside. All he had to do was make a wrong move somewhere. It had all happened so fast. I just couldn't believe it.
>
> But meeting Vaughan gave me a new life because I didn't know in what direction I was headed. I needed a totally new life and, in the environment I was in, it just wasn't there. Once I met him I was into his life and what he was doing and I really didn't need anything else. I

was totally absorbed by him and everything that was happening to him. This was what I needed. I needed some focus in my life. I could see his vision. I needed someone strong like that.

It changed my life completely because I didn't need anything else. I didn't need approval from other people.

It was still a double life with my home at the halfway house and spending the weekends with Portia, but we did what we had to do to make it work because we were in love.

Unfortunately the United Thank Offering grant was discontinued and I moved on to work for the Opportunities Industrialization Center (OIC's) national office where I was a director of an adult/youth offender program. There was a great deal of travel connected with this job as I was directing and managing 23 local affiliate programs of OIC throughout the state of Pennsylvania. I had to fly to Pittsburgh, Erie and other destinations and I clocked up thousands of miles on my car.

It was satisfying work because of the interaction and the opportunity to help people in the way I had been helped. I knew the importance of support systems for ex-offenders and I was uniquely qualified to understand and help them deal with life after crime and prison. I also had to conduct performance reviews and present leadership seminars.

At the weekends I would preach at various churches and I maintained an active participation in the ministry. But I was disappointed that I was not really taking the next major step I would need to become a priest.

When I went to see Bishop Ogilby about this, he told me that I needed to test my calling. "You were called, you know, under unusual circumstances in a controlled environment," he said to me. "Get a job. Let's see if you still have the calling after you have become involved in the business world, for example."

So they sent me to the Bernard Hall Dane Executive Counseling Service which is a testing and job hunting service. It is interesting that my highest score was as a clergyman, second highest was a salesman, and next was a social worker. My bishop wanted me to work in the private sector, so that is where I started.

At the time this was a tremendous disappointment. I felt I was being rejected and my progress was being blunted. But I did what he wanted me to do.

As the OIC job was disappearing in the rubble of President Reagan's budget cuts, I saw the handwriting on the wall and knew that I would soon be needing to look for another job.

There was a young man from Xerox Corporation whom I heard was working with ex-offenders, so I got in touch with him and started attending a program they were holding a couple of nights a week where people could come and see how corporate America functioned. They didn't make any commitments to hire anybody or anything. They had a program where we would learn to use the copiers and so on, but I was more interested in the sales side of it.

One day I said to them, "You know it's great that you're having all of us here, but wouldn't it be even better if you would hire some of us?"

"Put in your application," was the response.

I went to Xerox's main office in Philadelphia and submitted an application.

"Have you ever been convicted of a crime?" the application form wanted to know. I wrote, "Yes, and I would be happy to discuss it with the managers." Then I turned it in.

And that was my bid for a job in corporate America: the bid of an ex-lifer, murderer still in a halfway house and technically in prison, at least a full year away from the possibility of parole, with no recent experience in the business world.

How would Xerox respond to that?

CHAPTER ELEVEN

"Ask, and it will be given you; search, and you will find; knock, and the door will be opened for you."

(Matthew 7:7)

The best person to explain what went on within Xerox Corporation when that small bombshell hit them, is Arnett Spady, the man who had to make a decision about whether or not to hire me. At the time he was Regional General Manager for the Office Systems Division whose territory included Pennsylvania, although he has since continued to move up in the company. He recalls the problems connected with hiring a felon who was still not even out on parole.

> I had a sales force of I think six managers, each of whom had ten to twelve sales reps and analysts that covered the coastal region. At the time we had openings for three reps in the Philadelphia area.
>
> I received a call from the manager there who told me, "We have an individual here who has all of the selling skills to be successful and meet Xerox's objectives and customer requirements,

but for some reason nobody will hire him."

"What's the problem?" I asked him.

"Why don't you come up and we can go over it?"

I was tied up, but a couple of days after I got the call I went up to Philadelphia and interviewed Vaughan. I found an individual who was hungry. He was very polished, very aggressive. I felt he had all the characteristics of someone who would make a good sales rep. He had a "stick to it" attitude, very positive, very high energy level and he seemed to be results oriented.

Then when I looked at the bottom of the form I saw that he had a felon charge and that he had just gotten out of prison not long ago.

I told him, "Well let me get back with you." I needed a little time to assess it.

Then all of a sudden I started getting calls from other managers outside my division saying, "Arnett, you know, you may want to think about it before you hire him. You've got a very promising career ahead of you and you just want to be careful."

But I wasn't thinking about that too much. I was just looking at the individual to see if I felt he could make a contribution to the company.

I spent a lot of time, maybe three times as long as normal, during the interviewing process, because I wanted to get to know him. Vaughan went through in detail what had happened, when it happened, so I knew every step of the whole situation.

Even before I made the decision I had a session with him and his wife. I wanted to get to know her as well. I was really impressed with her. I thought, here was an individual who would always be there for him. I could tell from talking to her that if he ever stumbled or slipped, she would be right there to help hold him up and I felt good about that session I had with them. We had lunch and they invited me to their house and I got to know them.

Part of it was just for me so that I could feel more secure in my own mind that I was making the right decision. And she helped put enough security in my mind that I was. And let's face it, when you are making a decision like that, you are always looking for every avenue of support for the fact that you are making the right decision. She's a very positive individual and I felt, along with his strengths and her strengths, that they had a winning combination.

But again, I had to go back to the question: did he meet Xerox's criteria and my criteria for being successful in the job that I was interviewing him for? And that, to me, was the decision that I had to make.

Looking back on it, it was probably one of the most difficult decisions I have ever had to make at Xerox. I had to say to myself, "If I don't give him a chance, who will?" And I suppose my father and mother had instilled into me that if you can make the impact, don't wait—don't pass it on to someone else.

Also it was an opportunity for me to give something back, because although things are not perfect for me, I've had the opportunity to have what I believe is a good quality life. And it's hard, when you are downtown and you ride fifteen minutes away and see the conditions in the city. I can't forget that there are people there that we need to help. You can sit back and ignore it or you can get involved and make a positive contribution.

So I think this was also my way of saying, "Hey, you made a mistake, but I believe in my heart that if you were given an opportunity you would make the best of it."

I also discussed it with my father a little bit. Even though he is 83 years old, I still go to him and I get the lectures and we'll sit and talk. I've always talked to him, probably about most decisions, to get his input.

He said, "You've got to follow your heart. You've got to do what you think is right. You shouldn't judge him by the past. He made a mistake, but if he's paid his debt, how is the individual ever going to turn it around if you don't give him an opportunity?"

He confirmed the way I was leaning and reinforced my beliefs that it was the right thing to do. After I made the decision, I felt really good about it.

It still wasn't easy, because I had to be upfront with the other sales reps that he was going to be working with on a day-to-day basis, and sharing the office space with. I felt the right thing to do, although it wasn't something I had to do, was to be honest and up-front with those people he was going to be working with at that location.

I had a mixed reaction from the sales manager and his future peers. Some were concerned, some had fears, some had prejudged the individual. But overall they agreed that we had made the decision based on the qualifications and criteria we had for our sales reps.

I think everybody was walking on eggshells initially, but when they got to know him and looked at his character, his integrity and the leadership attributes that we look for in individuals, they found that he possessed quite a few of those. He was market driven, he was open and honest and had excellent interpersonal skills, and he was hard-working.

So it was that on November 18, 1981, I showed up for work at Xerox Corporation. Much of what had gone on behind the scenes was hidden from me at the time. I wasn't even sure whether the other people at Xerox knew about my background or not. They were very friendly and supportive. I was the new guy on the block and everybody was very helpful. They certainly didn't act like they knew, or rather if they did know, it didn't appear to make any difference.

Imagine coming out of prison and getting a job with a major corporation! Just think what that does to the ego. I began as an account representative and later moved up to being an account executive. I worked out of the Center City Philadelphia office, 1700 Market Street and we were up on the 30th floor. Interestingly enough, the headquarters of the Episcopal diocese were on the 26th floor of the same building and I would run into Bishop Ogilby; so he knew I was complying with his wish for me to test my call in the free world.

I spent much of my first day in personnel. I was given a booklet that gave the company's history and the code of ethics which the employees are expected to abide by and told me what I could and couldn't do and how to do business at Xerox.

Then I came out and met everybody on the team. And it really was a team. One became part of this exclusive community of corporate people who were working for this wonderful company.

The next step was to go through training. I wasn't going to

be selling copiers. This was the Office Products Division and we sold word processors and network systems. The next year they came out with their personal computer and the Star System, so I was selling sophisticated high tech equipment and systems.

Training involved going to Leesburg, Virginia, and this presented a problem. I had to get special dispensation to leave the state. Fortunately, this was granted. Leesburg was Xerox's international training center. There I met people from Rank Xerox in Europe, Xerox in Canada, Xerox from all over. The place is designed so that there are no corners in the building and there is some psychological reason for that. But the rooms were all painted in soft pastels which were conducive to learning. The lighting was perfect. There was a gym where you could go and work out. The food was excellent: you could have lobster for lunch, for example. The grounds were absolutely beautiful.

We had our own rooms. The company was also very family oriented and allowed you calls home so that you could stay in touch.

We were there to learn, and they taught us how to sell the products. When we left, we were expected to go back into the field and use everything we were taught and get results.

This I did. I remember going out and making my first sale which consisted of three of the new word processors to an engineering firm. I used all the sales tactics and the methods I had been taught and, when I got the sale, I thought, "Hey, this works!" It was exciting. We had our own territory and you could only sell within your territory. I had to do most of my own lead generation. Of course success is in direct proportion to hard work. I was cold calling and I did all the things I was supposed to do so the business was really coming in.

I am sure Arnett Spady, to whom I owed this wonderful opportunity, was watching with interest, if not concern, to see how I would perform.

I remember Vaughan only had six months to bring in his full year's plan. In Xerox in those days if you started in a new territory and you had six months minimum in the territory, you could still make President's Club. The President's Club is a recognition program for top performers in the country and we often have trips to reward those top performers. In those days the trip was to Hong Kong.

To qualify for the President's Club you had to write 150% of your business plan for the year. Well, Vaughan wrote his full year plan at President's Club level in six months, versus the twelve months that individuals normally have in which to overachieve. He made President's Club and along with that came the trip to Hong Kong for Portia and himself. He went on to make 185% of his first year's plan in that year.

Then I remember we ran into another bottle-neck because, under the state's pre-release program, you couldn't go out of the country. So everything was working and we were letting him know that he could get ready for the trip to take place, and then we found out that we had to get the Governor of the State of Pennsylvania to approve his leaving the country.

My manager for the area, Jack White and I went up to Harrisburg and met with the Lieutenant Governor to assure him that we would be responsible for Vaughan while he was away.

It really brought a lot of joy to us to see some-one do as well as Vaughan did, considering the situation and his past. I look back on it and think, "God, it was the right thing to do!" And I felt he played a great role in motivating his peers, the other sales reps to perform. Because I felt they would look at him and say, "With all that he's gone through, and the difficulty he had, he still has the dedication and the commitment to perform."

If you just listen to him and talk to him, it's always positive. I think he used the situation that occurred to psyche himself up and to motivate himself and that enthusiasm really trickled down to the other reps on the team.

Getting off to Hong Kong was not easy. I remember I was in Leesburg and I came back on a Friday, this was April 1982. Portia and I had our passports ready and our luggage was packed, but we still didn't know if I was going to be given permission to go. I was still living in the halfway house. We even had a contingency plan whereby Portia would go with another lady if I wasn't granted permission.

Portia met me at the airport on Friday and told me everything was approved and we had to go over and sign the papers. So it all worked out and we left early on Saturday morning.

This was my first time out of the country. We traveled, we went sightseeing, we had to do everything. Hong Kong is a big city, like New York or San Francisco. We stayed at the Shangri-La which was the sort of hotel where they changed the rugs in the elevator every day of the week: a Monday rug, Tuesday rug, and so on. The whole place was totally automated and there were Rolls Royces outside. It was like being rich for ten days.

The trip was well planned so that every night there was something different. We always had places to go and there were all sorts of perks. For example we would have tailors come to the hotel and I was fitted up for several suits. In three days my new three-piece suits were ready. They made us feel special, because we were special. We were acknowledged for really helping make the company go, and the general idea was, "Keep up the good work and we'll see you again next year."

I remember the first night they had a big opening reception for us and there was a band there from China that was playing "Dixie." These performers couldn't speak a word of English and yet they sang in English and could sound like anybody: the Temptations, the Supremes, you name it. Beautiful voices.

We also had a day trip to mainland China and that was very different. We were taken on a tour of the villages and countryside so that we could get an idea of what life was like. The houses were very small—I remember having to duck to go in the door. They must have had a couple of houses staged for the tourists because I remember seeing Dutch chocolate in the cupboard. We saw the people working in the rice paddies wearing their huge straw hats and the old, traditional Chinese clothes. They depend a lot on their old, black, sturdy bicycles for transportation. You'd often see three people on a bicycle.

They use water buffalo still. After 17 years of service the water buffalo is slaughtered and used for food. It is a very utilitarian society. And there was absolutely no sense of the modern world there. We saw the boat people living in their junks, went into a little apothecary shop where they were selling snake wine and all sorts of odd looking creatures in jars.

The Chinese struck me as being very industrious. You wouldn't see anyone not doing anything at any time. Little men carrying big sacks, ladies selling prawns, everybody busy. No one was on welfare.

At the checkpoint where our passports were inspected, the soldiers were kids, 15-year-olds. Apparently you could enter the army at 15. And the military was always present. Even if you couldn't see them, you could feel their eyes watching you all the time. The few motor vehicles we saw were military and we watched the soldiers doing military maneuvers in the fields around us.

I remember our last night in Hong Kong: Xerox hired the Pointer Sisters to entertain us. It was an excellent ending to a great trip. It was about as far from Graterford as one could get, in every respect.

And then I was back at the halfway house in Philadelphia, checking in with a smile on my face. I don't think the director was particularly happy that I was able to go to Hong Kong but that didn't matter. This wasn't supposed to be common knowledge, but someone always knows. So I went downstairs and the men asked me, "Did you have a good time in China?"

"I had a ball!" I told them.

Some of them were cheering because to them I was beating the system—rebelling—and they love to see that, even if they can't do it themselves. But I never saw it that way. My idea was not to get over on the system but to use the system, because that's what it is there for.

It wasn't too much later, October 23, 1982, that I was allowed out on parole—fifteen years after I had first gone to the Detention Center on that bleak morning. Now I only had to check in with my parole officer once a month and otherwise I was as free as anyone in society.

I learned to enjoy freedom a little bit at a time. I was still not out of the woods: I was still, and am still, on parole. In order to really appreciate freedom, I think you have to have lost that freedom at some point. I have a healthy respect for society, its rules and regulations. I love to interact with people. Every day for me is just a wonderful, life-giving experience because I am free. I can make decisions. I can do the things I want to do. I don't take anything for granted. Nothing is guaranteed. Every day is special to me and I start every morning thanking God for allowing me to wake up. I want to live every day to the fullest. I feel that freedom is relative and freedom has to come from within you. You can be out here in society and still be in prison.

Now I'm out here, I have a wonderful family, my wife, my

grandchildren, I'm working, I'm truly a blessed and happy person. What more can anyone want? That's what freedom meant to me then, and that's what it means to me now.

It was soon after we got back from China that I connected up more closely with my son Tawney. My contact with the children had been sporadic and, on the whole, brief since I first went to prison.

The first time I saw Kim and Tawney again, at a church where I was preaching while I was still in prison at Graterford, they didn't really know me, even though they knew I was their dad. It wasn't until after my release on parole that we began to renew the relationship.

When Kim was at high school I met with her counselor and she and I had lunch together. She lived with Alice and Billy and then for a while she was living with my mother. She did not want to come and live with us.

When I felt she was old enough I sat down and talked about the time when I had killed Angie, her mother. She asked me what had happened and I told her. She shared with me some of the anguish and agony that she had suffered growing up as a result of this.

There was no real connecting with them as their father. I was there and they were there, but the real connecting didn't happen. I think there was something of an attitude at times with my children, certainly to begin with, of "Well, you did this and you're going to pay for it." It was a bit of, "What can you do for me?" I didn't respond very well to that because it had an element of moral blackmail. It was a very difficult situation, especially as they were also under the influence of some of Angie's family members who were still angry.

I remember my older sister used to have conversations with Kim about that very relationship. Delphine discussed this in a recent interview.

Vaughan had Kim spoiled rotten when she was a kid. All she wanted was, "My daddy, my daddy, my daddy." Sometimes I used to say to her, "You have a mommy too, you know." But I think she did love her dad. He was, I suppose you could say, a hands-on father. He would play with her and give her a bath and all those things. I think he was a good father.

She was three when Vaughan went to prison. I remember because I gave her her fourth birthday party. I had told Angie I would, and I did. I had a cake made in the shape of a four.

Both children were raised by Alice, Angie's sister, and her husband Billy. They already had five children of their own and I thought she was a very special person to take on two more. But it was her feelings that she was going to raise her sister's children. She said they had already discussed that if anything ever happened, she would take care of them. The two of them were very close. Kim only learned as time went on what had happened to her mother.

The kids would come and visit so we kept in touch with them. Later on when she was in high school, Kim went to live with my mother for two years.

Kim was young and confused and she had heard a lot of stuff about Vaughan from her mother's side of the family which naturally was not favorable. So I don't think she liked him very much when she was growing up because of what she was told about him. That's all you could expect, really.

Then as time went on and he started coming out, he started visiting them and they would visit him. Both kids had an attitude but I don't think Tawney's attitude was the same as hers because he was younger and didn't have a full understanding.

I don't blame her because I understand how she felt and why, but I would get upset with her because as long as he had money or things to give her, it was fine. That's typical of kids: they will take. But I used to say to her, "If you don't like him, then you don't like his money, okay?" Because I don't believe in using people.

So she thought about that over a period of time, she was growing up too, and the relationship was trying to work. Later she started going to church and I think her whole attitude changed when she started to feel that she was a Christian. It was about trying to forgive and that's what helped the relationship to improve over time.

He tried hard with Tawney. I feel he tried really hard as a father dealing with a son, but again, Tawney was at that hard-headed age where you couldn't tell him anything. Vaughan tried to be there for him. He took him out of West Philadelphia, the city, out of the atmosphere that he was accustomed to, away from his friends and his mother's family who had raised him. It had to be hard.

Tawney was living with Alice and Billy in West Philadelphia. When we met again, he was working at the sandwich shop just around the corner from Xerox. He must have been about 14 or 15. He started coming around to my office and bringing his friends in to show them where his dad worked.

Portia's son, Pepi, was living with us in our apartment at the time. We had talked about Tawney coming and moving in with us, so when he expressed a desire to do so, I was delighted. Here was an opportunity to reestablish a relationship with my son.

We moved to a town house in Norristown where Pepi and Tawney were each able to have a room to themselves. They got on well together and acted like brothers would act.

Tawney was having difficulty with school. I was trying to hit the ground running as a father, which to me meant giving him some direction in terms of things he should and shouldn't do. I wanted to encourage him and get across to him the importance of education.

One time we sat down and discussed what had happened back in 1967 and he didn't seem to have any reaction to it. To him it was like taking in information. He never seemed to be angry with me for what I had done. It never came up again.

There were arguments because I wanted him to go to school and learn and to him it wasn't that important. He just wasn't performing well academically. I wanted to get to the heart of this so I had conferences with his teachers to find out if he needed special tutors or some other sort of help. But he just didn't seem to have any interest in education.

Portia has her own memories of life with Tawney in the house.

> Tawney and my son were two years apart. I had never had two children in the same house and Tawney was a little different. He was the type who would get on a bicycle and he'd come back and the bicycle would be wrecked.
>
> Later when Vaughan bought him a moped, he went out and had an accident. He was that kind of kid. He would ride into a wall. He really was a sweet kid but he was exposed to another side. He probably could have been like Vaughan but he never really had the chance. There was something

so sweet and good about Tawney but there was that bad side that he was attracted to.

By the time he came to live with us he was pretty much developed and he and Vaughan never really had a chance to have a good relationship. He wasn't really there long enough and in the summer and at weekends he always wanted to go back to Philadelphia.

I certainly never doubted that he was Vaughan's son because he looked just like him and the older he got, the more noticeable the resemblance became.

Tawney lived with us for about a year and a half before he decided to go back to live with Alice and Billy in the environment in which he had been raised. I felt, and I suppose he felt, that my rules and regulations and standards were being imposed on him, and he wanted to do things differently. His life was defined differently than I had defined it. I remember one time it was his birthday and he wanted me to buy him a case of beer. He was under age and I wouldn't do it. I tried to explain why but his response was, "Well, other kids' parents do it."

We were going to move to New Jersey and he decided he didn't want to come with us and after that, despite attempts to stay in contact and invite him to New Jersey, we lost contact with each other. I was afraid that the inner city would consume him and that is exactly what happened, but that was years later.

Life at Xerox continued to be a wonderful experience. The first year was the most spectacular, but things continued to go well even after that. In 1984 I was promoted to the Xerox Learning Systems Division in New York. The office was on 42nd Street and Third Avenue in Manhattan. For about a year and a half I was commuting to New York, which is how I ran up 230,000 miles on my car. Then we moved to Plainsboro, New Jersey, and it was less of a commute.

Here I was administering training programs such as Professional Selling Skills and Interpersonal Managing Skills, and I was also marketing the products. We would train people from other corporations such as American Express, AT&T and so on. Their sales force would come and learn how to sell. We had groups and we used interactive video and laser discs.

This continued until 1986 when Xerox sold the Learning Division and I left the company at that point after what were to me a wonderful four years.

Portia remembers another side to my life while I was at Xerox.

> Believe me, when he worked for Xerox, it was a lot of stress. The corporate world was very stressful. It changed him. He liked the idea of working in the corporate world for the big company and having company cars and talking about it and being in the President's Club and this and that—he liked it, but it wasn't really making him happy.
>
> I don't know if he really needed to go through it. Maybe he did. I'm sure it was part of God's plan to make him understand what his real mission was, although it wasn't his choice to go into the corporate world. It was his journey and it was very stressful.
>
> He always wanted to go to seminary and I guess they wouldn't allow him to go for a long time. When the bishop said he needed to go out into the corporate world, I thought to myself, "Well, I guess he's trying to tell you he isn't

going to ordain you, Vaughan." I think he
thought that too. I know it hurt him; it really hurt
him and he went through a slump there for a
while. He never said anything to me but I could
tell that it hurt him badly. He wanted to go to
seminary.

I felt sorry for him but it was easier for me to
accept it. I had fewer expectations. I couldn't see
how he could expect it. When he was in prison it
was a different matter. He wasn't going anywhere. I don't think they ever thought he was
going to get out. As far as they were concerned,
he was there for life.

There were other factors too. I mean there was
me. I often wondered why he had picked me. I
couldn't be an advantage. He would have done
better with someone connected with the church. I
wasn't part of that loop. There were other women
who could have helped him more politically. I
felt inadequate. But in spite of how I felt, things
were happening and I thought, maybe it will
work out.

What eventually did happen was really a
miracle.

During that period there was another man who didn't let
me forget my calling: Dick Swartout. He remembers it too.

I was off on a different ministry, at a parish in
New York, and when I left the prison ministry I
really left all those parishioners there, and
Vaughan was one of them. But Vaughan would
call me once in a while, every year or so. We'd
start talking and somewhere into the conversation
I would say, "Well, Vaughan, when are you going

to seminary? When are you going to complete this process that you started. You've played games long enough. Let's get to work on what your goals originally were when you were sitting in that jail cell back in Graterford."

Each time he would call, at some point I would say that to him. Then there was a period where I didn't hear from him at all.

But I had not forgotten my calling and I had not given up on my goals. The sale of the Learning Division by Xerox was the point where my own personal path and the path of corporate America began to diverge and I started to work my way back toward my real calling.

CHAPTER TWELVE

I will study the way that is blameless. When shall I attain it?

(Psalm 101:2)

When we moved to New Jersey, I spoke to Bishop Belshaw, the bishop of my new diocese, about becoming a priest. "Now you know you have to go back to school for three years," he said. I told him I did.

"If you do that, I will support you in your efforts to be ordained as a priest."

I was 35 when I gained my Bachelor's degree at Villanova and I would be 46 before I finally went back to school to resume my studies, this time at the Virginia Theological Seminary.

In 1986 when Xerox sold the Learning Division, I found a job as a substitute teacher and simultaneously began taking classes at the General Theological Seminary in New York. I had been out of school a long time, even though I had studied technical materials at Xerox, and I did not feel ready to jump back into the academic waters unprepared.

I began substitute teaching at New Brunswick High School, usually ending up with the special education students. I enjoyed that because I found I had a real knack for teaching them. I wasn't a softy, but I also wasn't really hard on them. I knew the importance of dignity and self worth and I tried to instill that into them. I could see with some of them that if they didn't change the direction their lives were going in, they would be ending up in the penitentiary. I had been with so many people like them.

It was a real challenge for me sometimes not to come right out and tell them, "Look, if you don't stop this, do you know what's going to happen to you?"

But I didn't. I couldn't very well tell them I had been in prison. I wanted to, but I thought it would probably get back to the Principal or the School Board—The Vice Principal knew my background, because she went to my church. But it would probably open a Pandora's box. Imagine the reaction of the parents if they found out their son or daughter was being taught by a murderer. People may wonder how I could teach in the public school system with a record. When I applied, they asked me if I had ever been convicted of child molestation, which I had not. They never asked me if I had ever been convicted of murder. It wasn't part of the requirements, I suppose.

I became what they call a permanent substitute teacher. I enjoyed it, the students and I seemed to get along well and the school authorities tried to encourage me to become a permanent teacher because they liked my style. But it wasn't something I wanted to do for the rest of my life.

I found that, as a teacher, I wasn't making the money we needed, so in 1987 I went to work for Sprint, marketing telecommunications out of their Princeton office. I told them that this was not a career move as I was on my way to seminary, and that was acceptable. My Xerox training came in very handy and we were able to save some money which we would need in order to get through the three years of seminary which lay ahead.

During that time we were members of Saint Alban's Episcopal Church in New Brunswick and I served there as a deacon on a voluntary basis, helping the priest at services. I would read the Gospel, assist with the Eucharist and also helped with Bible study and the youth group.

All the time I was getting closer and closer to making the break, going to the seminary, and following my true calling.

The road to becoming a priest in the Episcopal Church is not a broad highway on which everyone can travel and arrive without hindrance or constraint. On the contrary. It is more like a tortuous, winding path up a steep mountainside with checkpoints at every turn and plenty of opportunities to fall by the wayside. Rob Ross, who was to become my closest companion at Virginia Theological Seminary, described this process, and in particular how it related to my case, in a recent interview.

> In normal Episcopal processes the time frame is about two years from first indicating your interest in becoming a minister to the time you are admitted and actually arrive at seminary. There are lots of hoops you have to go through. You are likely to hear the expression "hoops" in the Episcopal church.
>
> First you have to approach the local priest, and then the local priest has to submit you to a parish screening committee of your peers; then you have to go and visit with the bishop; then you have to go before the bishop's committees; all this before you're even admitted to a program that which will eventually get you to seminary.
>
> In most dioceses, there are between twenty and twenty-five discrete steps in that process, at any one of which you can be turned down and the process, therefore, would stop. That includes just before you graduate from seminary for example. So if, just as you're graduating from

seminary, the seminary faculty decides to vote you unfit for ordination, then you cease in the process and you go back to work in the secular world. And the bishop says, "Sorry."

It's truly incredible. And it has happened to people I know. They felt awful, betrayed, like they'd given up years of their lives for nothing. But, to be honest, most of the people that I have known that had that happen to them shouldn't have been in the process, and should have been told much earlier that they were seen as unfit for the ministry. What often happens is that someone will say, "Well, the next group or person along the line will push the ejection button. I don't want to have to do it because it will be awkward for me to sit across the table and say to somebody, 'You're not fit.'"

You can try again after a period of time, but in every diocese there is a questionnaire that an applicant has to fill out. At the bottom it says, "Have you ever been denied, or dropped out of a process in any other diocese?"

I think it's a process that tends to keep out creative and interesting people and tends to promote homogenized people. That's why when people like Vaughan Booker get through the system you have to applaud and say, "Isn't this a miracle?"

I think a lot people don't even want to embark on it because they don't want to be subjected to that scrutiny. One hears about politicians saying, "I'm not going to run for office because I don't want my wife and my children to find out so and so, and I don't want that one bankruptcy that I had in the lemonade stand when I was a teenager

held against me." Well in the priestly process it's
even worse.

As Rob points out, it was a very involved process and I had
to once again come before the bishop's committees and be
subjected to the psychological examinations. Mine was a different situation than that of most of the people applying for
seminary. The normal procedure is to go through seminary,
then be ordained a deacon, serve for a period, usually six
months or so, as a deacon, and then be ordained a priest. But
I had already been an ordained deacon for 14 years when I
went to seminary. And of course, there was my background.
All the tests and interviews went well but I still needed to find
a seminary that would accept me.

In 1988, Portia, her granddaughter Tiera—who lived with
us then and still does—and I went down to the Virginia
Theological Seminary in Alexandria for an open house. We
spent the weekend there visiting the seminary, meeting the
professors and talking to the students. It was an orientation to
see if this was the place where we wanted to be.

It was at a conference at the Virginia Seminary early the
next year that I first ran into Rob Ross. He talks about the
first time we met, when I certainly didn't make a very good
impression on him.

> I met Vaughan for the very first time in February
> of 1989, at the Virginia Theological Seminary
> conference on ministry. It was an evening meet-
> ing that we all were invited to and my first
> impression of Vaughan was very negative. I was
> in the meeting on time, as most of us were, and
> about thirty minutes into the meeting, Vaughan
> and his wife came in. Vaughan was dressed to
> kill, with these extremely expensive khaki pants,
> with a crease that probably would never fade,

and he had these fancy shoes, probably Gucci, and was wearing a blue double-breasted blazer with a patch on it, probably a Ralph Lauren patch or something like that.

I turned to the person next to me and said, "Oh my God, look at that guy." He had more value in his clothing than my wife and I had in the car that we drove down in.

And he asked a couple of questions, and every time he asked a question he was just so full of himself, it was remarkable. He threw out his chest, and he puffed himself up, and he always delivered a small speech before every question. So my first impression of Vaughan was very negative.

It was an unusual beginning to what was to become a very close friendship which persists to this day. Rob was another one of those who helped me on the road. It seems that so many people contributed in so many different ways. But that was later. We were still in the throes of getting accepted by a seminary and making the move from secular to religious life.

Portia was amazed that we ever even arrived at the seminary. She remembers having fewer expectations, being more prepared for disappointment and therefore, perhaps, being more incredulous that things worked out the way they did.

Believe me, it's a miracle! First Vaughan went to a seminary in New York and then, when he decided to really go for it, he started applying to different seminaries.

I was really shocked, because he was accepted, and then we were here. We didn't have to do anything to get here. Everything was arranged. We got here, and I couldn't believe it.

He really has strong faith, he really does. He doesn't even think about the negative side or what if it won't happen. Sometimes I wonder what is he praying—what does he say? What is his relationship? How does he feel so comfortable praying?

But now I know that if he says he is going to do something, he will do it. If he says it can be done, it can. And he changed my life because I have a faith now that, before, life would not allow me to have. I had to deal with the cold reality: this was the way it was. But I learned that things don't have to be that way. You don't have to accept things. If you have faith, things can really change. It's all a matter of will. You really have to believe it. So now it's taught me that if I want to do something, I can. Before I always looked at things with the attitude of, "You can't do this because of that." So this has given me a new life.

We arrived at the seminary to find that Rob Ross and his wife were to be our neighbors. This turned out to be quite a shock to him, as he recalls quite vividly.

My wife and I moved down early from Boston so that she could look for a job when we relocated to seminary. We were put in a small neighborhood called Brookville, which is in the Landmark Valley of Alexandria, and we were on a little cul-de-sac. There was only one other seminary member who was going to be housed there and his name was Vaughan Booker. He was coming down from New Jersey and that's all I knew.

A lot of us were helping each other move in.

We were all filled with a Christian spirit of giving and caring, and we would get a case of Coke or orange juice or something, fill it with ice, and we'd go to meet the trucks as they came in. They were all U-Hauls because we were all moving ourselves: nobody had any money to move to seminary. We would all just unload people's boxes.

And so Vaughan pulls up in a big Ryder truck and we were moving this incredible furniture: beautiful, beautiful furniture, which is very atypical, because most of us were bringing in egg crate coffee tables and the like.

We were just about to lift up this bureau, and Vaughan and another seminary friend of mine, David, and I were in the truck together and we were perspiring badly so we decided to take a break. We all sat down on the few remaining boxes in the back of the truck.

Vaughan turned to both of us and said, "Hey, you know, you're going to find this out anyway, I'd rather have you find it out from me. But I murdered my wife many years ago and I served almost a dozen years in prison, and I'm out on parole. I was ordained a deacon in prison, and I worked for Xerox Corporation, and now I'm going to seminary. I just wanted to let you know that."

It was so funny because David and I looked at each other and said, "Oh, okay, well, you know, thanks, thanks, Vaughan."

And then I said, "Well, you get the other side of the bureau, Vaughan."

And all the while, inside, both of us are going, "Oh, my God. Oh, please." And he actually told us in some detail about the murder.

So we finished the move and we shook Vaughan's hand, we said good-bye, and David went off to his house and I went to mine, and I opened the door and said, "Honey," calling out to my wife.

"Yeah, what is it, dear?"

"We're living next door to a murderer," I said.

"What?"

"Yes, a murderer. And not only that, he's a black murderer."

My wife and I had both been agonizing about our racism, our kind of culturalized racism, being raised in affluent, suburban Boston. We knew how racist Boston was and we knew that we had that sin of racism in us and we were always trying to transcend it. So deep down inside there was a part of me that said, "You know, God put Vaughan next to me for a reason."

We ended up becoming incredibly fast friends very soon after that initial meeting.

When I first arrived in Alexandria, I was scared to death because there was no real contact at all between blacks and whites in Boston. I had no black friends. My exposure to blacks was minimal. In fact, I'm embarrassed to say that I knew my first black person when I was eighteen years old. I think that's humiliating and outrageous—an incredible indictment of the town that I grew up in. However, I do believe that God is a God that acts and I think that I was put in an apartment right next to Vaughan's for a reason, and that reason was two-fold—I think I helped Vaughan and I think he helped me.

We became a sanity check for each other. I mentioned that my first impression of Vaughan was that he puffed himself up a lot, and I think in the beginning Vaughan was nervous about being a graduate student and doing seminary education, because we had all heard rumors that it was going to be a difficult grind. There were students who had been doctors and lawyers who had all said that seminary was harder than medical school or law school.

So we were all nervous about that, and I think Vaughan was even more nervous, in part because he had earned his degree while he was in prison. As a result of that I think he tended to be defensive, and the way he was defensive was by posturing. In class he would raise his hand and he would say, "Professor, as a black man living in America today, I often face the tinge of racism, do you think that Moses perhaps could have faced that same difficulty?"

And I would look around at my fellow students and they would all be thinking, "Oh come on, please." Even if what Vaughan said had merit, which it very often did, he said it in such a way that it was off-putting. He spoke in a sort of fake voice. He and I would be talking normally and he would be saying, "Oh, yeah, Rob, that's great," and then all of a sudden he would raise his hand and he would say in a deeper voice, "Professor, I think that perhaps . . ." and he had this public speaking voice that I thought was artificial.

So on the way home from seminary I would say to him, "Vaughan, what are you doing that for? What's going on?" And we would talk it out. We would flush it out. And I think the way I tried to help Vaughan was to give him a sanity check as to what he was looking like.

One of the incredibly valuable things that you need when you're in ministry is you need a sanity check to say how you're coming off to people. Because you might think that you are being very humble, and a very good listener, when in fact people think, "Boy, he's just staring off into space and he's so full of himself." What you really need is people who love you enough to say, "Guess what, you're not coming off that way." That's what I tried to do for Vaughan.

Probably the biggest breakthrough in our relationship was when he told me in detail about the murder. He and I were commuting for about a month and I was just on egg shells the whole time. "I'm sitting next to a murderer," I would be thinking, wondering if he's going to take out a gun and shoot me, and finally I discovered that we were able to share real personal secrets and share things about our lives together, and we became confidants.

That's a slow process. I would share something with him about my personal life and then he would open up and share something with me and then I could then open up a little more. It was just a slow process of peeling away the onion and getting under each other's skin a little more and a little better.

I had always had a curiosity about prison life. I would see only what is portrayed in Hollywood or in the news, and I wanted to find out what it was really like. So that was the first big opening. I asked him, "What about a lot of the homosexuality that goes on in prison? What was your experience with that?" And he shared very, very graphic details about that, and how he prevented himself from being victimized by that and things of that sort.

That was probably the first pickle out of the jar, and then I finally asked him about the murder, "Vaughan, what was it like? What did it feel like? Why did you do it?" And that's when he told me the whole story. He was very, very open and very honest. I never once sensed any absence of complete remorse. He was never glib about his crime. I think he was grateful to have somebody that he could confide in, because I think he still had a lot of feelings about that. There are also certain things that happen to you as a black man in our culture that I think produced a lot of rage and a lot of anger in him, and I think it's important to have somebody you can talk to about that. I think in many ways I'm that person for Vaughan.

He talked to me also about things that led up to the murder. I didn't get the impression that their marriage was a particularly happy one or that they were particularly mature. Vaughan and Angie were kids. They were not using the normal methods to work out their difficulties. I think they were just screaming and tricking each other a lot.

I know for a fact, that if he had to do it all over again he would walk to his lawyer and get a divorce and not walk to the closet to get a bow.

And Vaughan did a lot for me. He let me into his home, he invited me to social events, he introduced me to black people and got me socializing with black people which is something I'd never done before.

Vaughan formed a black student association at

seminary which was something there had never been before, even though Virginia Seminary has a wonderful record of attracting American blacks and African blacks to it. There are more black students, both American and African, at Virginia Seminary than any other seminary, and that's true also on a percentage basis, not just because Virginia Seminary is so big. So when Vaughan started the black student association I said, "Gosh, Vaughan, I'd love to go to that." I just wanted to go and hear what their issues were and things like that. So he said, "Sure." And he welcomed me into that community and those became some of the best friends that I had at seminary, thanks to Vaughan.

As a result I developed a sensitivity for some of the more subtle expressions of racism in institutions. For example, there were always attempts to put together community activities at the seminary, and seldom would they concern themselves with what I would call Afrocentric sensibilities. They would put committees together to advise the Dean on certain issues, and they would hardly ever include black students. So Vaughan would say, "How many brothers, or how many sisters are on that committee?" and the people would all go, "Oops. That's right. We forgot."

Vaughan and many of the black students were aware that this seminary had once owned slaves, before the Civil War, and there were a lot of people who wondered if there wasn't still a lot of that residual racism in the community, and in and how they did business.

So he taught me, and he raised my consciousness regarding black concerns.

Vaughan was also very generous. He used to drive a black Pontiac Firebird; it was an old car and not worth very much, but the outer shell of the thing looked beautiful, because Vaughan had probably polished it with a Q-tip everyday. Well, the African students arrived and saw this man who had handsome clothes, because Vaughan always had handsome clothes, driving an impressive American sports car, even though looks are obviously deceiving, and they saw him as a successful black man, so they were naturally drawn to him because of appearances and also because he was so warm and inviting.

But once the appearances were transcended by the black students they then found out that his home was a home away from home for them. While at the seminary all the African students, like the rest of us, had to eat all three meals a day, twenty-one meals a week at an institution. And the institution was, I think, better than most, but it was still institutional food.

Every week or so Vaughan and Portia would grill up some African delicacy on his grill in the backyard, and he would invite all the African students over for a home-cooked meal. He would have these yams that reminded people of home; he would have this chicken in this kind of sauce that would taste very African, and he would grill it all, and he would find a way to get the extra twenty dollars necessary to buy eighty percent more food than he, Portia, and Tiera would eat, and he'd say, "Come on down."

So they would come down and would bring friends of theirs that were at seminaries in Georgetown, and at Howard, so his house became a Mecca for African students in the D.C. metro area. They all loved him because he was so generous and so giving. I'll never forget being at some of those sessions and I would say, "Gee, that's a great jazz cassette," and he would say, "Well, do you want it? Take it. Let me know when you're done." He's just incredibly giving. And it was just so genuine.

Portia also has memories of our time at the seminary which are not necessarily the same as my own, but help give a more complete picture of our life at this time.

The seminary was really challenging because here you are in a religious environment and these people are not what you would expect. It was a cold environment and I used to wonder, "Where is all the Christianity? Is it here? Where is this love thy neighbor?" It wasn't there. Some people would not look at me when they spoke, or acknowledge my presence.

I never had been farther south than Delaware, so coming to Virginia was really coming to the South. I knew all about racism but it was still a shock for me to see it right in the seminary.

Individually there were some nice people, but as a whole the environment was very cold. It wasn't everyone. There were some very nice people, and we had some very positive experiences. Overall, the seminary faculty and staff were quite cordial.

I remember introducing myself to the 18 or 20 students at my first class. The faculty there knew my background because the information was on my application form and had come up in interviews. But I don't think many of the students knew. Ted Gleason, my advisor, who happened to be Rob Ross's father-in-law, asked us all to talk a little about our lives by way of an introduction to the rest of the class. I told them about myself and my past, and obviously it was quite revealing because I told them my real background. The amazing thing was that no one was critical. What happened was that others started opening up and talking about secretive, painful aspects of their lives.

Ted always remembers that as being particularly meaningful to the rest of the class because it brought us close together at the very beginning. It was a catharsis. Here were all these priestly types doing a true confession, and it wasn't really intended for that. It was simply intended to tell the others a bit about yourself and it was usual to try and show your best side. It seemed that we told everything and it really did bring us closer together.

People trust you more when you are honest with them. Sooner or later in talking to someone, when we begin to talk about our lives, they're going to notice a void in mine from 1967 to 1977, so when it gets to that point, I usually share my past with them. I tell them the whole story, not just that I was in prison, but why. It usually takes them aback and often they will say, "Oh my goodness, you don't look like a murderer." My response is usually, "Well, how does a murderer look?" not to make light of it. Then they have to examine their preconceived notions of how a murderer looks, dresses and so on and it focuses their attention on the fact that people repent and can be renewed.

At the seminary we had chapel at 8:15 every morning and that went on until 9:00. Then my first class was Old Testament, followed by New Testament and then Greek and Hebrew. For lunch we would go over to the refectory where all the students had to eat, whether they lived on campus or off, along with the faculty and even the Dean. That was to help keep the community together. After lunch we would go back to our next class which was Systematic Theology. It was just like a college. I was on a three-year Master of Divinity, or MDiv, program for those who were going into parish ministry or expected to be ordained priests. This program was a requirement for ordination as a priest.

On Wednesdays we also had Eucharist, and then on Sundays most of us were assigned to churches. I was the only deacon in the class and had much more experience than anyone else there in terms of actually working in a church. That was a unique perspective for me because I was doing academic work like the others but I had a leg up in terms of experience. Consequently I was used as a resource at the seminary. I would be called upon to serve as a deacon and I was able to assist the priest with Eucharist and also preach at certain times. My classmates would also ask me to come and speak at outreach events about my work in prisons.

I feel I was treated the same as everyone else. If there were people with any bad feelings about my background, I suppose they just didn't hang around me. Most of the people I was with were very supportive and thought it was an unusual story of sin, repentance, forgiveness and renewal. It had some religious significance to them.

In the summer of my first year we had to do what we called Clinical Pastoral Education, which is field work carried out in a hospital or other institution under proper supervision. I did mine in Sibley Hospital, in Washington. There were eight or nine of us involved, including some Lutherans, Catholics and students of other denominations. We had to be at the hospital in the morning at about 8:00 and then each of us took a specific area. Some of us specialized in terminally ill patients and I spent some time with them.

We were trained in one-on-one counseling techniques and this helped build on skills I had acquired while in prison. Sometimes counselors tend to deal with their own problems—

they take their own baggage into the counseling session with them—and a good supervisor helps overcome these tendencies so that your counseling becomes more direct and helpful to the person being counseled.

I think my experiences in prison helped me understand patients better, because very often they are like prisoners, perhaps separated from their loved ones, and feeling helpless. There was one older lady who was a very difficult patient and I think my experience enabled me to help her. After a while, when anything would go wrong, she would call for me. I suppose I listened to her in ways that others didn't.

This was quite an intense program that lasted from May until I received my certificate in August. At some point in my career, I would like to go back and do some more work in Clinical Pastoral Education, perhaps becoming a supervisor. It was an enlightening experience.

In our second year we were required to propose and carry out a program of field work and this continued through to the end of the senior year. I chose to work at St. Timothy's, an Episcopal church in Washington, where my supervisor was Father Dalton Downs, a wonderful man who has been very supportive of me and my ministry. Still under him I went on to do my final year of field work at the D.C. jail, serving as a prison chaplain. One of the reasons I kept working in prisons is that I didn't want to become phobic about going back "inside." I can now go into prisons without any qualms because I know I'm no going to stay there.

It's interesting to note, however, that I was so much more comfortable at the VTS (Virginia Theological Seminary) than I had been at the General Theological Seminary in New York, because VTS had large, open grounds and lots of space, whereas at the General, I sometimes felt like I was back in my cell.

But working in the prison ministry, my background gave me credibility and enabled me to relate to the people I was ministering to. Before they knew that I had done more time than they were ever likely to, some of the inmates would try and put me on the defensive on the basis of, "Well, you don't know what it's like to be in here." But I quickly disabused them of that idea and a camaraderie developed between us. I became something of a role model for them and a source of inspiration. If Rev. Booker could redeem himself after committing murder and being sentenced to life in prison, then there was some hope for them.

My aim was not just to try to get the men and women to start going to church so that they could say or feel they were religious. Rather I tried to instill in them a more deeply encompassing way of life where they could love themselves and love others too, where they could interact with their fellows and live a positive life. There is little value in faith which exists on Sunday or Wednesday during a service but is lacking for the remainder of the week.

There were successes and there were failures. There were many who sincerely wanted to change their lives. But, for example, I met a juvenile at the D.C. jail who was there because he was going to be tried as an adult for a drive-by shooting in which he had killed an innocent bystander. I really tried to appeal to his heart. I said to him, "Suppose it had been your mother that you accidentally shot," and his attitude was, "She shouldn't have been there." He was very negative and very angry.

I realized that there are a lot of young men who don't have fathers bringing them up who are angry with their mothers because they are trying to be both father and mother at the same time. That is a very difficult thing to do. I don't think I got through to that young man at all. His attitude was, "If life is going to do this to me, I'm going to do it back to life," and I was the stupid one for trying to go along with the system.

There was another young man named Leonard, very bright, but he got involved in some criminal activity. He was already working towards his degree and he started to look at accepting

God into his life. He became tired of the old way and asked me to help him find some spiritual direction. I'm still in touch with him.

The work at the jail gave me a chance to return to the institution to give some of my experience back so as to help with the uplift and development of other human beings. There are people who are redeemable. It's a matter of putting the message out there like bait on a hook. Some will pick it up and some won't, and that's all you can ever ask for. Throughout this time St. Timothy's really supported me. They even put on a recital to help raise money for the prison ministry that I was conducting.

There were other aspects of life at the seminary, remembered here by Rob Ross, including the lighter moments and even some mild rebellion. After all, we were students.

> We were in the diocese of Virginia which runs down to Richmond, the headquarters of Dixie honor. So Vaughan and I in our early seminary years would love to throw bombs, just make inflammatory remarks aimed at the residue of Southern racism, and let the chips fall where they would. I think when you're a young student type you can get away with that.
>
> We also had a covenant. In the Old Testament there was a group of clergy, known as "the Jahweh" and so some seminarians, because they liked that part of the church history, called themselves the J Covenant. And they would gather together for some very conservative, old, ritualistic activities.
>
> Well, Vaughan and I called ourselves the C Covenant. The *C* stood for the grades that we averaged going through seminary. We actually were very deliberate about that because we found

that—we did better than *C* work, we probably did *B* work—but the truth was in order to get *A*'s you really had to sacrifice your family, and we both had a family, and neither of us were willing to make the sacrifices necessary to get *A*'s. That bothered some faculty members who thought that we should be monomaniacal in our approach to seminary education. In fact, we wanted to have a complete experience, which would be to be with our family, to be in our field work site learning the ministry first hand, and then studying the scholarly material.

So, we had the C Covenant, and it was a bit of a running joke. Every now and then when our grades would come out people would come up to us and say, "Vaughan, Rob, I'm joining your club." It was just a cute thing but it was also very symbolic of where we stood, and it infuriated a lot of people, particularly the scholarly types of the seminary who felt like we should place all the emphasis on studying.

There was a great deal of variety to seminary life and over-all it was a wonderful experience for me.

In the midst of that experience, however, there was tragedy.

Just when it seemed that my past really was behind me and I was building a completely new future, everything came pouring back with new pain. I suppose God felt a need to remind me that I had not yet arrived.

CHAPTER THIRTEEN

...you are my refuge in the day of disaster.

(Jeremiah 17:17)

As I said, when Tawney went back to live in Philadelphia after spending a year and a half with us, I was very uneasy about his future.

It was the 15th of September 1990, the beginning of my second year at VTS, that the phone rang. It was Kim.

"I have bad news for you . . . . Tawney was killed."

That hit me harder than any news I've ever received. Later I found out the details. Apparently he got into an argument with another man. I don't know if it was about a girl or what, but they claimed Tawney had a knife. I never knew Tawney to carry any weapon, but I suppose he might have had a knife. In any event, apparently the other man went home, got a gun and came back and shot Tawney in the stomach. He died in the hospital a few hours later.

The man who murdered him got five years. I suppose with the overcrowding of the jails coupled with the atmosphere created by the movies where this was just another young black man killed, that was considered enough. Not everyone by any means gets life for murder. I suppose if I talked to the young man who did it, it would be about the value of human life, not to try to get revenge for the murder of my son.

Again, Rob Ross recalls the events that immediately followed that terrible news. After my wife, he was the first person I spoke to and he was, as usual, a strong source of comfort during my grief.

> It was hard for me to imagine that anything worse could happen to Vaughan, and then it happened. I felt like God dealt him a very tough hand in life, and the rest of his life was going to be happy. I remember he called me late one night and said, "Tawney's been killed—gunned down."
>
> Vaughan was crying and he was telling me about how hard it was to convince his son that he should just stay away from the street life that was so dangerous. I forget what it was—one o'clock or two o'clock in the morning in a particularly rough neighborhood in Philadelphia—and he said, "You know nothing good is going to come from being there at that time, and more than likely something very bad." Well something very, very bad happened to him.
>
> I was still reeling from the news of the death. The first thing I did was to call up the chaplain at the seminary: "I've got some awful news for you, Vaughan's son has been murdered."
>
> If any of the other seminarians had had a murder occur in the family it would have been a horrendous tragedy, but the fact that it was Vaughan made it even worse. I was still stunned by the whole thing and I just put the phone down, and my wife and I sat in the living room and I cried for Vaughan.
>
> Then out of our living room window we saw this steady parade of seminary students coming by to pay their respects to Vaughan. At the time

there were probably 150 students at the seminary, I would say 75 or 80 as well as faculty members came by Vaughan's apartment just to say how sorry they were. It was just incredible. There was no wake or anything: they all just came in. Finally, I went over there and Portia had this buffet set up just to deal with the crowds.

When Tawney was killed it made it even more poignant for me, that Vaughan just wanted to be out of that inner-city environment that had been so harmful and destructive to his life and he didn't want that—not to run away from it at all, but rather to make it all go away. He just wanted to take the crime and the violence out of the ghetto— to take the pain out of the inner-city—and yet it wouldn't let him go. It killed his son. It was awful.

Portia also saw Tawney's death taking a toll on my life at the time.

When he lost Tawney it really affected him physically. It really ran his system down a lot and I know that was the reason. It really put a big strain on him physically.

I am sure he feels to this day that he is responsible for that happening. I don't know if he thinks about it, but I think he feels responsible.

I also believe that Tawney remembered somehow that his father had tried to strangle him when he was a baby. I don't think anyone ever told him, but I think somehow, unconsciously, he knew.

Because this boy had such a death wish that when he left the house you never knew what was going to happen.

The funeral was a tremendous ordeal. I was devastated by the loss and simply wanted to pay my respects to my son. And I was sad because we had not closed on a lot of issues, and I would never have a chance to do that now. I put my favorite cross in his coffin and that meant something to me. It was all I could do to say good-bye to him.

But at the funeral I had also wanted to try and bring about some reconciliation with the members of Angie's family, who were there, of course. There was a big risk of rejection going there and I even feared for the safety of my new family. Rob Ross had told me he wanted to come to the funeral but I asked him not to as I feared that he would be mistreated by those members of Angie's family who were still full of resentment and anger. As it happened, there was an attempt to start something. I tried to strike up a conversation with a young man there who I didn't even know. His response was, "I don't want you talking to me."

"I don't even know you," I said.

"Well, I know you," he answered with blatant hostility.

It was like a war beginning to fester. I didn't want to put my family at risk, so we left. It was strange that some of those family members who were angry were not even born in 1967 and a lot of them didn't even know me.

In an interview, some of Angie's family expressed their views on the funeral. They are included here because I want to try to present all sides of the story.

Linda Pickett, Angie's niece, said, "I resented his appearance at Tawney's funeral, crying over the coffin and so on. He was like an actor."

Geraldine Williams, Angie's sister, agreed, "He always knew how to get over."

Certainly they made their feelings clear at the funeral and it just added to my anguish.

I feel that if Tawney had been with me this might never have happened. I don't know how realistic that is. Hindsight is 20/20 vision. Perhaps in a different environment things would have been different. On the other hand both Portia and Rob saw that death wish streak in Tawney's nature. In any event, it was too late. There was nothing I could do that would change that reality. Tawney was dead.

You can imagine how I felt when Kim came to me when I was in my last year of seminary and asked me if I could help with her daughter, Eboni. Relations between us had been up and down and I had fervently hoped for a real reconciliation between us. She was working in early childhood education and there is not a lot of money in that. The private Christian school she was sending Eboni to closed down and Kim did not have the wherewithal to enroll her in a similar school.

I had always told Kim that if she was having difficulty and if I could help, I would. So I was ecstatic when she asked me if I could take Eboni. She was saying a lot of things. She was saying, "I trust you. I trust you with my daughter."

Eboni was about the same age as Tiera who had been living with us throughout this period. I knew there would be some bickering back and forth but they really liked each other and they have been like sisters. I knew it would be a good situation and it was never a hardship. We would be able to put Eboni in the sort of school Kim would want her in, so it was rewarding for me. She has been with us ever since, at least during school time.

The relationship with Kim has been one of partial reconciliation with upsets along the way. I believe she is torn between the natural love of a daughter for her own father, and the fact that I took her mother away from her when she was so young. Also she grew up with Angie's family and was exposed to the anger that some of them still felt. Fortunately she has become more and more involved with the church and I think this has helped heal her wounds.

I have tried to be supportive because I love her. Kim was the joy of my life until that grim morning in October 1967.

Now I try to listen to her. I remember a recent phone call where we must have been on the phone for two hours. I said, "Kim, tell me how you feel. If you're angry, you won't hurt my feelings. It's important. Let's talk." She did and we shouted at each other for a while and cried for a minute at the end and then we both felt better. These days we talk more and more about reconciliation. With Tawney no longer here, the relationship with Kim is even more important to me.

Tawney's death was a traumatic experience that brought the past right into the midst of my studies at the seminary. With the support of Portia, friends at the seminary, the faculty (who were most helpful even to the point of financial assistance with the funeral expenses) and through my own faith, I continued the program, perhaps even more determined to understand God, do His will and follow my calling. Somehow He kept reminding me that I could not sit back in complacency. My journey was still very much in progress.

May 16th, 1992 was graduation day at the seminary. We had a big green and white tent outside the building and the 65 members of the graduating class were all attired in black cassocks, ankle length white surplices and our scarlet, white and black academic hoods which symbolized the Master of Divinity degree. We had a class cross: everyone in the class wore the same type.

The dean and the bishop were there to hand out our scrolls, while beautiful music was playing in the background.

I was swamped by powerful and mixed emotions. The pride of accomplishment of three years of very hard study was mixed with the sadness of leaving the students and faculty. But above all there was the positive emotion: I was glad it was over and so happy that I was going on to be ordained a priest. When it was over I just broke down and cried.

I felt ready for the priesthood. Before those three years something would have been missing. At the seminary there was a constant interplay and dialogue about where we were going in terms of our ministry. And I felt prepared because the theological education is structured for formation of pastoral care, liturgy and all the other aspects of being a priest. Fulfilling the formal requirements was most satisfying.

In an interview, Dick Swartout, the man who was most instrumental in "holding my feet to the fire" throughout all those years since I had been ordained a deacon at Graterford, said, "I think Vaughan has grown tremendously over the years, and I think he grew more through going through the seminary process than he did at any other time."

One month and one day later we set off by car to New Jersey for what was to be, perhaps, the single most important event in my life. Although we had been living in Virginia for three years, I was still canonically resident in New Jersey and therefore under the authority of the bishop of New Jersey, the Right Reverend Mellick Belshaw. He had been true to his word and supported me on my road and now he was there to perform the final act of admission into the priesthood: my ordination.

It was a warm evening at St. Albans and it seemed that everyone I cared about in the world was there to share in my happiness: all the family; many friends; Dick Swartout and others within the clergy who had helped me along the way; friends from the seminary; Donald Vaughn, now Superintendent of Graterford penitentiary who had grown up in my neighborhood, had known me as a boy, and was one of the sergeants at Graterford when I arrived there; these and many, many others.

Donald Vaughn remembers the day.

> When I received the invitation to go to New Jersey for the ordination I had something planned for that date but I canceled it. I didn't even know where New Brunswick was and I thought it was going to take me an hour and a

half to get there.

"How far is it to New Brunswick?" I asked the woman at the toll booth.

"Oh, you're going up Near New York. Take Route 11."

"Well how long does it take? I have to be there by 8 o'clock," I said.

"You'll never make it," was the encouraging reply.

I admit that I broke the speed limit that day because I wanted to be there on time.

It was a good feeling. I hadn't seen or heard from Vaughan in years and hadn't even known where he was. I thought he was still working for Xerox.

I made it there that evening and eventually found the church after getting lost. I was happy to be part of that ceremony. I had cake and ice cream with Vaughan and his mother and his new wife. I must have been there until 11 o'clock that evening.

I brought some pamphlets away with me when I left because there were still people at Graterford who remembered him and who would be happy to learn of his achievements.

Dick Swartout remembers, and to him also the news came as something of a surprise.

I hadn't heard from Vaughan for about four years. I guess it was 1992 that I got a call from him and he said, "I'm graduating from Virginia Seminary and I wanted to share that with you."

I said, "Well that's fantastic. Too bad you didn't call me before, you know we're just across the bay."

Then he wanted me to come to his graduation which I couldn't do on such short notice. "But you will come to the ordination up in New Jersey because I want you to read the Gospel for the ceremony?" he asked.

So I did. That was a nice rounding off of the ministry because I'd closed out all the rest of it, probably 10 or 15 years ago.

Portia, as usual, was amazed.

So Vaughan got through seminary. I could hardly believe it. When they ordained him there was hardly any publicity at all. He did everything, he went through seminary, but I still wondered, "What else are they going to make him do?"

And then it was happening and I just couldn't get past that day. In my mind the world was going to end. I just couldn't believe that it was happening. It has changed our lives totally. I really believe in the power of God.

Perhaps what stands out for me the most were those questions put to the congregation to establish whether or not, even at this late stage, someone might object to my ordination.

Dear Friends in Christ,

You know the importance of this ministry, and the weight of your responsibility in presenting Vaughan Booker for ordination to the sacred priesthood.

Therefore, if any of you know any impediment or crime because of which we should not proceed, come forward now and make it known.

No one did come forward. No one there, apparently, saw the events of my past as an impediment or crime to preclude me from becoming a priest. That, to me, is forgiveness. I think that the bishop was really happy when no one came forward, because it's always difficult when that happens.

Then he asked, "Is it your will that Vaughan be ordained a priest?"

And the people said, "It is."

"Will you uphold him in his ministry?"

And they all said, "We will."

I recited my vows. The bishop and other ordained priests who were there laid their hands on my head and I was ordained a priest in the church of God.

I felt that God was holding me in His hands. I really did. Imagine having a dream like that come true. It's like saying to a genie, "I wish this could happen," and it happens. That's how I felt. It's what I had wanted more than anything else in my life and it happened. It actually happened.

Then the following week I said Mass at Saint Albans and it brought home to me that it really was worth the twenty years that it took me to get there. It takes most people about three or four years to enter the priesthood: It took me twenty. But even if it had taken me twenty-five, I would still be seeking ordination into the priesthood.

Being an ordained priest did not automatically put bread on our table. I had been teaching English as a second language part time for the last two years of seminary to help pay the bills. Now I began selling long distance services for Sprint while waiting for a job opportunity to present itself.

For ordination did not carry with it an assignment to a parish or any sort of job. I had been looking for a position for some time, starting even before graduation from VTS, but so far nothing had come my way. Priests have to market themselves, much the same as anyone else. You have to find out what opportunities are available, send out resumes and so on.

Some bishops have assignments already worked out for some of the students graduating seminary but that is increasingly rare. Many dioceses don't have budgets for new people and it is not unusual to begin your career as an assistant to a priest somewhere.

I also looked at the possibility of a chaplaincy. The Reverend Nathaniel Williams was retiring from Graterford penitentiary and I was offered a job there. My feelings were mixed. It was a real privilege even to be asked to submit an application, because it would have set quite a precedent for an ex-convict to be appointed as prison chaplain. On the other hand, I had a concern that if I was working for the state I would also be a custodian in a sense. I would have a key like everybody else and if something went wrong I would have to turn the key on the inmates just like any of the guards. It would have been a conflicting role for me. I have heard some horror stories about chaplains who are doubling as guards. Their commitment is to the prison first which means maintaining order. I didn't take the job at Graterford, though I felt honored to be asked.

Along with more than a hundred other aspirants I submitted an application to Meade Memorial Church in Old Town Alexandria. My only previous contact with that church had been the year before when, as a deacon, I had conducted a funeral there. I felt I was at a disadvantage because they had only seen me perform as a deacon, not as a priest.

Then I received a letter saying they had selected someone else and I was disappointed because I had really looked forward to being a priest there. It was a historically stable church and I would have been the first African-American priest in 30 years for what was a primarily black congregation. They had built a new building and were ready for someone to come and do a lot of creative, meaningful ministry there. I saw the potential for that.

It seems, however, that I was supposed to go to Meade Memorial Church after all.

CHAPTER FOURTEEN

"Look, the men whom you put in prison are standing in the temple and teaching the people!"

(Acts 5:25)

Before I had even had a chance to recover from the disappointment, I received a call from the church. Was I still interested in taking the position after all? I certainly was. I only found out later what happened. The story is best told by some of the members of the committee who are now my parishioners. Apparently I had not been the first choice but, when you think of how many people applied, to me it was almost the same as being first choice. I felt that although someone else may have been called first, it was I who was chosen.

The Senior Warden at the time of my selection by Meade was Lewis Forrest. Because Meade only had an interim priest, Lewis was administratively responsible for running the entire church. He explains the search process in general and recalls mine in particular.

> Choosing a priest in the Episcopal Church involves going through a search process. A Search Committee is selected and then we advertise

through the larger Episcopal Church out of New York.

The Search Committee consists of 12 members who work independently to the Vestry. The only time the Vestry becomes involved is when the candidate has been selected. The decision is submitted to the Vestry and the Vestry approves or disapproves.

You try to be objective. Everything that has impacted on someone's life comes into play, especially in Vaughan's situation. You have to do a lot of real soul searching because when you read his profile and his background it's quite shocking right from the beginning. I took the position that it was not up to me to judge his actions—that was up to the Supreme Being. I could only go on where he was at right now and where he was going.

For a person to have gone through all of that and still have his faith and be a deacon for that many years and then go through seminary to become a priest, I just thought he had a wealth of experience, knowledge and just plain life to bring to Meade church and I felt at that time that was what Meade needed.

I divorced all the other stuff of what he did when he was younger and just went on what I thought he could bring to Meade now.

One thing that stuck out in my mind was the question of whether everyone else would accept him the way I did, but I decided I couldn't worry about that too much because that's between those people and their God to decide. I had decided. I felt he was the choice at the time.

The first service went well. He was very well

received. We hadn't had a black minister in Meade church in over 27 years. We are 98% black. The minister before Vaughan, Jack Woodard, was our first full time minister in about 20 years.

I see things moving better than they were. We were always in flux. We'd get a part time minister and then that person would leave. When Woodard was hired we knew he was close to retirement and that we would have to go through the search process again.

I see a stability now that we haven't seen for a long time. I see a spirit in the church that we haven't had in a long time. Last Sunday we had a Gospel Truth concert with drums, bass, keyboard: that's something that's not traditional to Meade church. Everybody comes up for healing at the healing services. There's just a spirit there that hasn't been there before.

The church has grown. We have more baptisms and marriages. We're getting new people in. Some people have transferred from where he was before. New people have started to come. I can picture 10 or 12 families right off the top of my head. One of the things we wanted to see was growth in the congregation.

There were some ups and downs. There were some people who could not accept what he had done earlier in life and they were putting themselves in a position of forgiving and not forgiving and it's not in their hands. We did have some problems with that. There have been people who have wandered off but less than have come in.

He's made a very positive impact on the church and the congregation and the community.

His arrival was a relief for me. That particular
time without Jack Woodard and before Vaughan
came was a period of great turmoil for me and
when he came it was like a rock had been lifted
off my shoulders. It made a lot of difference. He
and I could sit down and talk and we understand
one another. Sometimes we might not say anything but we know what we're saying.

Vaughan is a people person. The experience he
brings is a definite plus. He preaches good sermons and that's what people want to hear. His
sermons are not high and lofty where people
can't understand what he's talking about. He par-
allels the Scriptures with what's happening right
here and now. We've had preachers who just
preached the Scriptures with no parallel of what's
happening now and people can't relate to that.

Pam O'Reilly, one of the members of the Search
Committee, remembers being concerned about my lack of
experience as a priest running a church.

I was not personally affected by Father Booker's
prison record or what got him there. He's been at
the heights and he's been at the depths and to see
him coming back so strong is a wonderful story.
It really tested the Christian belief in redemption
and forgiveness for the Search Committee, so it
was a leap of faith.

His background was a consideration but that
wasn't my own concern because my attitude was,
anyone can make a mistake. It's only through the
grace of God that I hadn't done something that
bad. This happened in the '60s. He had served
his time and carried out all this wonderful work

in prison and had done a fantastic job at Xerox where he proved himself as a top salesman.

My concern was more as to his experience as a priest and in running a church. He had just been ordained and he might have all the religion in the world, but could he successfully manage a church that was $700,000 in debt? Because we had the building fund mortgage to pay.

When I met him, I went in to the interview with reservations and I came away totally sold on him. It was amazing to hear him talk about his ministry at St. Timothy's and how he had run a prison ministry and had managed to obtain grants to fund it. I didn't feel like he was bragging: these were things he had done that he believed in. It was amazing and I don't know how he did it.

We had previously selected another man before Father Booker. He fit all our nice little stereotypes of what a pastor should be, so we disbanded. But then within a few days it was like the Lord saying, "You've made the wrong choice." The man we had chosen notified us that he wasn't going to accept the job. So we had an emergency reconvene session and all of us knew that we had made the wrong choice, that we had to make the right choice, and I think we knew what that was but it was a real leap of faith.

I compared it to when Pope John Paul I was elected and he was two or three months in office and then died. It was like God saying, "Let's go back and make the right choice." That's how I felt with Father Booker. God said, "OK, you made a logical choice but this is my will." It was a leap of faith but I think it's paid off.

When Father Booker arrived we had a church
that had been divided on feelings and issues and
we needed a healer. I think Father Booker is
healing. The focus has turned from the church
and all the discord to getting back on our feet
and rebuilding

The one thing that really impressed me and
reconfirmed my decision for me was the way he
was received by the congregation. The Search
Committee wondered how the congregation
would respond to this man because of his background. Again it was a leap of faith. But I felt we
were obviously on a course where these things
were happening for a reason and it would be
taken care of. Well, the first Sunday that he was
in front of the congregation I think the first thing
out of his mouth was, "Well, this is who I am,
this is my background," and he handled it so
beautifully. He had the congregation eating out
of his hand the first five minutes he was there.
And the congregation has been really supportive.
I don't talk to everyone but I never picked up that
there was anybody who was having reservations
about him. My impression is that there was no
animosity. It confirms our leap of faith. You have
to say, "Thank you." We did make the right decision.

Another thing that impressed me about Father
Booker is that he is not going to turn his back on
where he came from or on the people in prison.
He is going back into prison ministry and that to
me shows real strength of character that he is not
going to deny his background but is going to go
back and serve these people. And also he has a
real emphasis on youth. He's working with the

Scouts this afternoon so that the Cub Scouts can earn their religion badge. I've been here 7 years and he's the first priest that had any interest in doing that at all.

Some of the other members of the Search Committee were convinced that higher powers were at work in the selection of a new Rector for Meade.

Rosetta Tyree began going to Meade in the '40s when she was still a teenager, so she has seen our church change over the years with priests of all types coming and going. She was the spokesperson for the Search Committee.

Earlier on there weren't any black priests around to be had. In the seminary you'd only see one or two every year and they went back to where they were sent from. So we had white priests coming into Meade and we didn't realize there were black priests who were willing to come to our church.

Previously the diocese would send us someone to make do because we couldn't make up our minds among the white priests available to choose from. This time we had a choice of black priests and we didn't know which way to go because we weren't used to this. We were so excited.

We had narrowed it down to four black ones to choose from. There was one who had a heavy African accent and I don't think he was too pleased with Meade because he came out of a white, rich Episcopal church and we were poor. I think our ways and our accents and that type of thing made him feel that it wasn't his type of parish. So we said, "So long," to him.

We had already read all the papers that Father Booker had given us on his background ahead of time. We weren't even going to go as far as to call him because we had already read his record and we had chosen a Father Cobb.

I was the spokesperson for the Search Committee. We went in to face the Vestry, the leaders of Meade church, to tell them our decision. So I took my place at the head of the table, got my papers together and was ready to talk to them about Cobb, but I could not say anything about Cobb. I was sitting there like a dummy waving my hands and going, "Uh, uh, uh..." I thought I must be nervous, but I wasn't nervous. I was shaking my head and shaking my hands like I was trying to flush the chickens out or something.

I kept doing that and one of the other ladies who works on the Search Committee, Paula, was there and she saw I wasn't saying anything so she tried to step in for me. I kept making signs at her and we were making eye contact. She watched me and I was trying to encourage her when she said the right thing and shaking my head if it was wrong and so on. This is the way it went on until Paula finished with the item.

Eventually we did get Cobb accepted and the next morning Dana Lloyd was supposed to go and call him to let him know he had been chosen by the Meade people. When she called the man he was very angry. He didn't want the job. Some church had given him a scholarship to go back to North Carolina College. He didn't have time for this kind of thing. We don't know why the man was mad but my thoughts about it later were:

God sent Cobb away so there was no more Cobb and we had to go back to Vaughan Booker or we wouldn't have anybody.

When I talk about this I get so excited because this has never happened to me. I am not a Baptist: I'm one of these staid, high-nosed Episcopalians. But the next thing we knew, all of the bars were down and here was Booker, the one that I kept saying, "We cannot elect him because we're not just getting a priest for us here on the Search Committee. We're getting it for the whole church and then I would start naming off people: What is Miss So-and-so going to say? What's this other one going to say? They're not going to want Booker.

But then I wasn't able to say anything good about Cobb and then when we did get things together he didn't want the job...so this looked like the Lord's work to me.

I still don't really understand how he got there. He was the last man we put up. We had been through the other four. Booker was the last one we saw and the last one we chose. We really didn't know how we got Vaughan because really we did not want him, but we got him and everything is working out fine. So the Lord is still alive and working isn't He? This was a miracle.

Now some of the black people have tried to be snotty because of what he'd done. But I always know what to say to them when they say something about it to me. Because one time I was talking to Father Booker about what had happened, and I said to him, "It seems like you feel good about yourself," because this was a terrible thing that he had done.

He said, "God forgave me," and when he said that I was looking in his face and from the look on his face, I knew God had forgiven him. It was really a beautiful eye opener for me. So what I tell the people is, "You think you're smarter than God? God has forgiven him and we can't forgive him? I'd be afraid to close my eyes if I felt the way that you feel."

Blacks have a way of talking and saying things. With Father Booker I notice in some of his sermons we sit on the edge of our seats listening to what he is saying. He can throw some of those words in there and then we know he's not talking at us, he's talking to us. That makes a difference.

Now every other Sunday we have healing services. I'm 72 and I have arthritis and I go to the altar and kneel. When it's too bad to kneel he'll come down to where I'm standing to administer the anointing with oil and the laying on of hands.

He's a nice man and he knows how to get things done. Without him I don't know where we would have been by now, judging from the shape we were in before he came. At that time, members of the congregation weren't all that good friends. That's disappearing because people are getting different groups together to raise funds and help out. We have this big campaign going now to raise the money to pay for the mortgage.

More people are coming. The atmosphere in the church has changed. We have more visitors every Sunday who eventually join because of the warmth generated by Father Booker toward the congregation.

Sunday school has tripled. Many young families are joining the church and they can relate to the young priest and his wife and the grandchildren he's raising.

When we have baptisms, which is often, he will carry the young child around the church and introduce him or her to the congregation and tell us, "This is your new brother (or sister) in Christ."

He invites Sunday school kids to come into church during a baptism and sit near the front so that they can learn about being baptized. They really like that.

He visits incapacitated people more frequently than has been done in the past. The congregation feels like they are more friends to him than just sheep of his flock. It's personal feelings going on.

He's a good man. I don't know why and it's not my business to ask him why did this happen because he and the Lord have settled that. My family and I are very pleased and happy with him. I believe when I went to announce our choice of Cobb to the Vestry that I did lose my voice because I wasn't ready to take in one of God's children.

These are just a few of my wonderful new congregation. While these stories may seem flattering, they really reflect the love that exists at Meade, and my feelings for them are as positive as theirs for me.

Another person who was on the Search Committee and is also very active at Meade is Dana Lloyd, who has been going to this church for 16 years.

When I first came there was a white, interim priest. It was a nice little church, quaint, very

Episcopal, where if you listened to the sermon you nodded off once in a while. You didn't come to necessarily get close to God but because you knew it was the thing to do. I've seen about 6 or 8 come and go before Father Booker. Most of them were white except for a couple of the interim priests. One we asked not to come back.

The Search Committee narrowed the candidates down from 130 applicants—first to 11, then to 4. We wanted a black priest because we felt he could connect with our spirituality a bit better. We're probably about 95% black now.

Father Booker was very controversial. One thing that really bothered a lot of people was, would the parishioners accept someone who had come out of prison and, worse, who had murdered somebody? And how much of an embarrassment would this be in the neighborhood or to the community? We considered all this and he was not our first choice.

But as it turned out, the will of the Lord, as we came to believe, really showed through. Because the first person we chose we thought was everything we wanted. He was just a nice black person with a beautiful wife who could have been Miss America. They were just the cookie-cutter black family. He was just the thing to have. As it turned out, we chose him and then all of a sudden he gave a call and said, "By the way, I'm not coming," and didn't return any more phone calls.

We thought, "Well, maybe you weren't the cookie-cutter person we thought you were."

So we went back down the line and thought maybe we hadn't looked at this as well as we should have. Then after we met Vaughan it was like, "Oh, he's a nice person. I kind of like him after all."

And then, since he's been here, we feel we could not have made a better choice. Not only does he preach the Bible and forgiveness, he lives it. You can really see the spirituality of him and the love he has for other people. You do something wrong and it's not, "I'm going to beat you over the head with it," it's more, "OK, you goofed, let's try it again." He's a really loving, understanding person and an excellent counselor. And you can talk to him and know that he is sincere. It's not just veneer. So, he'd better not go anywhere!

I go to him when I have problems and I always feel better. It doesn't always necessarily fix up the problem completely but he'll give you suggestions on how to fix the problem. He won't fix it for you. He helped me when I wasn't sure what I really wanted to do. It took me 30 years to go back to college and he helped me through it. He even helped me apply for scholarships. He'd say, "Why don't you try this?" or "Your strengths are working with people," and he helped me work out how to go back to school when I was having financial difficulties: not by giving me money, but by helping me to try to work out the problems. The rest was mine to do. And he really stands behind you: "OK, are you still in school? What are you taking?" as far as giving you that moral support and that push that you need to keep going.

There isn't as much bickering within the church as there was at one point. He encourages us to love one another and he practices what he preaches. Most of his services leave you with something to think about afterwards and it's, "Wow, he said what we really needed to hear." He's a very dynamic speaker. He'll let you hear what you need to hear, not necessarily what you just want to hear.

Father Booker is also a good family man and he exhibits that. As in any culture, sometimes you have a priest who's not exactly above board. Vaughan's a very above board and upright person and is not going to be running around with Ms. So-and-so in the motel.

Portia's also a wonderful person and has her own strengths as far as her own counseling skills and her own listening abilities, quite in addition to him. I've talked to her many times.

Finally there is the voice of Charles McKnight who was the chairperson for the Search Committee. He too was interviewed recently.

I've been on the Search Committee before but this is my first time as a chairperson and I felt it was a most rewarding experience to be the person who chaired the committee for a new priest to come to our church and to serve the parishioners in good faith.

I had a wonderful crew with me and they backed me to the hilt. Everything was smooth sailing all the way.

Was I satisfied with the choice? You know the saying on the Pepsi ad, "Uh-huh." Can I say that? I was most satisfied. I can say without any reservation, I am truly pleased that I was part of this organization that chose this intrepid man to come to this organization.

There have been drastic changes since he's been here. We noticed the growth of the church as far as people coming in, the growth of our Sunday school, and our membership.

I had strong feelings that he was going to be one of the ones in the running and near the top. My wife, Edmonia, is like a psychic. The things she reveals always come true. She met Vaughan when he came to our house. Something within her told her that he was the man. She wasn't even on the Search Committee.

One thing about Father Booker, he is a true Christian and a man of God in every respect. The parishioners are very fond of him. They love him.

His past did not faze me one bit. He was in this position and so was Paul and Paul came out victoriously and this man did and will. I strongly believe that God is with this man and will continue to stay with him.

I thank God that I was chosen by the Vestry to be the Search Committee chairperson. We did it in a Christian way. There were times that there was disagreement. Sometimes there were heated discussions and I thank God that we came through victoriously. There was one lady who, when things got really heated, would say, "Wait," and I was glad that she was there because she would say, "Let's have a prayer." We would stop and join hands and have prayer and ask God to bring us close together and let these things iron out.

We still pray to God for this man being with us. Vaughan Booker was and is an inspiration to Meade church.

The net result of this process is that there I was, and here I am, Rector of Meade Memorial Church, where our theme is renewal of the spirit. At the first service I preached I told everyone about my life, that I'd been in prison and why. I had assumed that everyone already knew but I found out later that this was not the case. I preached it in the context of those protagonists in the scriptures who had sinned, turned away from God and God used them as vessels of His grace. I think people were better able to understand it in that context rather than just giving them a biographical sketch. That was the beginning of my writing and delivering credible, Scripture-based sermons that people could identify with and relate to.

Sermon time is often time to read the church bulletin, take a nap and do other things. But I must say that I'm really blessed that people listen. There's eye contact. I see people looking right at me and listening to what I'm going to say next. I like to get people involved. There are times when levity is really important because the message of repentance and forgiveness is a heavy message. Sometimes I just need to lighten it so I'll interject a bit of levity.

Recently I told them a story about a homeless man who came into the church and the ushers ran right over to him and escorted him out. He was outside on the sidewalk, sitting with his head in his hands, when Jesus walked by, saw him, and said, "Don't worry, my friend, they wouldn't let me in either." It's not always seriousness that gets the message across.

I preach about domestic violence and other issues which the church often shies away from. I tell them you can't go to church, take Communion, and go home and beat your wife or abuse your children. I know that is kind of bold to be saying up in the pulpit but we have to understand that this does happen among religious people of all denominations. I feel that, as the moral voice of the community, the church has a responsibility to address these issues.

We have a new Vestry which is our leadership group. I

have some good, young, progressive people in it and it is a very cooperative group. They're excited about coming and doing things to make the life of the church a lot better.

We are addressing the practical issues of day to day living. Meade had a huge debt—a $700,000 mortgage—and I think one of their reasons for calling me was my experience as a businessman, including fund raising and grant proposal writing. We're beginning to pay off this debt. Dr. Jerry Mites, the Senior Warden, came up with the idea of sacrificial giving. We're asking them to sacrifice that pizza or that video rental. It comes out to about $12 per month per family member. Every month I submit my $48 because if I'm going to ask people to do it, I'm going to do it myself. Now there are some people who are tithing. Our budget next year will be significantly higher than it's been and I suspect that most of that will be coming from pledges.

We have a lot of different activities centered in the church. We recently had our homecoming weekend which included a dance on Friday and a picnic on Saturday at a park that had a swimming pool and playground. This was for people coming back after summer vacation and people who had been away from the church and who were coming back and recommitting themselves to Christ. Next Sunday we have a fashion show. The Gospel Choir and the Senior Choir are really thriving. People are very much involved. You can come to the church almost any night of the week and people will be there engaged in some activity.

Outreach is very important and we have programs designed to reach out into the community. For example, we feed from 40 to 60 people a day. This used to be held at Hopkins House around the corner but they shut down and the program transferred to Meade. What better form of ministry than to feed the hungry? My friend Rob Ross, who is at a church nearby, remembers how this program started at Meade.

I have always had a particular interest in Vaughan's ministry at Meade Memorial, and I was lucky because I secured a position about eight blocks from Meade Church, and so Vaughan and I have lunch once a month, or so. He's harder to get a hold of than I am, because I think he's busier than I am, since he's the Rector there.

I always go around and ask people, "How's he doing?" I ask parishioners that I run into, I ask former Rectors, and I get the impression that he's still giving a hundred and ten percent. There are many, many people who would be content to spend their first year just securing their position as Rector of a church like Meade—an old and established black church, a magnet church for black churches all around the area—but he was not content to do that. He went out and started a ministry of outreach to former prisoners and he's developed a whole array of new programs that have extended that church's ministry by two or three hundred percent. Where somebody else would have said, "I've got to consolidate, I've got to secure my position, I've got to be careful the first year of my ministry," he did the opposite and said, "Let's reach out, we've got a lot of gifts here at Meade."

For example, Saint Paul's is one of eight churches that had a bag lunch program for homeless people on a rotating basis. Every eight weeks, Saint Paul's would put together eighty bag lunches, consisting of a sandwich, an apple and a snack, or something like that. I got a call one day from the parishioner who was coordinating the lunch program at Saint Paul's and she said, "The facility that we've been doing the lunch program out of is giving us three weeks notice to get out." They had been doing a particular type of outreach ministry and they decided that homelessness was not where they wanted to put their energy anymore. They could have given us more time, but they had also given us three or four years of free rent, so we were only mildly unhappy but we were caught because we had three weeks to put together an alternate site. Otherwise, the safety net was really going to have huge holes in it—in many cases this was the only meal these people were getting during the day. Ronald Reagan talked about the safety net— no one would fall through the safety net. Well, I can tell you that if you are a homeless person who has not yet been able to get a grip on some form of substance abuse there are almost no private or public social service agencies to help you right now and so therefore you're ostracized from city and private shelters because you're a drunk, or you're an addict. It's a tragedy. It's a huge tragedy. So much for the safety net.

The bag lunch program was going to go away and we had no other way to solve the problem. So I thought to myself that this facility was about three or four blocks away from Vaughan's church and I knew Vaughan had a big parish hall, so I called him, and said, "Vaughan, the bag lunch program has got three weeks to get out this place, is there anyway that we can do it at Meade?"

Vaughan said, "Oh, I would love to have it at Meade. That would be great for this parish. Wonderful."

I said, "Vaughan, don't you need to get some approval?"

So he convened his Vestry and obtained all the necessary approvals, and without missing a beat, we left this place on the Friday that they had thrown us out and started up on Monday at Meade. We had signs up all over the neighborhood, all through Old Town, "The bag program is now at Meade Memorial," and without missing a day, we just made the transition right into Vaughan's church, and people have been fed there for the last year thanks to Vaughan and Meade.

Vaughan could have said, "Well, I'm doing so many outreach things," or, "I don't think it would be right to be the only black church—why don't we have it at a white church?" There were many things he could have said, but he didn't, he said, "I'll do it, I'd love to do it, it would be great."

That's how that particular program started. One Sunday my sermon was about, "If these same people that we feed wanted to come into the church, where would they sit? How will we minister to them beyond just filling their bellies?"

I want to design more spiritual programs. I don't believe that at the church it can be good works just for the sake of good works. I believe there has to be a spiritual motivation and to do it for the sake of doing it is not a good enough reason.

We have two services on Sunday: 8:30 Eucharist and 11:00 Eucharist. Every second Sunday we have the gospel Choir singing and every last Sunday we have the Men's Choir. We have a Youth Choir singing on the fifth Sunday of every month that has five Sundays. We have youth running the service, reading the lessons and doing almost everything except preaching. They feel good about it. I believe we have to prepare them for a life in the church. We have a new, Episcopal curriculum and it's excellent. And we have some committed teachers.

We also have a nursery school so that when people come who have infant children, there's a safe haven for those children, under supervision, while their parents worship.

We're preparing for a health fair. Physical health is directly related, I believe, to spiritual health, and so we're going to do diabetic testing, high blood pressure testing and address other physical problems which afflict African Americans in particular. We need to address these things and deal with them and be healthy if we want to live and we have to have a reason to live—that's where the spiritual side comes in. We need to love our neighbors as ourselves, but we sometimes fall short in loving ourselves so the love we extend to our neighbors is not so wonderful.

We have a fairly long list of sick and shut-ins and part of our ministry is a healing ministry. We have a healing service every third Sunday and every Wednesday at noon. That includes the Eucharist, anointing with oil and laying on of hands. I have a regular schedule for visiting those people who are sick and shut in and who are unable to come to church. I take Communion to them and have a regular service that I do in their home or in the hospital. They have relatives and we can sit around together and go through an abbreviated service. We do these three or four times a week sometimes. People will call before or after an operation. It's a very meaningful service. People want prayer and they want healing and I consider it a priority ministry.

For another program, we have trained ten volunteers from the parish to teach ex-offenders employability skills. There are currently thirteen men and women in the group. We show them a film on how to interview for jobs, which is one of the most difficult things for inmates, because they have to explain having been in prison. Then there are classes which teach them very basic skills: how to print properly and fill out application forms, posture during an interview, what to wear, what to say. We put them on video so they can see and hear themselves which is very revealing and encourages them to improve.

An official at the US Park Service recently hired two men from our program. They work from March to November and make $8.75 an hour, which is not bad for someone just out of jail.

One young man, a Muslim, was in prison for 13 years but is out now and is making a tremendous adjustment. A member of my congregation suggested to him that he come over and talk to me and we hit it off right away. Now he has his own business. He has overcome his feelings of inadequacy and has been able to become the breadwinner for his family, even owning his own business. He's happy as a lark although he knows it is still a challenge..

As a Muslim he too has a spiritual life. Anyone who comes to me, no matter what his or her religious persuasion, I am going to minister to with the love of Christ. We can profess Jesus Christ and then live in a very un-Christlike way. I'm talking about people who feel good about themselves, they love themselves, they love the world and they love each other. That's Christlike. My concern is for the person.

I have a young man, 16 years old, who is doing a community program here. He killed his cousin. It was an accident but the court is holding him responsible. I've been working with him in terms of his repentance. We go in the chapel and pray together. At 16 how do you understand that God can forgive you for doing such a terrible thing? He read my story and he feels good being here and I can see he's feeling better about himself.

My assistant in the ex-offender program just got out of a halfway house. He's an ex-offender too. One thing he had in his favor was that when he got out he had somewhere to go and something to do. Based on our success so far, we have applied for another $10,000 to enhance the ex-offender program.

We also have a computer program, teaching computer skills as a component to the employability skills program. I applied for and received a $5000 grant from the Episcopal Church Fund for Human Need. We bought 4 multimedia, 486, CD-ROM, Packard Bell systems with printers and individual workstations, and started our computer program. In addition to the ex-offenders, we also have 20 people signed up from the parish who are taking the course which is delivered by volunteers from the parish who make their living working with computers.

In addition to church services, and outreach and other programs, I have many other demands on my time which come with the job—at least for me they do. For example, there has been an attempt to abolish parole in Virginia and I was asked to speak before the Governor's Task Force, asking them to retain parole as an incentive for men and women who are in prison—a motivation for them to change their lives and get back into society. I'm on the Board of Directors of a number of organizations: OAR (Offender Aid and Restoration) and Virginia CURE (Citizens United for the Rehabilitation of Errants). They asked if I would testify because of my background.

I'm also on the Board of Advisers for the George Washington Bank and am the clergy representative for housing in Alexandria.

The chaplain and superintendent at Graterford asked me to come and preach there. I was delighted at the opportunity to go back and see some of my old friends and preach the Word, bringing some hope. The system is so different now than it was in my day. There is a different class of inmates—much younger, more violent, less educated. There are fewer programs. Many kids of teenage, drug-addicted parents and grandparents have had to raise themselves and live in communities where the value systems are very different. In some communities if someone disrespects you ("disses" you) you can kill them and it's alright. In the prison system those values loom heavily. So even the older inmates don't like associating with the younger ones because they're so volatile. What we have to do is go in and preach love: love for self and others and the value of life.

We have a lot of plans at Meade. We want to get this mortgage paid off and we would like to set up a school. Our African American students are dropping out of high school at a phenomenal rate, even down to the junior high level. We need to have an alternative education. I would like to set up an after school tutoring program, a place where young people can come and be tutored by volunteers from the parish.

Rob Ross and I have been discussing the possibility of setting up an African-American art center: finding suitable premises and bringing in instructors to teach dance, fine arts, and other art forms with the idea of turning that into an academic curriculum and having a school for the arts. It's a vision.

I've been invited to many of the local churches to speak. It's been a wonderful experience interacting with the other churches of the other denominations in the area.

I have been invited to historic Christ Church in Alexandria where George Washington and Robert E. Lee worshiped to deliver seminars for three straight weeks. The subjects of the seminars were, "From Prison to Pulpit," "Taking the Spirit of the Eucharist With You," and "How to Deal With Anger."

I have also become a supervisor for seminarians who are completing their required field work so I am able to return some of the help I received from St. Timothy's when I was in my last two years at Virginia Theological Seminary. I have a student from the seminary, Cyril White, who has been a deacon for 12 years. He was a schoolteacher and is now in his senior year at seminary and I am able to help prepare him for ordination.

One of the most beautiful things about my life now is that I have a real, loving family that has meant so much to me. I don't think I could be where I am, doing what I'm doing, without that nucleus of a loving family. I've been blessed, I've had another chance and here I am. I have a new wife,and two beautiful grandchildren.

This situation has not just come about overnight. Tiera, Portia's granddaughter has been living with us for years. Eboni, my daughter Kim's daughter, came to us more recently. In a recent interview, Tiera, who is 11, explained what it was like for her to find out about my past.

> My grandmother didn't want us to know at an early age. Finally one day she says "Girls, I have to tell you something," and Eboni asked "What's it about?" And Mom Mom goes, "Pop Pop, and how his life was before he married me," and Eboni goes, "Oh, I know this one."
>
> I was like, "What?" and I was crying and everything, and I said, "Mom Mom, you have to tell me." Eboni's mother told her when she was 6 or 7 years old and she was hiding it from me, and everybody had been hiding it from me. I never knew and I was kind of pretty angry when I found out. This was when I was 9.
>
> I was like, "You lied to me all these times," but I finally understood why: because if you were of a young age and you found out you were living with somebody who was in jail like 20 years ago and you never knew about it you would get pretty mad—so I was.
>
> I was like, "Oh my gosh, he murdered some-one." I knew he was my grandpa and all, and I knew he was nice but I started to get scared.
>
> He usually took me to a toy store, just me and

him together, but I was scared and I said, "Mom Mom, come with us," because I was so scared that I didn't want to go to a toy store or anywhere else with him by myself. If he wanted to go somewhere I would ask Mom Mom if she could come with us. Then he said, "Why do you want Mom Mom to come?" I would say, "I just want her to come so she knows what we are doing. She misses us a lot whenever we go away." I never told him I was scared. He still doesn't know.

Finally, I stopped feeling that way when my grandma finally sat me down one night and said, "Why do you want me to go everywhere with you? Before you knew how this incident happened, you always wanted to go everywhere with Pop Pop and just leave me at home."

So I said I got scared and she said, "Oh."

I said, "Mom Mom, you can't tell Pop Pop," and she said she wouldn't. So she went into her room and shut the door and I thought, "Oh, no she's going to tell him." I acted like I was asleep and they came out, usually to get medicine because the medicine cabinet is right by our room, and I was acting like I was asleep so he wouldn't come in my room and say, "Now were you scared all these times?" I was so worried, I was nervous. I just stayed in bed and while he was getting his medicine I went, "Phew." And he said, "What were you phewing about?" and I said, "Oh nothing, I was just having a dream."

It changed when I read the articles. Then Mom Mom started telling me that he's not a bad man anymore. "Do you see that he's a priest and once you're a priest you can't do mean things like that again or else you're disobeying God."

So I said, "Okay, I will try to calm down." And then she was at work and I almost started crying because he had to pick up his clothes from the cleaner and then he said where do you want to go and I said, "Shopping, as usual." He said, "Okay," and I was like "Gosh, can Mom Mom come?" Then he said, "You want Mom Mom to come?" and I said, "Yes, yes!"

Then he remembered, "She works until 9:00." And I didn't want to say we should go home because we were halfway to the mall already. So we went into the mall and it was just fun. Once I started getting outfits and stuff I forgot all about it. Then I just got over it and then Mom Mom gave me a talk and I got over it completely. I adjusted. It hardly ever goes through my head that I'm living with a man who was in prison.

With Tiera and Eboni I am having a second chance to raise two children, something which my actions prevented me from doing with my own children. I count this as just one more blessing in my life.

As to the future, I am not looking beyond Meade. These people went out on a limb to hire me and I want to be true to them and to my calling as a priest. I'd like to see them up and going. I don't see myself going anywhere else. I don't feel restless. There is still so much to do. I love this place and I love the people and what I do.

But while it is easy for me to exist happily in the present, with an eye to a wonderful future, I believe it is also necessary to look at my whole story, not forgetting the past which I have come from.

Different people have different views of this unusual story, some of them not nearly as positive as mine.

CHAPTER FIFTEEN

"For I have come to call not the righteous but sinners."

(Matthew 9:13)

I could end this book with a philosophical dissertation about sin and forgiveness, repentance and renewal. I would rather try to paint a picture of my entire story as seen through the eyes of many different people from my past and my present. The many different points of view of these events I have described raise questions which, if this book is to be of any value, you will need to ask yourself.

None of these words were spoken to me. They were spoken about me in recent interviews which I did not attend, and I am sure they are therefore quite candid opinions and feelings.

The first of these voices is that of The Reverend Richard Winn. He was one of my three tutors when I was a candidate studying to be a deacon, while a resident at the state penitentiary. He is no longer certain that I should have been ordained a deacon or even allowed out of prison.

> I have had a continuing long time friendship with Vaughan both inside and outside. When his father died I performed the funeral service and I married Vaughan to his wife Portia who

belonged to my parish in Norristown, not far
from Graterford prison. Portia's family has been
with my church forever and I knew all her sisters.
Vaughan's brother-in-law, Chris Northington
who is a Baptist preacher, married Portia's sister
Rebecca, and he is one of my protégés of whom I
am very proud. When they were still laymen I
used to hang around with them to a certain
degree. Vaughan and I always had a friendship
outside of that tutoring in the jail and the other
tutors didn't.

I must admit I was curious when I heard that
there was to be a book about Vaughan. I wondered, "Why him?" It seems to me that his
accomplishments are really the culmination of
the work of a lot of people and he got a lot of
breaks that most people don't get. He happened
to have a lot of good fortune, some of which he
drew to himself.

But why should one have to go do anything as
horrible as a murder, particularly the murder of
one's wife and the mother of one's children—and
a perfectly hideous murder, a murder that quite
frankly astounds my imagination?

At the time when I first met Vaughan I was
certainly a lot less familiar with the whole subject of domestic violence and its consequences
than I am at the present time. Now I am a child
protective service worker and I live with the consequences of domestic violence every day.

Probably I and the others who were involved
in Vaughan's tutoring were not looking at the circumstances that brought us into that process with
the clarity that certainly I do now. I was very
young and much of my own thought was very

unformed and not taken out to its completion. I am not at that same place today.

I have a personal affection for Vaughan but I am astounded at the horror of anyone murdering the mother of his own children. I don't think people think of it in those terms. It's more like, "Oh, you killed somebody. Right. Well, we all occasionally run through stop signs." No! This is much, much more serious than that. It's not even like, I get in an argument with somebody about a parking space and shoot them, and I don't know them from Adam. No, I know these people.

I suppose, however, that we do need to feel that there is some possibility of redemption.

I first knew Vaughan when he was at Graterford. My understanding was that he would be remaining in prison for the rest of his life. And when Bishop DeWitt originally agreed to his ordination I am sure there was no expectation, at least as I understood it, that Vaughan was ever going to be released. The idea was that he was going to spend his life in prison serving others from a particular religious ministry. But that he was going to be released in the way that he was released and ultimately have as much run of the society as you and I, was certainly not a possibility I had considered at the time.

On the other hand, there have been some other inmates with whom people have worked just as hard and they have not turned out as well. They have, after years of alleged upward mobility, turned around and murdered someone and ended back in jail or something like that.

I was taken with Vaughan because he was a very apt student and I've always liked reading and studying and discussing so I was very much attracted to him because he has a keen mind. He has a keen mind and he is a very, very bright student and that had been one of my great peeves with clergy and clergy training—that there's too much stupidity there.

At the time of Vaughan's ordination to the diaconate there was a great strong controversy you understand. It was not at all well received. Bishop DeWitt and I disagree violently on a lot of things but he is a man of great integrity and great courage, and he's a man of great conviction and I admire him greatly because of that. He did what he thought was right.

I'm not really certain that I would have participated in this program if I had known that he was going to get out. I was always happy for him to be out and I was a sponsor for furloughs and things like that. But it's very hard, because I never really faced the pain and so on. I sort of masked that over in my own mind. I was dealing with Vaughan and here was a man who was in chains and who had a quest for Holy Orders. I was dealing with it at that level, not at the level of "what if...?"

We're talking about a period in time when the lambs were going to lay down with the lions. We're talking about before Reagan, which was another world. I think the horrors of the Reagan years have sobered a lot of us in terms of how little we accomplished because we dreamed great dreams but we didn't cut out this monster at the roots.

I certainly participated in the program willingly. What we were talking about doing was something completely different than how it turned out. In truth, I probably would have done what I did anyway, because I was at the time of the idea that everyone in jail ought to be turned loose in the streets.

There has been some recent work done on that sort of thing in the church because of the fact that more and more people who are victims of horrible crimes and horrible events are saying that the church has always had this wonderful idea of ministry to the perpetrators. They are saying that we have always thought, "Oh we must embrace the thief when he turns around and repents." We turn to the victims and say, "You must forgive this person." We don't really have compassion for the victims' pain and we don't address their pain in any kind of realistic fashion.

It's very seldom that you hear any talk about divine justice. It's more about: "In the end we're going to get off one way or another because, after all, we're all stupid and we didn't quite know what we were doing and it had to do with our toilet training." I've come a long way from feeling that. I've had to deal much more with people who are the victims of violence and my agency takes just the totally opposite view. We identify the perpetrators but we take no responsibility for what happens to them. Our only purpose is to exclude them from the scene.

At first that seems kind of cruel but the reality is we can't deal with both sides of the equation with the resources we've got and these people had no reason to be hurt. Their existence was greatly damaged by the pain that was caused, and in the case of Vaughan, the pain that's been caused to his own children.

I was in the "receiving the prodigal son" mode. I wasn't dealing with the realities of what had gone on. I think had we all known his children and had we all known his wife, our attitudes might have been quite different.

I'm not saying this to hurt Vaughan. I direct these questions basically to myself. I'm not so sure I did a good thing.

I really don't know if I feel he should still be in jail. I think it's up to him in many ways to say how he redeems his acts and it's up to God to say whether that's enough. I don't have enough insight. I just question whether what I did was right. We thought we were doing good, of that I am sure. But I'm not sure all the time, particularly the more I study the history of the church, that a lot of the time when we thought we were doing good might not have been when we were doing the worst.

It has been the church that has done more to encourage family violence than almost any other institution around. We are the people who have, for as far back as I can remember, told abused women that they must return to their husbands and put up with that abuse in the name of the sanctity of marriage and the preservation of their families and for the "good of their children." That has been the church's lie.

I think Vaughan was sincere in becoming a priest and I had no reason to believe that he ever thought at that time that he would ever be functioning outside jail or in any capacity other than as an internal chaplain in a real sense.

I have too much respect for him to think that he tried to pull some sort of an elaborate con. I think when doors opened, he used those doors and I don't blame him a bit for that. Whether those were the best choices or not, I have to leave that to somebody who's got more information than I have.

I'm still fully ordained as a priest, but I'm not firmly aligned with the Episcopal Church, because I feel they have run off the rails on several points. I certainly believe in the Christian religion and what I believe to be the catholic faith. Now whether that is what the Episcopal Church is talking about I'm not at all certain.

Another of my tutors was The Reverend Paul Washington. He is now 73 and he has retired from his work as Rector of the Church of the Advocate in North Philadelphia and on the bishop's panel for community concerns. But he is still active in his favorite ministry: what he refers to in the title of his recently published book, as the "other sheep" he has: the homeless, welfare groups, peace groups, lesbian and gay groups and so on. He remembers our time together at Graterford quite vividly.

The bishop approached me to be one of his tutors. I think Vaughan had the privilege of coming out on Sundays and I believe he chose the Church of the Advocate as the church he would attend, maybe not exclusively, but perhaps more so than others. That was my church at the time.

It seemed natural that I would be asked. I had been involved in ministering in county as well as state prisons. Since I knew him, once he was accepted for Holy Orders, it seemed natural that I should be one of his tutors.

I felt it was perhaps a great statement made by the church which is supposed to forgive and redeem and I was quite pleased about his being accepted for Holy Orders.

He impressed me then as he impresses people today. He is quite affable and I think he has a charm. I can only describe the feeling I had when I first got to know him as a very satisfying one. I certainly had no question in my mind as to whether he would be suited for the ordained ministry. There was no question in my mind about that at all.

At that time we didn't know whether his sentence would be commuted. However, in my experiences I had met many inmates who carried on a real ministry to other inmates. They weren't necessarily seeking ordination but they had the kind of character, temperament and personality, they offered a certain understanding and stability, that caused other inmates to seek them out almost as much as they would seek out one of the chaplains. So I think I felt at that time that he could carry on a ministry right there at Graterford.

There is one incident that stands out in my mind. I do recall asking him during one of our meeting together if he had any kind of special, different feelings when he looked back at the crime that he committed. I think I was probing to see if he had experienced any real agony and pain or just what. He answered that he felt he had been forgiven and if he was forgiven then he should certainly leave that behind and deal with the present and the future. I remember that in particular because I was wondering how much he was haunted by the memory of the period.

The answer surprised me and I can respond to that only in terms of my own personal experiences. There are things in the past which I have done and of which I am guilty and I am absolutely sure that I have been forgiven and yet when I think of those things I am pained.

His response was quite different from my own experience. He did not speak of any pain or any suffering and I realized that that was quite different from my own experience.

I felt there should have been feelings there that weren't, but that may be just my own personal ideas and whether or not that is justified in terms of our understanding of forgiveness and all that that should mean—I don't know if I've even thought that through yet. Does forgiveness mean that the past has been forgiven and erased? I know that it is erased as far as God having forgiven us, but my real question is, can it be erased from one's memory and from one's emotions?

I also remember that Vaughan accepted this great privilege that was being bestowed upon him of being ordained a deacon as though it was something to which he was entitled and I don't know that he felt any greater sense of accomplishment, satisfaction or joy upon being ordained than any other person. It was something that seemed very natural to him.

I would have thought that someone in his position might feel a greater joy and satisfaction and for him it was just a matter of course. When I described the day of his ordination it was as though the past had gone. This was another day and he was as anybody else.

Looking back on the merit of what we did in conducting Vaughan's personal seminary at Graterford, I must believe in the forgiveness of sins. I think we have a way of putting sin on a kind of a scale: this is a real bad sin and then on up to white lies. I have a feeling that when we are not faithful and not obedient and when we depart from God's will that God doesn't say, "Well, that was a white lie so that was alright, and this was a crime of passion and that's terrible." I feel that sin is sin.

Therefore I would say, "Let him who is without sin cast the first stone."

For someone to say, "Vaughan's sins are greater than mine," might be man's way of looking at it, but I don't know if God would look at it that way.

Rob Ross, of course, remains a close friend to this day, but he knows my entire story as well as anybody and he saw me go through my years of seminary and to the position I now hold as Rector at Meade Memorial Church. He is a thinker and expresses his thoughts quite freely.

One of my favorite stories of Vaughan's was: Prisoners would always come to him and say, "You think God can get me out of this if I pray hard enough? Will I get out? Can God free me?" And Vaughan would always say to the prisoner, "I have one piece of advice for you: pray as hard as you want, but get yourself a good lawyer."

And that advice, I think, has translated into his nonprison ministry as well. He has a sense of the pragmatic, along with the spiritual, which I really admire, because that's an aspect of my ministry that I feel strongly about. I'm sure he would say, "Oh, yes, we are going to be able to feed the poor if we pray to God. But God will also remind us to go to Safeway and buy the sandwich meats and the bread." That's his approach.

I think the Episcopal Church, for too long, was bringing people in who had no pragmatic sensibility. That's not just my opinion. I think that there are a lot of people who feel that the church became a place where you went to run away from the real world. So I think that there's a whole generation of priests in the Episcopal Church who are not particularly good at some of the real world challenges that are facing the church. I think that Vaughan is the antithesis of that; he's really good at that.

Vaughan is also a man who is incredibly generous; overly generous I think. He's a man who had a lot of time to work on his rage, and so he's extremely articulate at understanding his own anger. I think that came from therapy in prison and from his own inner-work, his reflection with clergy and others. So he's very self-effacing; he's humble.

I don't think he is an angel. I think that one of the things that Episcopal priests need to be is human beings, because we all are, and I think Vaughan is extremely good at being aware of those limitations of himself as a human being. He likes nice cars, he likes nice clothes, he's very proud of his appearance, he is an excellent orator. I think he genuinely likes people from all classes and all races, which I feel is rare. He moves comfortably in those circles and I think that he has learned a lot about not needing to be defensive. All that puffery I noticed earlier when we first met at the seminary doesn't go on anymore.

Just to give you one example, we were at a big diocesan gathering about six months ago, and he stood up in front of all of the clergy of the dioceses of Virginia, five hundred of us, and he asked the most pointed and wonderful question about a budget cut that was going to be made in a scholarship to a black college. Now instead of delivering this speech that would make him seem important, he spoke very poignantly about the loss, on a real grass roots level, to the student that would lose the scholarship. It was a small grant, maybe four thousand dollars, but it meant that some black student wasn't going to have four thousand of the money that he was going to need to go to school. And Vaughan talked about that lost opportunity in a very touching way. I went up to him afterwards and I gave him a big hug, in part because the first time I'd ever met him he had puffed himself up and he had said, "Well, you know, in America where the races are constantly struggling . . . " and instead he was just so direct and so honest, and I just realized that he had come such a long, wonderful way.

I don't think that Vaughan is an angel. I think he's a human being with a lot of the same foibles that most of us have, but he's incredibly willing to admit that on a regular basis, and I think that there is no better example of the incarnation of the theology of redemption, anywhere in the world, than is embodied in Vaughan Booker. I feel like he's a work in progress and he just keeps getting better and better.

Arnett Spady, another man who played an important role in helping me back into society, gives his viewpoint, that of a successful African American who worked his way into the higher levels of the corporate world, but never kicked away the ladder that helped him get there.

> I really was proud of the success Vaughan has experienced. I think we spend too much time in the media with all the negative stories about crime and problems. You look at the front pages of the newspapers and magazines and there are always negative crime type situations, but never the positive kinds of things that this individual has experienced.
>
> And I think, when you look at that, Vaughan can be a role model for those who have had problems in the past, maybe who have taken the wrong path. His story says that if you commit yourself to turn things around, you can have the same kind of results that Vaughan has had. And that's the good part. In fact, I travel around and speak to a lot of college students, and even church groups and often talk about positive kinds of things, such as the idea that just because you may feel that you're in trouble today, or you may have had trouble in the past, it's never too late to turn it around. And I often use Vaughan as an example of an individual who has turned it around.
>
> It's just positive. I feel really good about what has happened, for him especially. And another thing too, you've got to admire his wife, because she really stuck by him. I know that was a difficult time and she has a lot of class, a lot of character, and I think they became best friends.

When I hear people complain about how difficult things are, and how difficult things can be—
and most of us have been around people who are
always negative and always complaining and this
is always happening to them and nobody else—
but when you sit down and you talk to Vaughan,
it makes you understand and realize that whatever your goal is, if you focus on it and dedicate
your time and your actions to achieving those
goals, it can be done. He's a living proof that it
can be done.

And I just think there are a lot of Vaughan
Bookers out there. We have a lot of crime in the
country today, and we have a lot of individuals
who feel they have no chance of making it. And I
think that if we can get out in front of those individuals, more individuals, like a Vaughan
Booker, can be turned around. Then I think we'll
start improving some of the problems and some
of the individuals who say, "I've just given up in
life." The more we can get out there in front of
them with role models like Vaughan Booker, the
more I think it will start turning things around for
a whole lot of people who feel there's no opportunity for them—who have given up.

It's kind of hard to just sit back and say, "Well,
hey, I can ignore a lot of things." I think a lot of
people in America today are doing that. You have
to get involved. It would have been easier for me
to say, "Hey, I'll play it safe and leave this decision to somebody else." But you can't do it that
way because you have to get involved.

There are a lot of people who, if you take the
time like we did with Vaughan Booker, could turn
it around. It doesn't have to be in a penitentiary

type of environment. There are people down-town, and in inner-cities, or in some of the rural areas, that if people would just take time and work with them, work with the kids and the youth, and give people a second chance, would take it.

I think Vaughan is doing what you hope every-body else will do: he is now putting back into the society some of the benefits that he may have had from someone giving him a second chance. So he's not just sitting back. He spends a lot of time working with the youth, a lot of time work-ing with the individuals who are incarcerated. And when you look back, you think, "That's what it's supposed to be about."

And people that you help out in that type of situation, or a similar situation, do get back and they make a positive contribution. I just think he's a great individual, and he has my best wish-es, and I wish him continued success.

Bishop Robert DeWitt, who as the bishop of the Pennsylvania diocese opened the door for me to take my first steps on the road to becoming a priest, sees my story as being very much in the Christian tradition.

It all hinges on the fundamental concept in the Christian tradition and the love of God for His creatures, which involves and embraces the con-cept of forgiveness. There is a Russian novel and one of the characters in the book is talking to another one about this concept of forgiveness and he said that if Judas Iscariot, even in that very last moment, had repented what he had done, betraying Jesus of Nazareth...[then], "I say to you that the first drop of Jesus' blood was shed for Judas Iscariot."

It's a very central concept in the Christian tradition, and it's very largely what the story of Vaughan Booker is all about in terms of his ordination and his going on to the ministry. He was under this cloud of a conviction of murder which in typical society puts him just on the outer shades, beyond any recognition or anything else; banished from society; in prison for life. And yet the Christian doctrine is that the love of God is much greater than the sins of Man. God therefore, because of his love, will forgive people if they repent of what they have done. And this is the rock, I think, on which Vaughan Booker has stood and is standing—on which his ministry rests.

So that no one can say of him, "What right does he have to be preaching the Gospel?" Well, he has every right in the world, because we are all forgiven sinners, and he had his sins and you and I have ours, and we're all standing under the same condemnation until the love of God forgives us.

Another individual who has watched my progress, my sister Delphine, has gone through stages ranging from initial anger and dismay to being glad that things have turned out the way they have.

I think, even though this tragedy happened, basically the Giggle that we knew, that soft, gentle person was there and I think that this came out in him even when he was in prison.

He was still very much interested in going to

school, and wanting to pursue more education. The average prison inmate is not interested in doing this. A lot of people will say, "Oh, he went into the religion as an excuse." But I don't feel religion is something you play with and I feel that Catholic, Episcopalian, those religions, you have to study, you have to prove yourself to be able to get to the point of showing the authorities that you're really ready. It's not just something you decide, "Oh, I'm going to be a minister today."

And, evidently, he was supposed to do this, because he's there now. He's home free. Even when he got out of prison it was a shock to me. I said, "I thought he got life?" And, then when he was being released on the work-release program, I said, "Wow, the guy is something." Because how did he work that? I'm not saying that it's magic or anything, but it was the person that he was, and the sincerity that he had to show over the period of years that he was really determined to do this.

I'm not saying he's so great and so on, but it was different. It's not your average, run of the mill, "I go to prison, get a life sentence, and get out." It doesn't happen here today. This is when I realized that this is a special situation here. Evidently God wants it. He's going to bring it around and it has worked its way through. It amazes me still. I was there to see him ordained, but it just has amazed me, even though he's my brother. The whole situation from the beginning to now has amazed me. And I'm a Christian. I go to church every Sunday and I know what God's powers are, but it's still not your run of the mill situation. And I said, "Well, God must have had a plan for him."

The good part about it is that he has come through this and can be put in a position that we can even call an example. He's a person who is an example, if anybody's paying attention. Because young people do things today and as many people that go to jail, get killed, do all the things that they do, there are still those dummies who come out and still do it over again.

My mother expressed herself in fewer words. She simply said to me, "God had you in the palm of His hand."

The Reverend Dick Swartout helped me an enormous amount and has been instrumental in keeping me pointed in the right direction. He has seen a great deal of my life and the lives of other inmates and also has his own feelings about the penal system.

Some of my wisdom from criminal justice prison ministries is that rehabilitation ministry isn't going to change anybody. Even if they change in the institution, when they hit they street again, they're not changed. That piece of time is as if it was just wasted out of their life. They go back—I wouldn't say everybody, but many of the inmates that I worked with—they were this person when they were incarcerated and when they were released, they were the same person on the other end. And everything in between was forgotten when they walked out of the gate. No matter what it was. And I saw that over and over and over again.

And I think we've got the whole idea wrong in this country: we're locking up way too many people. This country is going to be like Russia was in a little while.

Graterford, when I was there, had a population of 1500 and then they doubled up on the cells. Now they have over 4000 men in that place. And I used to walk that place and I felt safer with Vaughan next to me than I did with a guard next to me.

As far as Vaughan is concerned, I think he has grown by maturing, settling down and getting a perspective for his life. As he would say, from early childhood when he went with his uncle as an acolyte, he's wanted to be a priest. Once you realize that, you can never say "No." Eventually you have to say "Yes" to God's calling. It happened to me, it's happened to all kinds of people. I took off and went in the Navy for three years and then I was in college studying to be an electrical engineer at the University of Albany. I was involved in what was called the Canterbury Association, which was a national group for Episcopal college students.

My studies were just getting all screwed up and I wondered, "What is going on here? Maybe I'm in the wrong course of study."

So I called my priest up in Lockport, New York, where I grew up and I said, "Russ, I've got to talk with you about something."

He said, "Are you ready to go into the priesthood?"

"Yep."

And he said, "Okay, come on up, let's talk." And so we talked. He had already made an appointment for the bishop to preliminarily talk with me and then we went from there and that was 33 years ago.

You say, "Yes." And Vaughan eventually said, "Yes." And now he's happy and he's enjoying it. But he needed that, that space too from prison to really say yes.

And I am really pleased that Vaughan is doing as well as he is.

There is also the voice of Donald Vaughn, now Superintendent of Graterford, who was there throughout my entire period of incarceration at the penitentiary.

Vaughan, in growing up, was different. I recognized him and saw him to be different because of the way that I grew up and saw the individuals that lived in our neighborhood. He was intelligent and he was smart—and you can be intelligent and not be smart. And there were certain traits about him that separated him from the other inmates here as there were certain traits that separated him in his growing up. He was a quiet individual. He was a positive person. And when I first heard he was going into the ministry, I thought, "Well that's the type of person he is. He's going into something now that I feel that he's suited for."

A lot of inmates come in and religion is an avenue that they may get involved in to help put themselves in a more positive setting, and to be recognized in a different light. That's true.

In my career I haven't had anyone else who has gone to the point that Vaughan went to. I don't think that had a total bearing on his release. And even when he was released, he went on with his life and he could have just kept on going with

Xerox or whatever, because of the person he is.
He backed up at some point and realized where
he really belonged and what he should be doing,
and changed his life. I think you can make much
more money doing what he was doing with
Xerox than you can make in the area that he's in.

So this is not something that he did for a profit
or to make a good showing. I think it's something within him that is telling him, "You are the
chosen one to carry this message, and to deliver
the Word." And some people look at men and
human beings as being God and that's not so.
He's just the message carrier. And I see him as a
message carrier. I see him as someone working
for God to carry the Word. I think that he has
recognized his calling and I think he'll do well.

The other thing too is that he hasn't forgotten
where he's come from and he's always coming
back. Not too long ago he came to visit me and
he remembered a lot of people here that he wanted to see while he was here. He didn't come just
to see me. He wanted to see some of the inmates.

A lot of them write him and talk to him. The
people here still remember him because I do
have a lot of people that are doing life that were
here when he was here. And they are glad to see
him making it the way he's making it.

I don't think there is anyone here that would
ever say, "He just used the system," because they
don't see it that way. They see him as an individual who had his calling and that Someone is
using him—that God is using to him to carry that
message.

He is a role model. He is someone that other
inmates can look and say, "Well, you know, he's

been through this horrible system that we live
within, and he's made it."

We feel good about a person like Vaughan
who has been through the system, had a life sentence, did time here, and has gone out to help
other people. That is what he is doing. He is somewhat preaching, not just to his congregation, but to
the world.

Much more on the negative side there is the voice of Linda
Pickett, Angie's niece, who probably represents the feelings
of those members of Angie's family who are still angry and
who have not forgiven me.

He is being made out to be this super individual
who was able to commit a crime, rehabilitate
himself and move on to do these wondrous
things. But what about the other people who suffered? What about his own flesh and blood who
are still here suffering?

David Kairys, who helped me so much with the legal side
of my life, in addition to being a friend, looks at my case as it
reflects on the entire justice system and society's relationship
to people charged with crimes.

Vaughan's case in particular makes us face some
basic questions about crime and violence. If you
look at all of the statistics, and the commutation
board was aware of this, the lowest repeat rate
has been for these same kind of "all American"
murders. They did not go marry someone else
and kill them. That is incredibly, incredibly rare.
Whatever it is that led them to the first one, after
this happens once, when they eventually get out

they don't do it again. They are not serial killers—that's a whole different phenomena.

So there was a low risk, and there was no good reason to keep him in that long. These days, who's to say? We keep everybody in. But that wasn't true back then. Other people were getting commuted sooner.

Vaughan is such an obvious example of that, and the contrast between his successes, his middle class life and what he did to his wife, is striking. Here's somebody who was gainfully employed, pretty solidly in a the middle-class existence and kills his wife in this usual scenario.

I view Vaughan as a friend at this point and probably did way back, but I don't think that colors my view. There is a level on which the criminal is not that different from the rest of us. I question this whole notion that there are normal people and then there are criminals and criminals are these vicious, horrible, deformed people.

Sometimes that even gets translated into, "You can tell them when you see them," and all those genetic theories. There are some pretty awful people: there are serial killers, for instance, and even them, you see their pictures on television and you think, "Oh my God, I wouldn't recognize that guy for a murderer if I saw him."

But these sorts of murders are too frequent and too similar to view as just isolated, individual problems. You grieve for the victims and rightly hold the murderer responsible, but it's willful ignorance not to notice that as young boys we are taught to react with violence to several sets of circumstances. And if you don't, you are not a man. It's not just that such violent behavior is not put down, it's encouraged. There are certain situations where as a young man you are supposed to commit an act of violence or you are weak. This is the oft-repeated message of prime time TV. And when you react with violence you could kill a loved one and it's there the rest of your life, which of course is the case with Vaughan.

But these are just regular people to me. That night could have gone a little differently for those two and there might not have been a murder: less drink, different words said, comes home a little later, doesn't see this man leaving—lots of things could have happened and maybe there would have been counseling the next week for the two of them and nothing like this would have happened.

Or maybe they would have decided that they needed a divorce and that's it. It would be over. Certainly, there were, and we have no way of knowing the numbers, but there would have been many thousands, maybe hundreds of thousands of other couples who had terrible arguments that night where it didn't go this far. But they are lucky, many of them, because it could have.

So a certain amount of this is going to happen in this culture. And I don't mean it is happenstance and I certainly don't mean that the people who do it aren't responsible for it—they are totally responsible for it and they should pay the price—but we've now got this notion that criminals are this distinct horrible group of people and somehow if we can find enough of them and put them in jail forever, we'll be fine.

It's wrong and it's hurting us. For a good

twenty years, we've been thinking this way and we have the highest imprisonment rate in the world right now. We surpass South Africa and the Soviet Union—who used to be the world leader in the proportion of their population that was in prison—and now we lead the world, smashing all records.

We are spending a fortune on prisons, police, lawyers and courts, giving up on huge portions of our people. We seem to have lost a sense of compassion or cohesion in this society, and all the money spent and lives wasted in prisons haven't even made us safer.

Tom Stachelek remembers the time, not that long ago, when I went up to Graterford for a job interview, before I joined Meade Memorial.

We invited him up to interview for a contract chaplain's position. We very much would have liked to hire him as contract chaplain for Graterford but unfortunately he had another job offer. He really impressed the interview committee and I think he could have done a lot for the inmate population.

Many different voices from my past and present. But I suppose that I am entitled to the last word in this book.

At Meade, we're building and we're growing. We're making our parish financially solvent; we want to increase our outreach programs which we're doing; we have the feeding program at the church, the ex-offender program at the church, we have people coming in because of our outreach.

I want other people to be happy, too. I want them to know that God is there for them, and in their lives, and that there is nothing, nothing that can keep them from the knowledge and love of God, if they truly want him in their lives. Our theme at the church is, "Renewal of the Spirit." So we want to renew everyone's spirit. If you to come to our church, we're going to renew your spirit.

It's been a journey, and it's still a journey. I thank God every day, first of all that after going through such a tragedy in my life, I can still feel good about myself and other people. I think that's a gift from God. To be able to reach out in love—I really love all of God's creation, and not just people.

I feel good about everything, and it isn't just an escape from reality, it's an escape into reality. I believe that this is the way we are supposed to be, and that's the relationship we're supposed to have with God. I believe that God is always there just waiting for us to come home, so to speak, and when we do, we're blessed, and the blessings keep going on and on, and on, and on, and on. But it's a lot of hard work too.

The words from the sermon Paul Washington preached at my ordination as a deacon come back to me: "Much is expected from those to whom much is given." And I am finding that out.

I preach a lot about relationships: How you can't come to church and worship God and then go home and beat your wife. It happens. I think the church now is being courageous enough to speak out on domestic violence, child molesting, and homosexuality in the church and all those issues. We have to. Because the church can't put its head in the sand and not deal with them anymore. We are the moral voice of society. I think it is up to the church.

Of course, my focus is that we can't be hypocritical about things like forgiveness and repentance. It's all through our prayer book: "Forgive us our sins, as we forgive the sins of others." We say that in the Lord's Prayer. And in our baptismal vow, we talk about forgiving sins, during the Eucharist we talk about, "This is my blood, which is shed for you for the remission of sins." We say that, but it's hard for people to really live it, to be forgiving, even when they haven't been personally hurt by someone.

In a case like mine there are people who have a difficult time forgiving me for something that happened twenty-eight years ago. But part of the journey is moving from a point where you can't forgive, to a point where you can. And I understand that for a lot of people who can't forgive me, it may not have anything to do with their forgiveness of me; it may have more to do with their own issues—maybe something that they've done for which they can't forgive themselves. Or something that they're holding on to that they can't let go of. But if they truly want to be able to forgive, then they have to let it go and they have to, as we call it, take it to the foot of the cross—take it to God in prayer.

I think many religions tell us that we as human beings are weak and frail, and, in and of ourselves, don't have the ability nor the capacity to change. But if we understand that there is a much larger force in our lives, the force that we call God—the Muslims call Him Allah, Yahweh in the Jewish faith—if we can understand that, then it adds to the quality of our lives. It makes us better people.

I really believe that there is hope for the world. I believe that if we get involved and help young people who have no parents, have no direction, that we can change their lives right now, by getting involved, not just sitting back and criticizing. We can sit back and say what a terrible thing it is that all these people coming out of prison keep going back to prison, and that's easy to say, if you don't have to help them find a job, or help them to feel good about themselves, or re-establish themselves with their families. But if we do those things, and we help them, we can feel good knowing that there are couple of them who don't fall back into that same situation.

It's an ongoing struggle, that's why it's a journey. And it

goes on and on. It isn't saying, "Okay, I've arrived." Unfortunately we have so many self-righteous people who feel that way. "Well, I'm here, and it's us against you."

I don't happen to believe it's that way. We have to constantly give God thanks for helping us. For me the freedom was gradual and I appreciate it, every little gradual bit of it: every little morsel. You maximize whatever you have.

Maybe it seemed like a little thing to others, but to me it was a big thing: a little bit of freedom, going out on the weekend, big thing, freedom. You go out and you're successful on the weekend, and you go out for two weekends, successful with that, then you do what's next. It's growing.

So I'm still on the journey, and I know I'll never stop until I can't journey any more.